CHOCTAW BY BLOOD

ENROLLMENT CARDS

1898-1914

VOLUME XI

TRANSCRIBED BY

JEFF BOWEN

NATIVE STUDY
Gallipolis, Ohio
USA

Other Books and Series by Jeff Bowen

1901-1907 Native American Census Seneca, Eastern Shawnee, Miami, Modoc, Ottawa, Peoria, Quapaw, and Wyandotte Indians (Under Seneca School, Indian Territory)

1932 Census of The Standing Rock Sioux Reservation with Births And Deaths 1924-1932

Census of The Blackfeet, Montana, 1897- 1901 Expanded Edition

Eastern Cherokee by Blood, 1906-1910, Volumes I thru XIII

Choctaw of Mississippi Indian Census 1929-1932 with Births and Deaths 1924-1931 Volume I

Choctaw of Mississippi Indian Census 1933, 1934 & 1937, Supplemental Rolls to 1934 & 1935 with Births and Deaths 1932-1938, and Marriages 1936-1938 Volume II

Eastern Cherokee Census Cherokee, North Carolina 1930-1939 Census 1930-1931 with Births And Deaths 1924-1931 Taken By Agent L. W. Page Volume I

Eastern Cherokee Census Cherokee, North Carolina 1930-1939 Census 1932-1933 with Births And Deaths 1930-1932 Taken By Agent R. L. Spalsbury Volume II

Eastern Cherokee Census Cherokee, North Carolina 1930-1939 Census 1934-1937 with Births and Deaths 1925-1938 and Marriages 1936 & 1938 Taken by Agents R. L. Spalsbury And Harold W. Foght Volume III

Seminole of Florida Indian Census, 1930-1940 with Birth and Death Records, 1930-1938

Texas Cherokees 1820-1839 A Document For Litigation 1921

Choctaw By Blood Enrollment Cards 1898-1914 Volumes I thru X

Visit our website at **www.nativestudy.com** to learn more about these and other books and series by Jeff Bowen

Originally published:
Baltimore, Maryland
2016

Reprinted by:

Native Study LLC
Gallipolis, OH
www.nativestudy.com

Library of Congress Control Number: 2020911767

ISBN: 978-1-64968-014-3

Made in the United States of America.

This series is dedicated to
Mike Marchi,
who keeps my spirits up.

CREEK CENSUS.

SECOND NOTICE.

Members of the Dawes Commission will be present at the following times and places for the purpose of enrolling Creek citizens, as required by Act of Congress of June 10, 1896:

At Muskogee, Nov. 8 to 30, 1897, inclusive.
At Wagoner, Nov. 8 to 13, " inclusive.
At Eufaula, Nov. 8 to 13, " inclusive.
At Sapulpa, Nov. 15 to 20, " inclusive.
At Wetumpka, Nov. 15 to 20, " inclusive.
At Okmulgee, Nov. 22 to 30, " inclusive.

All persons who have not heretofore enrolled before the Dawes Commission should appear and enroll. Parents and guardians can enroll their families and wards.

TAMS BIXBY,
FRANK C. ARMSTRONG,
A. S. McKENNON,
THOS. B. NEEDLES,
Commissioners.

The above illustration is similar in nature to what was found throughout Indian Territory for different tribes as far as postings on bulletin boards, public centers, or wherever they could be read so people would be notified of where and when they needed to be for enrollment with the Dawes Commission.

This is a picture of the Dawes Commission at Camp Jones in Stonewall, Indian Territory on September 8, 1898.

The images below are of two of the original cards given on the microfilm. The cards given in this book have been formatted to fit on one page and still give all the information found on the original cards.

Introduction

This series of Choctaw Enrollment Cards for the Five Civilized Tribes 1898-1914 has been transcribed from National Archive Film M-1186 Rolls 39-46.

The series contains more than 6100 Choctaw enrollment cards. All of the cards list age, sex and degree of blood, the parties' Dawes Roll Numbers, and date of enrollment by the Secretary of Interior for each person. The contents also give the enrollee's parents' names as well as miscellaneous notes pertaining to the enrollee's circumstances, when needed. Most entries indicate whether or not a spouse is an Intermarried White, with the initials I.W.

Enrollment wasn't as simple a process as most would think just by going through these pages. The relationships between the Five Tribes and the Dawes Commission were weak at best. There were political battles going on between the tribes and the U.S. Government as it was, but the struggles didn't stop there. Each tribe had its own political factions pulling it from every direction. On top of everything else, people from every corner of the United States were trying to figure how to get in on the spoils (Money and Land Allotment) by means of political favor. Kent Carter, author of *The Dawes Commission*, describes the continuous effort required to enroll the different tribes and the pressure the Commission incurred from people all over the country who tried to insinuate themselves into the equation:

"In May 1896 the Dawes Commission Returned To Indian Territory for its third visit, establishing its headquarters at Vinita in the Cherokee Nation. It now had to process applications for citizenship in addition to negotiating allotment agreements; these circumstances make the narrative of events more confusing because the commission attempted the two tasks concurrently. The commissioners resumed making their usual speeches to tribal officials and public gatherings to promote negotiations, but now they inevitably had to respond to questions about how the application process for citizenship would work. They also began receiving letters from people all over the United States asking how they could 'get on the rolls' so they could 'get Indian land'."[1]

For the actual process of Choctaw enrollment, "A commission was appointed in each county of the Choctaw Nation under an act of September 18 to make separate rolls of citizens by blood, by intermarriage, and freedmen; it was to deliver them to recently elected Chief Green McCurtain by October 20, but he rejected them even before they were completed because of charges that people were being left off for political reasons. On October 30, the National Council authorized establishment of a five-member

---

[1] *The Dawes Commission* by Kent Carter, page 15, para. 1

commission to revise the rolls within ten days and then directed McCurtain to turn them over to the Dawes Commission on November 11, 1896. The Choctaws hired the law firm of Stuart, Gordon, and Hailey, of South McAlester to represent the tribe at all proceedings held by the Dawes Commission,"[2] another indication that throughout the Commission's efforts there was always controversy between the tribes and the negotiators.

When completed, this multi-volume series will contain thousands of names, all of them accounted for in the indexes carefully prepared by the author. Hopefully this work will help many researchers find their ancestors and satisfy the questions that so many have had about their Native American heritage.

Jeff Bowen
Gallipolis, Ohio
NativeStudy.com

---

[2] *The Dawes Commission* by Kent Carter, page 16, para. 5

Choctaw By Blood Enrollment Cards 1898-1914

POST OFFICE: LeFlore, I.T.	COUNTY. **Choctaw Nation**	**Choctaw Roll** (Not Including Freedmen)	CARD NO. FIELD NO. 3001

Dawes' Roll No.	NAME	Relationship to Person Named	AGE	SEX	BLOOD	TRIBAL ENROLLMENT		
						Year	County	No.
8796	1 Winlock, Brazil 67	First Named	64	M	1/2	1896	Sugar Loaf	12897
8797	2 ~~Lena~~ DIED PRIOR TO SEPTEMBER 25 1902	~~Wife~~	~~45~~	F	~~Full~~	~~1896~~	" "	~~12898~~
8798	3 Kincade, Alice 18	G.Dau	15	"	3/4	1896	Towson	7527
8799	4 " Kizzie 16	"	13	"	3/4	1896	" "	7528
8800	5 ~~Hampton, Louisiana~~ DIED PRIOR TO SEPTEMBER 29 1902	"	~~14~~	"	~~7/8~~	~~1896~~	~~Sugar Loaf~~	~~5253~~
8801	6 Jones, Israel 15	S.Son	12	M	3/4	1896	" "	6545
	7							
	8							
	9							
	10							
	11							
	12							
	13							
	14	ENROLLMENT						
	15	OF NOS. 1,2,3,4,5,6 HEREON						
	16	APPROVED BY THE SECRETARY						
	17	OF INTERIOR JAN 17 1903						

TRIBAL ENROLLMENT OF PARENTS

	Name of Father	Year	County	Name of Mother	Year	County
1	Tom Winlock	Dead	Non Citz	Amy Winlock	Dead	Towson
2	~~Impson Sexton~~	"	~~Sugar Loaf~~	~~Susan Sexton~~	"	~~Sugar Loaf~~
3	Jos Kincade	"	" "	Mary Kincade	"	" "
4	" "	"	" "	" "	"	" "
5	~~Simeon Hampton~~	"	" "	~~Selina Hampton~~	"	" "
6	Norris Jones	"	" "	Lena Jones	1896	" "
7						
8	No.4 – Duplicate enrollment of Sissie Kincade, Roll No 2581.					
9						
10	~~No2 on 1896 roll as Layon Winlock~~					
11	~~No5 " 1896 " " Lucy Ann Hampton~~					
12	Oct 7/99: #3&4 on roll as Alice & Kizzie Kincade					
13	~~No.2 died April 15, 1902; Enrollment cancelled by Department July 8, 1904~~					
14	For child of No3 see NB (Mar 3-1905) Card #204					
15					Date of Application for Enrollment.	
16					6/21/99	
17						

1

Choctaw By Blood Enrollment Cards 1898-1914

RESIDENCE: Sugar Loaf COUNTY. **Choctaw Nation**   **Choctaw Roll** CARD No.
POST OFFICE: LeFlore, I.T.   *(Not Including Freedmen)* FIELD No. 3002

Dawes' Roll No.	NAME	Relationship to Person First Named	AGE	SEX	BLOOD	TRIBAL ENROLLMENT		
						Year	County	No.
8802	1 Sexton, Esias ~~DIED PRIOR TO SEPTEMBER 25 1902~~		41	M	Full	1896	Sans Bois	11115
	2							
	3							
	4							
	5							
	6							
	7							
	8							
	9							
	10							
	11							
	12							
	13							
	14							
	15							
	16							
	17							

ENROLLMENT
OF NOS. 1 HEREON
APPROVED BY THE SECRETARY
OF INTERIOR JAN 17 1903

TRIBAL ENROLLMENT OF PARENTS

	Name of Father	Year	County	Name of Mother	Year	County
1	Impson Sexton	Dead	Sugar Loaf	Susan Sexton	Dead	Sugar Loaf
2						
3						
4						
5						
6						
7		On 1896 roll as Esiah Sexton				
8						
9						
10						
11						
12						
13						
14					Date of Application for Enrollment.	
15						
16					6/21/99	
17						

Choctaw By Blood Enrollment Cards 1898-1914

RESIDENCE:	Sans Bois	COUNTY.						CARD No.	
POST OFFICE:	Sans Bois, I.T.	**Choctaw Nation**			**Choctaw Roll** (Not Including Freedmen)			FIELD No. 3003	

Dawes' Roll No.	NAME		Relationship to Person	AGE	SEX	BLOOD	TRIBAL ENROLLMENT		
			First Named				Year	County	No.
8803	1 Garvin, Louis	46	First Named	43	M	Full	1896	Sans Bois	4611
8804	2 " Sopha	51	Wife	48	F	"	1896	" "	4612
8805	3 " Simpson	14	Son	11	M	"	1896	" "	4613
	4								
	5								
	6								
	7								
	8								
	9								
	10								
	11								
	12								
	13								
	14	ENROLLMENT							
	15	OF NOS. 1, 2, 3 HEREON							
	16	APPROVED BY THE SECRETARY OF INTERIOR JAN 17 1903							
	17								

TRIBAL ENROLLMENT OF PARENTS

Name of Father		Year	County	Name of Mother	Year	County
1	John Garvin	Dead	Nashoba	Mollie Garvin	Dead	Red River
2	Jack McCurtain	"	Wade	Mariah McCurtain	"	Sugar Loaf
3	No1			No2		
4						
5						
6						
7						
8						
9						
10						
11						
12						
13						
14					Date of Application for Enrollment.	
15						
16					6/21/99	
17	Eagle Point 11/1/04					

Choctaw By Blood Enrollment Cards 1898-1914

RESIDENCE: Sugar Loaf   COUNTY. **Choctaw Nation**   **Choctaw Roll**   CARD No.
POST OFFICE: Red Oak, I.T.   *(Not Including Freedmen)*   FIELD No. 3004

Dawes' Roll No.	NAME		Relationship to Person	AGE	SEX	BLOOD	TRIBAL ENROLLMENT		
							Year	County	No.
8806	1 Jefferson, Sam	27	First Named	24	M	Full	1896	Sans Bois	6414
	2								
	3								
	4								
	5								
	6								
	7								
	8								
	9								
	10								
	11								
	12								
	13								
	14								
	15								
	16								
	17								

ENROLLMENT
OF NOS. 1   HEREON
APPROVED BY THE SECRETARY
OF INTERIOR   JAN 17 1903

TRIBAL ENROLLMENT OF PARENTS

	Name of Father	Year	County	Name of Mother	Year	County
1	Nicholas Jefferson	1896	Sans Bois	Sarah Wesley	Dead	Sans Bois
2						
3						
4						
5						
6						
7						
8						
9						
10						
11						
12						
13						
14						
15						
16				Date of Application for Enrollment	6/21/99	
17						

Choctaw By Blood Enrollment Cards 1898-1914

RESIDENCE: Tobucksy
POST OFFICE: Krebbs, I.T.

COUNTY. **Choctaw Nation**

Choctaw Roll
(Not Including Freedmen)

CARD NO.
FIELD NO. 3005

Dawes' Roll No.	NAME	Relationship to Person First Named	AGE	SEX	BLOOD	TRIBAL ENROLLMENT		
						Year	County	No.
✓	1 Blake, Emma		48	F	1/4			
	2							
	3							
	4							
	5							
	6							
	7							
	8							
	9							
	10							
	11							
	12							
	13							
	14							
	15							
	16							
	17							

ENROLLMENT
OF NOS. .... HEREON
APPROVED BY THE SECRETARY
OF INTERIOR ....

TRIBAL ENROLLMENT OF PARENTS

	Name of Father	Year	County	Name of Mother	Year	County
1	Jonathan Lowe	Dead, Non Citz		Susan Lowe	Dead	Choctaw
2						
3						
4						
5						
6	No1 Denied by Com in 96 Case #197					
7	Admitted by U.S. Court, Central District					
8	Sept 9/97 Case No 92 as Emma Butteroff					
	As to residence, see her testimony					
9	Judgment of U.S. Court admitting No1 vacated and set aside by Decree of Choctaw Chickasaw Cit Court Dec 17 02					
10	No1 [illegible] C.C.C.C. Case #					
11	No1 denied by C.C.C.C. March 21 04					
12						
13						
14						
15					Date of Application for Enrollment.	
16					6/21/99	
17						

DENIED CITIZENSHIP BY THE CHOCTAW AND CHICKASAW CITIZENSHIP COURT

5

Choctaw By Blood Enrollment Cards 1898-1914

RESIDENCE: Sugar Loaf COUNTY. **Choctaw Nation** **Choctaw Roll** *(Not Including Freedmen)* CARD NO.
POST OFFICE: LeFlore, I.T. FIELD NO. 3006

Dawes' Roll No.	NAME		Relationship to Person	AGE	SEX	BLOOD	TRIBAL ENROLLMENT		
			First Named				Year	County	No.
8807	1 Jones, James	54	First Named	51	M	Full	1896	Sugar Loaf	6552
8808	2 " Selissa	30	Wife	27	F	"	1896	" "	6553
8809	3 " Kitzie	19	Dau	16	"	"	1896	" "	6554
8810	4 " Morrow	9	Son	6	M	"	1896	" "	6555
	5								
	6								
	7								
	8								
	9								
	10								
	11								
	12								
	13								
	14	ENROLLMENT							
	15	OF NOS. 1,2,3,4 HEREON							
	16	APPROVED BY THE SECRETARY OF INTERIOR JAN 17 1903							
	17								

TRIBAL ENROLLMENT OF PARENTS

	Name of Father	Year	County	Name of Mother	Year	County
1	Laymon Jones	Dead	Sugar Loaf	Ah-le-ha-ma	Dead	Gaines
2	Men-ko-shuffie	"	Gaines	Lottie Jones	1896	Sugar Loaf
3	No1			Lizzie Jones	Dead	" "
4	No1			No2		
5						
6						
7						
8			No2 on 1896 roll as Sillis Jones			
9			For child of No3 see NB (Apr 26-06) Card #852			
10						
11						
12						
13						
14					Date of Application for Enrollment.	
15					6/21/99	
16						
17						

6

RESIDENCE: Sugar Loaf   COUNTY. **Choctaw Nation**   **Choctaw Roll** CARD No.
POST OFFICE: Le Flore, I.T.   *(Not Including Freedmen)*   FIELD No. **3007**

Dawes' Roll No.	NAME		Relationship to Person	AGE	SEX	BLOOD	TRIBAL ENROLLMENT		
							Year	County	No.
8811	1 Adams, James	26	First Named	23	M	Full	1896	Skullyville	54
8812	2 " Sallie	27	Wife	24	F	"	1896	Sans Bois	6397
8813	3 DIED PRIOR TO SEPTEMBER 25, 1902 " Gertie		Son	5mo	M	"			
4									
5									
6									
7									
8									
9									
10									
11									
12									
13									
14									
15	ENROLLMENT OF NOS. 1,2,3 HEREON								
16	APPROVED BY THE SECRETARY OF INTERIOR JAN 17 1903								
17									

TRIBAL ENROLLMENT OF PARENTS

	Name of Father	Year	County	Name of Mother	Year	County
1	Sam Adams	Dead	Sugar Loaf	Sillen Adams	1896	Sugar Loaf
2	Jackson Webster	"	Sans Bois	Anoranna Webster	Dead	Skullyville
3	No1			No2		
4						
5						
6						
7						
8			No2 on 1896 roll as Sallie Jackson			
9			No.3 died Oct. 25, 1901: Enrollment cancelled by Department July 8, 1904			
10			For child of No.1 see NB (March 3, 1905) #1395			
11						
12						
13						
14					Date of application for Enrollment.	
15						
16					6/21/99	
17						

Choctaw By Blood Enrollment Cards 1898-1914

RESIDENCE:	Sugar Loaf	COUNTY.						CARD NO.	
POST OFFICE:	Le Flore, I.T.	**Choctaw Nation**				Choctaw Roll (Not Including Freedmen)		FIELD NO. 3008	

Dawes' Roll No.	NAME		Relationship to Person	AGE	SEX	BLOOD	TRIBAL ENROLLMENT		
							Year	County	No.
8814	1 Hudson, Henry	29	First Named	26	M	1/4	1896	Sugar Loaf	5243
8815	2 " Irie	26	Wife	23	F	Full	1896	" "	5244
	3								
	4								
	5								
	6								
	7								
	8								
	9								
	10								
	11								
	12								
	13								
	14	ENROLLMENT							
	15	OF NOS. 1 and 2 HEREON							
	16	APPROVED BY THE SECRETARY OF INTERIOR JAN 17 1903							
	17								

TRIBAL ENROLLMENT OF PARENTS

	Name of Father	Year	County	Name of Mother	Year	County
1	Joel Hudson	Dead	Eagle	Margaret Hudson	1896	Non Citz
2	Sweeny Brashears	"	Kiamitia	Liza Brashears	Dead	Kiamitia
3						
4						
5						
6						
7			No2 on 1896 roll as Issie Hudson			
8						
9			As to marriage of parents of No1			
10			see enrollment of Margaret McFerrin.			
11						
12						
13						
14					Date of Application for Enrollment.	
15						
16					6/21/99	
17						

8

Choctaw By Blood Enrollment Cards 1898-1914

RESIDENCE: Tobucksy COUNTY. **Choctaw Nation** **Choctaw Roll** CARD NO.
POST OFFICE: South MᶜAlister I.T. *(Not Including Freedmen)* FIELD NO. 3009

Dawes' Roll No.	NAME	Relationship to Person First Named	AGE	SEX	BLOOD	TRIBAL ENROLLMENT		
						Year	County	No.
✓ ✓	1 Brazell, James ✳	Named	31	M	1/16			
DP	2 " Maggie	Wife	24	F	I.W.			
	3							
	4							
	5							
	6							
	7 No2 not in Judgment of C.C.C.C. Why?							
	8							
	9							
	10 #2 DISMISSED							
	11 MAR 18 1905							
	12							
	13							
	14							
	15							
	16							
	17							

TRIBAL ENROLLMENT OF PARENTS

	Name of Father	Year	County	Name of Mother	Year	County
1	John Brazell	1896	Non Citz	Jennie Brazell	1896	Tobucksy
2	Frank Burks	Dead	" "	Susan Burks	Dead	Non Citz
3						
4	DENIED CITIZENSHIP BY THE CHOCTAW AND					
5	CHICKASAW CITIZENSHIP COURT					
6	No1&2 denied in 96 Case #6					
7	Admitted by U.S. Court Central District					
8	Aug 24/97, Case No 96					
9	No2 was admitted by the U.S. Court as an Intermarried Citizen					
10	As to residence, see testimony of No1					
11						
12						
13						
14						
15				Date of Application for Enrollment.		
16				6/21/99		
17						

Choctaw By Blood Enrollment Cards 1898-1914

RESIDENCE: Sugar Loaf   COUNTY. **Choctaw Nation**   **Choctaw Roll**   CARD NO.
POST OFFICE: Le Flore, I.T.   *(Not Including Freedmen)*   FIELD NO. 3010

Dawes' Roll No.	NAME		Relationship to Person	AGE	SEX	BLOOD	TRIBAL ENROLLMENT		
							Year	County	No.
8816	1 Blue, Willy	31	First Named	28	M	Full	1896	Sugar Loaf	805
8817	2 " Melvina	23	Wife	20	F	1/4	1896	" "	806
8818	3 " Daniel	6	Son	2	M	5/8			
8819	4 " Eli	2	Son	6mo	M	5/8			
	5								
	6								
	7								
	8								
	9								
	10								
	11								
	12								
	13								
	14	ENROLLMENT							
	15	OF NOS. 1,2,3,4 HEREON							
	16	APPROVED BY THE SECRETARY OF INTERIOR JAN 17 1903							
	17								

TRIBAL ENROLLMENT OF PARENTS

	Name of Father	Year	County	Name of Mother	Year	County
1	William Blue	1896	Sugar Loaf	Nancy Blue	Dead	Sugar Loaf
2	Joel Hudson	Dead	Eagle	Margaret McFerren	1896	white woman
3	No1			No2		
4	No.1			No.2		
5						
6						
7			As to marriage of parents of No2,			
8			see Card of Margaret McFerren			
9			No.4 Enrolled July 19, 1901			
10						
11			For child of Nos 1&2 see NB (Apr 26-06) Card #457			
12			" " " " " " " (Mar 3-05) " #1165			
13						
14						
15				#1 to 3		
16				DATE OF APPLICATION FOR ENROLLMENT.	6/21/99	
17	PO Bengal IT 4/19/05					

10

Choctaw By Blood Enrollment Cards 1898-1914

RESIDENCE:	Sugar Loaf	COUNTY.						
POST OFFICE:	Red Oak, I.T	**Choctaw Nation**			**Choctaw Roll** *(Not Including Freedmen)*	CARD NO. FIELD NO. 3011		

Dawes' Roll No.	NAME	Relationship to Person First Named	AGE	SEX	BLOOD	TRIBAL ENROLLMENT Year	County	No.
8820 1	Colbert, Martin DIED PRIOR TO SEPTEMBER 23? 1902		24	M	Full	1896	Sugar Loaf	2218
2								
3								
4								
5								
6								
7								
8								
9								
10								
11								
12								
13								
14								
15	ENROLLMENT OF NOS. 1 HEREON							
16	APPROVED BY THE SECRETARY							
17	OF INTERIOR JAN 17 1903							

TRIBAL ENROLLMENT OF PARENTS

	Name of Father	Year	County	Name of Mother	Year	County
1	Mack Colbert	1896	Sugar Loaf	Elsie Colbert	Dead	Skullyville
2						
3						
4						
5						
6	No1 Died April 7" 1902· Proof of death filed Dec.r 23rd 1902					
7						
8						
9						
10						
11						
12						
13						
14						
15					Date of Application for Enrollment.	
16					6/21/99	
17						

Choctaw By Blood Enrollment Cards 1898-1914

RESIDENCE: Sugar Loaf	COUNTY.								
POST OFFICE: Le Flore, I.T.	**Choctaw Nation**					Choctaw Roll (Not Including Freedmen)	CARD NO. FIELD NO. 3012		

Dawes' Roll No.	NAME		Relationship to Person	AGE	SEX	BLOOD	TRIBAL ENROLLMENT		
							Year	County	No.
8821	1 LeFlore, Mack H	47	First Named	44	M	Full	1896	Sugar Loaf	7804
I.W 279	2 " Bertha	(38)	Wife	36	F	I.W.	1896	" "	14748
8822	3 " Sallie	19	Dau	16	"	1/2	1896	" "	7805
8823	4 ~~DIED PRIOR TO SEPTEMBER 23 1902~~ Mannie K	"	13	"	1/2	1896	" "	7806	
8824	5 " Mat H	12	Son	9	M	1/2	1896	" "	7807
8825	6 " Ethel W	6	Dau	3	F	1/2	1896	" "	7808
8826	7 " Virginia	4	"	1	"	1/2			
8827	8 " Willie T	1	Son	2mo	M	1/2			
9	ENROLLMENT								
10	OF NOS. 2 HEREON								
11	APPROVED BY THE SECRETARY OF INTERIOR SEP 12 1903								
12	ENROLLMENT								
13	OF NOS. 1,3,4,5,6,7,8 HEREON								
14	APPROVED BY THE SECRETARY OF INTERIOR JAN 17 1903								
15	No4 died Jan 20, 1901 En-								
16	rollment cancelled by								
17	Department July 8, 1904								

TRIBAL ENROLLMENT OF PARENTS

	Name of Father	Year	County	Name of Mother	Year	County
1	Wallace LeFlore	Dead	Wade	Judie LeFlore	Dead	Sugar Loaf
2	J. C. Kennedy	"	Non Citz	Sallie Kennedy	"	Non Citz
3	No1			No2		
4	No1			No2		
5	No1			No2		
6	No1			No2		
7	No1			No2		
8	No.1			No.2		
9						
10						
11						
12	No1 on 1896 roll as M. H. LeFlore			For child of Nos 1&2 see NB (Mar3,1905) #813		
13	No2 " 1896 " " Bertha N. "					
14	Evidence of marriage to be supplied. Exhibited 6/22/99, found to be in due form, but					
15	No.7 Affidavit of birth to be supplied. Recd 6/22/99					
16	not in condition to be filed				Date of Application for Enrollment.	
17	No.8 born Jany 12, 1902: enrolled March 28, 1902				6/21/99	
	No4 died January 20, 1901; proof of death filed Dec 19 1902					
	Nos 1-2: Evidence of marriage filed Dec 24, 1902					

Choctaw By Blood Enrollment Cards 1898-1914

RESIDENCE:	Sugar Loaf	COUNTY.	**Choctaw Nation**	Choctaw Roll	CARD NO.	
POST OFFICE:	Fanshaw, I.T.			*(Not Including Freedmen)*	FIELD NO.	3013

Dawes' Roll No.	NAME		Relationship to Person	AGE	SEX	BLOOD	TRIBAL ENROLLMENT		
							Year	County	No.
8828	1 Sockey, Ned	32	First Named	29	M	Full	1896	Sugar Loaf	11201
8829	2 " Malinda	29	Wife	26	F	3/4	1896	" "	11202
8830	3 " Mary	8	Dau	5	"	7/8	1896	" "	11203
8831	4 " Eli	6	Son	3	M	7/8	1896	" "	11204
8832	5 " Myrtle	2	Dau	6m	F	7/8			
8833	6 " Irene Maree	1	Dau	3wks	F	7/8			
	7								
	8								
	9								
	10								
	11								
	12								
	13								
	14								
	15	ENROLLMENT OF NOS. 1,2,3,4,5,6 HEREON							
	16	APPROVED BY THE SECRETARY							
	17	OF INTERIOR JAN 17 1903							

TRIBAL ENROLLMENT OF PARENTS

Name of Father	Year	County	Name of Mother	Year	County
1 Willis Sockey	Dead	in Mississippi	Martha Sockey		Mississippi
2 Solomon Harris	"	Sugar Loaf	Mamie Harris	1896	Sugar Loaf
3 No1			No2		
4 No1			No2		
5 No 1			No 2		
6 Nº1			Nº2		
7					
8					
9	No1 admitted by act of Choctaw Council of April 9, 1891				
10					
11	No.5 Enrolled January 25, 1901				
12	Nº6 Born May 9, 1901, enrolled May 29, 1902				
13	For child of Nos 1&2 see NB (March 3, 1905) #1130				
14					#1 to 4
15				Date of Application for Enrollment.	
16				6/21/99	
17					

13

Choctaw By Blood Enrollment Cards 1898-1914

RESIDENCE: Sugar Loaf	COUNTY. Choctaw Nation	Choctaw Roll (Not Including Freedmen)	CARD NO.
POST OFFICE: Le Flore, IT			FIELD NO. 3014

Dawes' Roll No.	NAME	Relationship to Person First Named	AGE	SEX	BLOOD	TRIBAL ENROLLMENT		
						Year	County	No.
Dead 1	Adams, Simon	Named	44	M	Full			
8834 2	" Sarah ⁴⁷	Wife	44	F	"			
DP 3	" Sam	Son	11	M	"			
4								
5								
6	No3 DISMISSED							
7	FEB 4- 1907							
8								
9	No. 1							
10	ORDER OF HEREON DISMISSED UNDER							
11	FIVE CIVILIZED TRIBES OF JULY 18, 1905.							
12								
13								
14								
15	ENROLLMENT OF NOS. 2 HEREON							
16	APPROVED BY THE SECRETARY							
17	OF INTERIOR JAN 17 1903							

TRIBAL ENROLLMENT OF PARENTS

	Name of Father	Year	County	Name of Mother	Year	County
1	Jos. B. Adams	Dead	Sugar Loaf	En-la-te-ma	Dead	Sugar Loaf
2	John Wilson	"	Skullyville	Sallie Wilson	"	Skullyville
3	No 1			No 2		
4						
5						
6	No1 died Oct 27 1899· Proof of death filed August 11, 1906					
7						
8	No.2 also on 1896 roll; page 2; No 53 as Selia Adams					
9	No1 on 1896 roll as Simon Adam					
10	No2 " 1896 " " Sarah "					
11	No3 " 1896 " " Sam "					
	Correct given name of No.2 is Selia – 12/16 '02					
12						
13						
14						
15				Date of Application for Enrollment.	For Nos 1&2	
16					6/21/99	
17				No3 enrolled Dec 5/99		

Choctaw By Blood Enrollment Cards 1898-1914

RESIDENCE:	Sans Bois	COUNTY.						CARD NO.	
POST OFFICE:	Sans Bois, I.T.	**Choctaw Nation**		Choctaw Roll *(Not Including Freedmen)*				FIELD NO.	3015

Dawes' Roll No.	NAME		Relationship to Person	AGE	SEX	BLOOD	TRIBAL ENROLLMENT		
							Year	County	No.
I.W. 280	1 Vance, Rus	(37)	First Named	34	M	I.W.	1896	Sans Bois	15132
8835	2 " Clarissa	39	Wife	36	F	1/4	1896	" "	12590
8836	3 Pickens, Edna	18	Ward	15	"	1/2	1896	" "	10040
	4								
	5								
	6								
	7								
	8								
	9								
	10	ENROLLMENT OF NOS. 1 APPROVED BY THE SECRETARY HEREON OF INTERIOR SEP 12 1903							
	11								
	12								
	13								
	14	ENROLLMENT OF NOS. 2 and 3 APPROVED BY THE SECRETARY HEREON OF INTERIOR JAN 17 1903							
	15								
	16								
	17								

TRIBAL ENROLLMENT OF PARENTS

	Name of Father	Year	County	Name of Mother	Year	County
1	John Vance	Dead	Non Citz	Adaline Vance	Dead	Non Citz
2	Israel LeFlore	"	Red River	Phoebe LeFlore	"	Red River
3	Levi Pickens	"	Chickasaw	Adaline Pickens	"	Sans Bois
4						
5						
6						
7						
8						
9		For child of No.3 see N.B (Apr 26-06) No. 800				
10						
11						
12						
13						
14					Date of Application for Enrollment.	
15						
16					6/21/99	
17						

RESIDENCE: Sugar Loaf COUNTY. **Choctaw Nation** Choctaw Roll CARD NO.
POST OFFICE: Summerfield I.T. *(Not Including Freedmen)* FIELD NO. 3016

Dawes' Roll No.	NAME	Relationship to Person	AGE	SEX	BLOOD	TRIBAL ENROLLMENT		
						Year	County	No.
DEAD	1 Sexton Thompson D ~~DEAD.~~	First Named	65	M	Full	1896	Sugar Loaf	11167
DEAD.	2 ~~Barns Lillie P~~	Wife	39	F	I.W.			
8837	3 Harris Nellie N. 21	Dau	18	"	1/2	1896	" "	11169
8838	4 Sexton Charles D 19	Son	16	M	1/2	1896	" "	11168
8839	5 " Joseph R 15	"	12	M	1/2	1896	" "	11170
8840	6 " Berta M 13	Dau	10	F	1/2	1896	" "	11171
8841	7 " Irene J 11	"	8	F	1/2	1896	" "	11172
8842	8 " Lela J 9	"	6	F	1/2	1896	" "	11173
8843	9 Harris, Lilly E 1	G.Dau	2mo	F	1/4	No1 On 1896 roll as Thompson Sexton		
	10					No2 Certificate of marriage exhibited,		
	11 dated May 6th 1880, duly signed and sufficient, but not in condition to be filed, admitted							
	12 by Dawes Com, as intermarried citizen as Lilly P Sexton Case No 813							
	13 No.3 is now the wife of James F. Harrison Choctaw card #5708							
	14 No.1 died in January, 1900.							
	15 No.2 is now the wife of George Barnes a non-citizen							
	~~See statements of James F. Harris of Jany 11th 1901~~							
	16							
	17							

TRIBAL ENROLLMENT OF PARENTS

	Name of Father	Year	County	Name of Mother	Year	County
1	~~David Sexton~~	~~Dead~~	~~Miss~~	~~Ish-le-mil-lay Sexton~~	~~Dead~~	~~Skullyville~~
2	~~J. C. Kennedy~~	"	~~Non Citz~~		"	~~Non Citz~~
3	No 1	No. 1 and 2 HEREON DISMISSED UNDER		No 2		
4	No 1	ORDER OF THE COMMISSION TO THE FIVE		No 2		
5	No 1	CIVILIZED TRIBES OF MARCH 31, 1905.		No 2		
6	No 1	ENROLLMENT		No 2		
7	No 1	OF NOS. 3,4,5,6,7,8,9 HEREON		No 2		
8	No 1	APPROVED BY THE SECRETARY OF INTERIOR JAN 17 1903		No 2		
9	Thompson Sexton					
10						
11	No3 On 1896 roll as Nellie Sexton					
12	No4 " 1896 " " Charlie "			N°9 Born Nov. 6, 1901; enrolled Jan 11, 1902		
13	No5 " 1896 " " Joseph "			Father of N°9 is James F Harris, non-citizen		
	No6 " 1896 " " Berta "			Mother of N°9 is N°3		
14	No7 " 1896 " " Irene "			Nos 4-8 inclusive are wards of Thomas J Sexton		
15	No8 " 1896 " " Lela "			Choctaw card #2256		
16	No2 died Aug 16, 1902; proof of death filed Dec 19 1902			Date of Application for Enrollment	6/21/99	
17	For child of No5 see NB (Apr 26-06) Card #731				→1 to 8	

" " " No3 " " (Mar 3-05) " #1477

Choctaw By Blood Enrollment Cards 1898-1914

RESIDENCE: Gaines COUNTY.	Choctaw Nation	Choctaw Roll	CARD NO.
POST OFFICE: Wilburton I.T.		(Not Including Freed...)	FIELD NO. 3017

Dawes' Roll No.	NAME	Relationship to Person First Named	AGE	SEX	BLOOD	TRIBAL ENROLLMENT		
						Year	County	No.
8844	1 Wall Wrimie 17	First Named	14	F	Full	1896	Gaines	12971
	2							
	3							
	4							
	5							
	6							
	7							
	8							
	9							
	10							
	11							
	12							
	13							
	14							
	15							
	16							
	17							

ENROLLMENT
OF NOS. 1 HEREON
APPROVED BY THE SECRETARY
OF INTERIOR JAN 17 1903

TRIBAL ENROLLMENT OF PARENTS

Name of Father	Year	County	Name of Mother	Year	County
1 Jesse Wall	Dead	Gaines	Nancy Wall	Dead	Gaines
2					
3					
4					
5					
6					
7					
8					
9					
10					
11					
12					
13					
14				Date of Application for Enrollment.	
15					
16				6/21/99	
17					

RESIDENCE:	Sugar Loaf	COUNTY.					CARD NO.	
POST OFFICE:	LeFlore, I.T.	**Choctaw Nation**			Choctaw Roll *(Not Including Freedmen)*		FIELD NO.	3018

Dawes' Roll No.	NAME	Relationship to Person	AGE	SEX	BLOOD	TRIBAL ENROLLMENT		
						Year	County	No.
8845	1 Jones, Lottie ~~DIED PRIOR TO SEPTEMBER 25, 1902~~	First Named	45	F	Full	1893	Gaines	508
8846	2 " Benjamin 21	Son	18	M	"	1896	"	6596
8847	3 " Henry 18	"	15	"	"	1896	"	6597
8848	4 " Moltsey 16	Dau	13	F	"	1896	"	6599
8849	5 " James 12	Son	9	M	"	1896	"	6598
8850	6 " Ellen 11	Dau	8	F	"	1896	"	6600
	7							
	8							
	9							
	10							
	11							
	12							
	13							
	14							
	15	ENROLLMENT						
	16	OF NOS. 1,2,3,4,5,6 HEREON APPROVED BY THE SECRETARY						
	17	OF INTERIOR JAN 17 1903						

TRIBAL ENROLLMENT OF PARENTS

	Name of Father	Year	County	Name of Mother	Year	County
1	Tobley	Dead	Gaines	Sha-ho-yo	Dead	Gaines
2	Johnson Jones	"	"	No1		
3	" "	"	"			
4	" "	"	"	No1		
5	" "	"	"	No1		
6	" "	"	"	No1		
7						
8						
9						
10	No1 on 1893 Pay Roll, Gaines Co, Page 54, No 508, as Lottie Sealy					
11	No4 " 1896 roll as Matsey Jones					
12	No6 " 1896 roll as Eley Ann "					
13	~~No.1 died July 1901: Proof of death filed Dec 24, 1902~~					
14	No.2 is now the Husband of Kizzie Laman, Choc Card #2921					
15	For child of No 3 see NB 973 (Act Apr 26 '06)					
16				Date of Application for Enrollment.	6/21/99	
17						

18

Choctaw By Blood Enrollment Cards 1898-1914

RESIDENCE:	Gaines	COUNTY.	**Choctaw Nation**	**Choctaw Roll** (Not Including Freedmen)	CARD NO.
POST OFFICE:	Featherstone, I.T.				FIELD NO. 3019

Dawes' Roll No.	NAME		Relationship to Person	AGE	SEX	BLOOD	TRIBAL ENROLLMENT		
							Year	County	No.
8851	1 Lewis, Artemissa	23	First Named	20	F	1/2	1893	Wade	512
8852	2 Carney, Serena	1	Dau	1	"	3/4			
14784	3 " David	2	Son	2	M	3/4			
	4								
	5								
	6								
	7								
	8								
	9								
	10								
	11								
	12								
	13								
	14								
	15								
	16								
	17								

ENROLLMENT OF NOS. 1 and 2 HEREON APPROVED BY THE SECRETARY OF INTERIOR Jan 17, 1903

ENROLLMENT OF NOS. 3 HEREON APPROVED BY THE SECRETARY OF INTERIOR MAY 20 1903

TRIBAL ENROLLMENT OF PARENTS

	Name of Father	Year	County	Name of Mother	Year	County
1	Wiley McKinney	1896	Colored	Lucy	Dead	Sugar Loaf
2	Jonas Carney	1896	Gaines	No1		
3	" "			No.1		
4						
5						
6			No1 on 1893 Pay Roll, Wade Co, Page 69, No 512, as Artemus White			
7			No3 Born Feby. 27, 1901: Proof of birth filed Dec 23, 1902			
8			For child of No.1 see NB (March 3, 1905) #1231			
9						
10						
11						
12						
13						
14						
15						
16				Date of Application for Enrollment.	6/21/99	
17	P.O. Quinton I.T. Dec 23. 1902					

Choctaw By Blood Enrollment Cards 1898-1914

RESIDENCE: Skullyville	COUNTY.	**Choctaw Nation**	**Choctaw Roll**	CARD NO.
POST OFFICE: Lodi I.T.			(Not Including Freedmen)	FIELD NO. 3020

Dawes' Roll No.	NAME		Relationship to Person First Named	AGE	SEX	BLOOD	TRIBAL ENROLLMENT		
							Year	County	No.
8853	1 Lewis. Cyrus	35	First Named	32	M	Full	1896	Sugar Loaf	7769
8854	2 " Easter	7	Dau	4	F	"	1896	" "	7771
8855	3 ~~Josephine~~ DIED PRIOR TO SEPTEMBER 25, 1902		~~Dau~~	~~1~~	~~F~~	~~"~~			
	4								
	5								
	6								
	7								
	8								
	9								
	10								
	11								
	12								
	13								
	14								
	15	ENROLLMENT OF NOS. 1, 2, 3, HEREON							
	16	APPROVED BY THE SECRETARY OF INTERIOR JAN 17 1903							
	17								

TRIBAL ENROLLMENT OF PARENTS

	Name of Father	Year	County	Name of Mother	Year	County
1	James Lewis	Dead	Skullyville	E-ma-cha-ia-ho-ke	Dead	Sugar Loaf
2	No 1			Bessie Lewis	Dead	" "
3	No 1			" "	"	" "
4						
5						
6						
7						
8	Nº 1 is now the husband of Sis Martin on Choctaw card #2223 Sept 6, 1902					
9						
10						
11	No3 died Feb 2, 1900; proof of death filed Dec 19 1902					
12	No3 died Feb 2, 1900; Enrollment cancelled by Department July 8, 1904					
13						
14					Date of Application for Enrollment.	
15						
16					6/21/99	
17						

Choctaw By Blood Enrollment Cards 1898-1914

RESIDENCE: Sugar Loaf	COUNTY.	Choctaw Nation	Choctaw Roll (Not Including Freedmen)	CARD NO.
POST OFFICE: Red Oak, I.T.				FIELD NO. 3021

Dawes' Roll No.	NAME	Relationship to Person First Named	AGE	SEX	BLOOD	TRIBAL ENROLLMENT Year	County	No.
8856 ₁	Brashears, John ³⁵		32	M	1/4	1896	Sugar Loaf	801
I.W. 281 ₂	" Minnie ⁽³⁸⁾	Wife	36	F	I.W			
₃								
₄								
₅								
₆								
₇								
₈								
₉	ENROLLMENT							
₁₀	OF NOS. 2 HEREON APPROVED BY THE SECRETARY							
₁₁	OF INTERIOR SEP 12 1903							
₁₂								
₁₃								
₁₄								
₁₅	ENROLLMENT OF NOS. 1 HEREON							
₁₆	APPROVED BY THE SECRETARY							
₁₇	OF INTERIOR JAN 17 1903							

TRIBAL ENROLLMENT OF PARENTS

	Name of Father	Year	County	Name of Mother	Year	County
₁	Turner Brashears	Dead	Skullyville	Kate Brashears	Dead	Non Citz
₂	Levi Moore	"	Non Citz	Amy Moore	1896	" "
₃						
₄						
₅						
₆						
₇		As to marriage of parents of No1,				
₈	see testimony of R. O. Edmonds					
₉	No.2 admitted by Dawes Commission in 1896 as an					
₁₀	intermarried citizen. Choctaw case #883. no appeal.					
₁₁						
₁₂						
₁₃						
₁₄						
₁₅					Date of Application for Enrollment.	
₁₆					6/21/99	
₁₇	12/17/02 – PO Wilburton IT					

Choctaw By Blood Enrollment Cards 1898-1914

RESIDENCE:	Skullyville	COUNTY.							CARD NO.	
POST OFFICE:	Lodi, I.T.	Choctaw Nation				Choctaw Roll (Not Including Freedmen)			FIELD NO. 3022	

Dawes' Roll No.	NAME		Relationship to Person	AGE	SEX	BLOOD	TRIBAL ENROLLMENT		
							Year	County	No.
8857	1 Lewis, Woodson	50	First Named	47	M	Full	1896	Sugar Loaf	7767
8858	2 " Selina	33	Wife	30	F	"	1896	" "	7768
	3								
	4								
	5								
	6								
	7								
	8								
	9								
	10								
	11								
	12								
	13								
	14								
	15	ENROLLMENT OF NOS. 1 and 2 HEREON							
	16	APPROVED BY THE SECRETARY							
	17	OF INTERIOR JAN 17 1903							

TRIBAL ENROLLMENT OF PARENTS

Name of Father	Year	County	Name of Mother	Year	County
1 James Lewis	Dead	Sugar Loaf	E-ma-chi-a-ho-ke	Dead	Sugar Loaf
2 Daniel Bell	1896	Tobucksy	Sallie	Dead	Gaines
3					
4					
5					
6					
7					
8		No2 on 1896 roll as Silinie Lewis			
9					
10					
11					
12					
13					
14				Date of Application for Enrollment.	
15					
16				6/21/99	
17					

22

Choctaw By Blood Enrollment Cards 1898-1914

RESIDENCE: Sans Bois COUNTY.			**Choctaw Nation** (Not Including Freedmen)				Choctaw Roll	CARD NO.	
POST OFFICE: Hoyt I.T.								FIELD NO. 3023	

Dawes' Roll No.	NAME		Relationship to Person First Named	AGE	SEX	BLOOD	TRIBAL ENROLLMENT		
							Year	County	No.
8859	1 Taylor John	56	First Named	53	M	1/8	1896	Skullyville	11948
I.W. 282	2 " Alice V	43	Wife	40	F	I.W.	1896	" "	15090
	3								
	4								
	5								
	6								
	7								
	8								
	9								
	10								
	11	ENROLLMENT OF NOS. 2 HEREON APPROVED BY THE SECRETARY OF INTERIOR SEP 12 1903							
	12								
	13								
	14								
	15	ENROLLMENT OF NOS. 1 HEREON APPROVED BY THE SECRETARY OF INTERIOR JAN 17 1903							
	16								
	17								

TRIBAL ENROLLMENT OF PARENTS

	Name of Father	Year	County	Name of Mother	Year	County
1		Dead	Non Citz	Hester A Taylor	Dead	Ark.
2	Samuel Nelson	"	" "		"	Non Citz
3						
4						
5						
6						
7						
8						
9						
10	No2 Admitted by Dawes Com as intermarried citizen Case					
11	No 277 as Alice Taylor. Also on 1896 roll as Alice Taylor.					
12						
13						
14					Date of Application for Enrollment.	
15						
16					6/21/99	
17						

Choctaw By Blood Enrollment Cards 1898-1914

RESIDENCE:	Sans Bois	COUNTY.	Choctaw Nation	Choctaw Roll	CARD NO.	
POST OFFICE:	Featherstone I.T.			(Not Including Freedmen)	FIELD NO.	3024

Dawes' Roll No.	NAME		Relationship to Person	AGE	SEX	BLOOD	TRIBAL ENROLLMENT		
							Year	County	No.
8860	1 Bench Matilda	27	First Named	24	F	1/32	1896	Sans Bois	690
8861	2 " Isaac	6	Son	2	M	3/64		" "	
	3								
	4								
	5								
	6								
	7								
	8								
	9								
	10								
	11								
	12								
	13								
	14								
	15	ENROLLMENT OF NOS. 1 and 2 HEREON APPROVED BY THE SECRETARY OF INTERIOR JAN 17 1903							
	16								
	17								

TRIBAL ENROLLMENT OF PARENTS

	Name of Father	Year	County	Name of Mother	Year	County
1	Samuel Quentin	Dead	Non Citz	Elizabeth Quentin	1896	Sans Bois
2	Samuel Bench	1896	Sans Bois	No 1		
3						
4						
5						
6						
7			For child of No.1 see NB (March 3, 1905) #1321			
8						
9						
10						
11						
12						
13						
14					Date of Application for Enrollment.	
15						
16					6/21/99	
17	PO Quinton IT 4/28/05					

RESIDENCE:	Sans Bois	COUNTY.	**Choctaw Nation**			Choctaw Roll	CARD No.	
POST OFFICE:	Featherstone					*(Not Including Freedmen)*	FIELD No.	3025

Dawes' Roll No.	NAME		Relationship to Person First Named	AGE	SEX	BLOOD	TRIBAL ENROLLMENT		
							Year	County	No.
8862	1 Quinton James	32	First Named	29	M	1/16	1896	Sans Bois	10648
I.W. 1516	2 " Sallie		Wife	25	F	I.W.			
8863	DIED PRIOR TO SEPTEMBER 25, 1902 3 James F Son			5mo	M	3/32			
14785	4 " Avery	1	"	21"	"	3/32			
	5								
	6								
	7								
	8								
	9								
	10								
	11								
	12								
	13								
	14								
	15								
	16								
	17								

ENROLLMENT OF NOS. ~~~~ 2 ~~~~ HEREON APPROVED BY THE SECRETARY OF INTERIOR NOV 27 1905

ENROLLMENT OF NOS. 4 HEREON APPROVED BY THE SECRETARY OF INTERIOR MAY 20 1903

No. 3 died Sept - 1899 Enrollment cancelled by Department July 8, 1904

ENROLLMENT OF NOS. 1 and 3 HEREON APPROVED BY THE SECRETARY OF INTERIOR JAN 17 1903

Evidence of marriage between Nos 1 and 2 filed Jany. 17, 1903

GRANTED OCT 4- 1905

TRIBAL ENROLLMENT OF PARENTS

	Name of Father	Year	County	Name of Mother	Year	County
1	Samuel Quinton	Dead	Non Citz	Elizabeth Quinton	1896	Sans Bois
2	Tuck Bench	1896	Ark	Martha Pool	Dead	Non Citz
3	No 1			No 2		
4	No. 1			No. 2		
5						
6				For child of Nos 1&2 see NB (Mar 3-05) Card #1174		
7				" " " " " " (Apr 26-06) " 685		
8						
9						
10				No2 Evidence of marriage of father and mother to be supplied		
11				No3 Affidavit of birth to be supplied. Recd July 27/99		
12				No2 Father and mother said not to have been lawfully married		
13				No3 Died Sept. 1899: Proof of death filed Dec 23 1902		
14			Sept 8th 1899	No2 illegitimate child of Tuck Bench		
15				Choctaw by Martha Poole white woman		
16				Above enrollment erroneous. She is not on any		
				Choctaw roll.	Date of Application for Enrollment	
17	No2 PO Quinton 2/25/03			No.4 Born March 28, 1901: Proof of birth filed Dec 23/02		6/21/99

| RESIDENCE: Sans Bois | COUNTY. Choctaw Nation | Choctaw Roll | CARD No. |
| POST OFFICE: Enterprise I.T. | | *(Not Including Freedmen)* | FIELD No. 3026 |

Dawes' Roll No.		NAME		Relationship to Person	AGE	SEX	BLOOD	TRIBAL ENROLLMENT		
								Year	County	No.
8864	1	Young, Jeff	41	First Named	38	M	1/16	1896	Sans Bois	14192
I.W.997	2	" Catherine	40	Wife	37	F	IW			
8865	3	" William B	19	Son	16	M	1/32	1896	" "	14193
8866	4	" Eli D	17	"	14	M	1/32	1896	" "	14194
8867	5	" Robert	15	"	12	M	1/32	1896	" "	14196
8868	6	" Matilda E	13	Dau	10	F	1/32	1896	" "	14197
8869	7	" Levi	7	Son	4	M	1/32		" "	
8870	8	" Lizzie	6	Dau	2	F	1/32		" "	
8871	9	" Jesse	4	Son	3mo	M	1/32		" "	
14786	10	" Dollis	2	Dau	2	F	1/32			
	11									
	12	ENROLLMENT OF NOS. ~~~ 2 ~~~~ HEREON APPROVED BY THE SECRETARY								
	13	OF INTERIOR OCT 21 1904								
	14									
	15	ENROLLMENT OF NOS. 1,3,4,5,6,7,8,9 HEREON								
	16	APPROVED BY THE SECRETARY								
	17	OF INTERIOR JAN 17 1903								

TRIBAL ENROLLMENT OF PARENTS

	Name of Father	Year	County	Name of Mother	Year	County
1	Ben Young	Dead	Non Citz	Elizabeth Young	1896	Sans Bois
2	Bill Warefield	"	" " "		Dead	Non Citz
3	No 1			No 2		
4	No 1			No 2		
5	No 1			No 2		
6	No 1	ENROLLMENT OF NOS 10 HEREON		No 2		
7	No 1	APPROVED BY THE SECRETARY		No 2		
8	No 1	OF INTERIOR MAY 20 1903		No 2		
9	No 1			No 2		
10	No 1			No 2		
11	No3 On 1896 roll as Will Young					
12	No4 " 1896 " Douglass Young					
13	No6 " 1896 " Martha Young					
14	No2 As to marriage of herself and Jeff see his testimony and that of Elizabeth Quinton					
15	Nos 8 and 9 Affidavit of birth to be supplied.				Date of Application for Enrollment.	
16	No10 Born Dec' 27' 1900: Evidence of Birth filed Dec' 23 1902				6/21/99	
17	PO Quinton I.T. 12/28/02		For child of No6 see NB (Apr 26'06) Card No 1300			

" now Russellville, I.T. 12/24/02   " " " Nos1&2 " " (Mar 3 '05) " " 646

Choctaw By Blood Enrollment Cards 1898-1914

RESIDENCE:	Sugar Loaf	COUNTY.			
POST OFFICE:	Le Flore I.T.				

Choctaw Nation

Choctaw Roll *(Not Including Freedmen)*

CARD NO. FIELD NO. **3027**

Dawes' Roll No.	NAME	Relationship to Person	AGE	SEX	BLOOD	TRIBAL ENROLLMENT		
						Year	County	No.
8872	1 Burns Henry F 30	First Named	27	M	1/2	1896	Sugar Loaf	810
8873	2 " Jane 26	Wife	23	F	1/4	1896	" "	811
8874	3 DIED PRIOR TO SEPTEMBER 25 1902 " William	Son	15mo	M	3/8		" "	
8875	4 " George Dewey 3	Son	3mo	M	3/8			
14787	5 " Robert Lee 1	Son	3mo	M	3/8			
	6							
	7							
	8					ENROLLMENT		
	9					OF NOS. 5 HEREON APPROVED BY THE SECRETARY		
	10					OF INTERIOR MAY 20 1903		
	11							
	12							
	13							
	14							
	15 ENROLLMENT OF NOS. 1,2,3, 4 HEREON							
	16 APPROVED BY THE SECRETARY							
	17 OF INTERIOR JAN 17 1903							

TRIBAL ENROLLMENT OF PARENTS

	Name of Father	Year	County	Name of Mother	Year	County
1	Buckner Burns	1896	Non Citz	Isabelle Burns	Dead	Sugar Loaf
2	Watty Winlock	1896	Sugar Loaf	Sally Winlock	"	Red River
3	No 1			No 2		
4	No 1			No 2		
5	No 1			No 2		
6						
7	No1 On 1896 roll as Henry Burns					
8	No3 Affidavit of birth to be supplied. Recd 11/1/99					
9	No5 born August 30 1902: enrolled December 1, 1902 No3 Died Oct 11th 1900. Proof of death filed Dec 23 1902					
10	No3 died Oct 11, 1900. Enrollment cancelled by Department July 8, 1904					
11						
12	No4 Enrolled June 25, 1900 For child of Nos 1&2 see NB (Apr 26-1906) Card #412					
13						
14						
15					Date of Application for Enrollment. 6/21/99	

27

Choctaw By Blood Enrollment Cards 1898-1914

RESIDENCE: Skullyville	COUNTY. **Choctaw Nation**	**Choctaw Roll** *(Not Including Freedmen)*	CARD No.
POST OFFICE: Lodi I.T.			FIELD No. 3028

Dawes' Roll No.	NAME		Relationship to Person	AGE	SEX	BLOOD	TRIBAL ENROLLMENT		
							Year	County	No.
8876	1 Jackson Robin	50	First Named	47	M	Full	1896	Skullyville	6466
8877	2 " Winey	48	Wife	45	F	"	1896	"	6467
8878	3 " Joseph	22	Son	19	M	"	1896	"	6469
8879	4 " Arthur	15	"	12	M	"	1896	"	6470
8880	5 " John	9	"	6	M	"	1896	"	6471
8881	6 Colbert Selena	18	Niece	15	F	"	P R 1893	Gaines	64
	7								
	8								
	9								
	10								
	11								
	12								
	13								
	14								
	15	ENROLLMENT OF NOS. 1,2,3,4,5,6 HEREON APPROVED BY THE SECRETARY OF INTERIOR JAN 17 1903							
	16								
	17								

TRIBAL ENROLLMENT OF PARENTS

	Name of Father	Year	County	Name of Mother	Year	County
1	William Jackson	Dead	Skullyville	Ona Jackson	Dead	Skullyville
2	"	"	Tobucksey[sic]		"	Gaines
3	No 1			Mollie Jackson	"	Skullyville
4	No 1			" "	"	"
5	No 1			" "	"	"
6	Reuben Colbert	Dead	Gaines	Sukey Colbert	"	Gaines
7						
8						

9	No1 On 1896 roll as Robert Jackson
10	No2 " 1896 " " Winnie Jackson
	No6 On page 7 No 64, 1893 Gaines Co. payroll as Lena Colbert
11	No.3 is now husband of Lizzie Jacob, Choc Card #2997
12	For child of No3 see NB (March 3, 1905) #970
13	" " " No6 " " " " " #1172
14	
15	
16	Date of Application for Enrollment. 6/21/99
17	

28

Choctaw By Blood Enrollment Cards 1898-1914

RESIDENCE:	Gaines	COUNTY.							CARD NO.	
POST OFFICE:	Wilburton, I.T.	**Choctaw Nation**				**Choctaw Roll** (Not Including Freedmen)			FIELD NO. 3029	

Dawes' Roll No.	NAME	Relationship to Person First Named	AGE	SEX	BLOOD	TRIBAL ENROLLMENT			
						Year	County		No.
8882	1 Adams, Willy 25	First Named	22	M	Full	1893	Gaines		20
	2								
	3								
	4								
	5								
	6								
	7								
	8								
	9								
	10								
	11								
	12								
	13								
	14								
	15								
	16								
	17								

ENROLLMENT OF NOS. 1 HEREON APPROVED BY THE SECRETARY OF INTERIOR JAN 17 1903

TRIBAL ENROLLMENT OF PARENTS

	Name of Father	Year	County	Name of Mother	Year	County
1	John Adams	Dead	Sugar Loaf	Seal Adams	Dead	Gaines
2						
3						
4						
5						
6						
7			First enrolled June 21/99 and re-enrolled			
8			Aug 2/99 and tribal enrollment changed			
9			by suggestion of Com. McKennon.			
10						
11						
12						
13						
14						
15					Date of Application for Enrollment	
16					June 21/99	
17						

RESIDENCE:	Sugar Loaf	COUNTY.							CARD NO.	
POST OFFICE:	Le Flore I.T.	**Choctaw Nation**					Choctaw Roll (Not Including Freedmen)		FIELD NO.	3030

Dawes' Roll No.	NAME		Relationship to Person	AGE	SEX	BLOOD	TRIBAL ENROLLMENT		
			First Named				Year	County	No.
8883	1 Jack Martin	31	First Named	28	M	Full	1896	Sugar Loaf	6528
8884	2 ~~Caroline~~ DIED PRIOR TO SEPTEMBER 25 1902		Wife	25	F	"	1896	" "	6529
8885	3 ~~Callie~~ DIED PRIOR TO SEPTEMBER 25 1902		Dau	9	F	"	1896	" "	6530
8886	4 ~~Rhoda~~ DIED PRIOR TO SEPTEMBER 25 1902		"	2	F	"		" "	
8887	5 " George	11	Neph	8	M	"	1896	" "	6540
	6								
	7								
	8								
	9								
	10								
	11								
	12								
	13								
	14								
	15	ENROLLMENT OF NOS. 1,2,3,4,5 ~~HEREON~~							
	16	APPROVED BY THE SECRETARY							
	17	OF INTERIOR JAN 17 1903							

TRIBAL ENROLLMENT OF PARENTS

	Name of Father	Year	County	Name of Mother	Year	County
1	Columbus Jack	Dead	Sugar Loaf	Winnie Jack	1896	Sugar Loaf
2	~~Josie~~	"	~~Miss~~	~~Stama~~	~~Dead~~	~~Miss~~
3	~~No 1~~			~~No 2~~		
4	~~No 1~~			~~No 2~~		
5	Jon Jack	Dead	Sugar Loaf	Mina Jack	Dead	Sugar Loaf
6						
7						
8	No 5 On 1896 roll as Georgia Jack					
9						
10	No 2 died Aug 12, 1901; proof of death filed Dec 19 1902					
11	~~No 3 " in 1900,~~					
	~~No 4 " in 1900; " " " " " "~~					
12	No.1 is now husband of Louisa Adams Choc. #2892					
13	~~No 2 died Aug 12, 1901; No 3 died - - 1901; No 4 died - - 1901; Enrollment cancelled by Department July 8, 1905~~					
14	For child of No.1 see NB (March 3, 1905) #1180					
15						
16					Date of Application for Enrollment.	6/21/99
17						

Choctaw By Blood Enrollment Cards 1898-1914

RESIDENCE:	Sans Bois	COUNTY.	**Choctaw Nation**		**Choctaw Roll**	CARD NO.	
POST OFFICE:	Stigler I.T.				*(Not Including Freedmen)*	FIELD NO.	**3031**

Dawes' Roll No.	NAME		Relationship to Person	AGE	SEX	BLOOD	TRIBAL ENROLLMENT		
							Year	County	No.
8888	1 Webster Wallen	29	First Named	26	M	Full	1896	Skullyville	12819
8889	2 ~~Minnie~~ DIED PRIOR TO SEPTEMBER 25, 1902		~~Wife~~	~~21~~	~~F~~	"	~~1896~~	"	~~12820~~
8890	3 " Daniel	5	Son	2	M	"			
	4								
	5								
	6								
	7								
	8								
	9								
	10								
	11								
	12								
	13								
	14								
	15	ENROLLMENT OF NOS. 1,2,3 HEREON APPROVED BY THE SECRETARY OF INTERIOR Jan 17 1903							
	16								
	17								

TRIBAL ENROLLMENT OF PARENTS

	Name of Father	Year	County	Name of Mother	Year	County
1	Jackson Webster	Dead	Sans Bois	Ana-yi-ma	Dead	Skullyville
2	~~Leonidas Thomas~~	~~1896~~	~~Skullyville~~	~~Sibbela Thomas~~	"	" "
3	No 1			No 2		
4						
5						
6						
7						
8	No2 died on last day of May, 1902: proof of death filed Dec 20 1902					
9	No.2 died May 31, 1902: Enrollment cancelled by Department Sept. 16, 1904					
10						
11						
12						
13						
14						
15				Date of Application for Enrollment.		
16						6/21/99
17						

RESIDENCE: Sugar Loaf COUNTY. **Choctaw Nation** **Choctaw Roll** CARD No.
POST OFFICE: Red Ok I.T. *(Not Including Freedmen)* FIELD No. 3032

Dawes' Roll No.	NAME		Relationship to Person First Named	AGE	SEX	BLOOD	TRIBAL ENROLLMENT		
							Year	County	No.
DEAD.	1 Loman Jack	DEAD		53	M	Full	1896	Sugar Loaf	7792
8891	2 " Sillis	50	Wife	47	F	"	1896	" "	7793
	3								
	4								
	5								
	6								
	7								
	8								
	9								
	10								
	11	No. 1 HEREON DISMISSED UNDER							
	12	ORDER OF THE COMMISSION TO THE FIVE							
	13	CIVILIZED TRIBES OF MARCH 31, 1905.							
	14								
	15	ENROLLMENT OF NOS. 2 HEREON							
	16	APPROVED BY THE SECRETARY OF INTERIOR JAN 17 1903							
	17								

TRIBAL ENROLLMENT OF PARENTS

	Name of Father	Year	County	Name of Mother	Year	County
1	Ey a ka tab e	Dead	Towson		Dead	Towson
2	Lewis Perry	"	Sugar Loaf	Pisa-chi-ho-na	"	Sugar Loaf
3						
4						
5						
6	No.1 Died June 10, 1900. Proof of death filed Dec 24 1902					
7						
8						
9						
10						
11						
12						
13						
14						Date of Application for Enrollment.
15						6/21/99
16						
17						

Choctaw By Blood Enrollment Cards 1898-1914

| RESIDENCE: Sugar Loaf | COUNTY. **Choctaw Nation** | | | **Choctaw Roll** *(Not Including Freedmen)* | | CARD NO. |
| POST OFFICE: Bengal I.T. | | | | | | FIELD NO. 3033 |

Dawes' Roll No.	NAME	Relationship to Person First Named	AGE	SEX	BLOOD	TRIBAL ENROLLMENT		
						Year	County	No.
I.W 1116	1 Ollar Sarah E. 41	Named	38	F	IW			
	2							
	3							
	4							
	5							
	6							
	7							
	8							
	9							
	10							
	11							
	12							
	13							
	14							
	15							
	16							
	17							

ENROLLMENT HEREON OF NOS. ~~ 1 ~~ APPROVED BY THE SECRETARY OF INTERIOR NOV 16 1904

TRIBAL ENROLLMENT OF PARENTS							
Name of Father	Year	County	Name of Mother		Year	County	
1 Jay Rice	Dead	Non Citz	Minerva Rice		Dead	Non Citz	
2							
3							
4							
5							
6							
7	Admitted by Dawes Commission as intermarried citizen						
8	Case No 1160						
9							
10							
11							
12							
13							
14						Date of Application for Enrollment.	
15							
16						6/21/99	
17							

Choctaw By Blood Enrollment Cards 1898-1914

RESIDENCE: Tobucksy COUNTY. **Choctaw Nation** **Choctaw Roll** CARD No.
POST OFFICE: So. McAlester I.T. *(Not Including Freedmen)* FIELD No. 3034

Dawes' Roll No.	NAME	Relationship to Person First Named	AGE	SEX	BLOOD	TRIBAL ENROLLMENT		
						Year	County	No.
✓ 1	Brazell Jennie	※	50	F	1/8			
✓ 2	" May	※ Dau	17	F	1/16			
3								
4								
5								
6								
7								
8								
9								
10								
11								
12								
13								
14								
15								
16								
17								

TRIBAL ENROLLMENT OF PARENTS

	Name of Father	Year	County	Name of Mother	Year	County
1	Cyrus Wilson	Dead	Miss	Sarah Wilson	1896	Non Citz
2	John H Brazell	189_	Non Citz	No 1		
3						
4						
5						
6						
7						
8	No 1&2 denied in 96 Case #6					
9	Nos 1 and 2 Admitted by U.S. Court So. McAlester Aug 24					
10	1896, Case No 96. As to residence see her testimony					
11	Nos 1&2 made by O.F.M.... Court 96					
12						
13						
14						
15					Date of Application for Enrollment.	
16					6/21/99	
17						

Choctaw By Blood Enrollment Cards 1898-1914

RESIDENCE: Sugar Loaf COUNTY.
POST OFFICE: Le Flore I.T.

Choctaw Nation

Choctaw Roll (Not Including Freedmen)

CARD NO.
FIELD NO. 3035

Dawes' Roll No.	NAME		Relationship to Person First Named	AGE	SEX	BLOOD	TRIBAL ENROLLMENT Year	County	No.
8892	1 Going Lilly	23	First Named	20	F	Full	P R 1893	Sugar Loaf	14
14788	2 McCurtain, Silas	2	Son	2	M	"			
	3								
	4								
	5								
	6								
	7								
	8								
	9								
	10								
	11								
	12								
	13								
	14								
	15								
	16								
	17								

ENROLLMENT
OF NOS. 2 HEREON
APPROVED BY THE SECRETARY
OF INTERIOR MAY 20 1903

ENROLLMENT
OF NOS. 1 HEREON
APPROVED BY THE SECRETARY
OF INTERIOR JAN 17 1903

TRIBAL ENROLLMENT OF PARENTS

	Name of Father	Year	County	Name of Mother	Year	County
1	Wilson Going	Dead	Sugar Loaf	Susan Amos	Dead	Sugar Loaf
2	Thomas McCurtain			Nº1		
3						
4						
5						
6		On page 2 No 14, 1893 P.R. Sugar Loaf Co				
7		Nº2 Born Nov. 4, 1900. Enrolled Dec. 24, 1902.				
8		For child of No.1 see NB (March 3, 1905) #1395				
9						
10						
11						
12						
13						
14					Date of Application for Enrollment.	
15					6/21/99	
16						
17						

Choctaw By Blood Enrollment Cards 1898-1914

Choctaw Nation

Choctaw Roll *(Not Including Freedmen)*

CARD NO.   FIELD NO. 3036

Dawes' Roll No.	NAME	Relationship to Person	AGE	SEX	BLOOD	TRIBAL ENROLLMENT Year	County	No.
8893	1 Jack, Winnie ⁷⁶	First Named	73	F	Full	1896	Sugar Loaf	6543
	2							
	3							
	4							
	5							
	6							
	7							
	8							
	9							
	10							
	11							
	12							
	13							
	14							
	15							
	16							
	17							

ENROLLMENT
OF NOS. 1 HEREON
APPROVED BY THE SECRETARY
OF INTERIOR JAN 17 1903

TRIBAL ENROLLMENT OF PARENTS

	Name of Father	Year	County	Name of Mother	Year	County
1	Pis-a-ta-e-ka	Dead	Miss	Sally	Dead	Miss
2						
3						
4						
5						
6						
7						
8						
9						
10						
11						
12						
13						
14						
15						
16						
17						

Date of Application for Enrollment. 6/21/99

Choctaw By Blood Enrollment Cards 1898-1914

RESIDENCE:	Sugar Loaf	COUNTY.	**Choctaw Nation**		**Choctaw Roll**	CARD NO.	
POST OFFICE:	Le Flore I.T.				*(Not Including Freedmen)*	FIELD NO.	3037

Dawes' Roll No.	NAME		Relationship to Person First Named	AGE	SEX	BLOOD	TRIBAL ENROLLMENT		
							Year	County	No.
8894	1 Baker Thompson	DIED PRIOR TO SEPTEMBER 25 1902		54	M	Full	1896	Sugar Loaf	772
8895	2 " Lucy	38	Wife	35	F	"	1896	" "	773
8896	3 David Viney	18	StepDau	15	F	"	1896	" "	774
8897	4 Baker Noel	9	Son	6	M	"	1896	" "	775
8898	5 " Mattie	7	Dau	4	F	"	1896	" "	777
8899	6 Isaac William	16	Neph	13	M	"	1896	" "	6251
8900	7 " Lela	14	Niece	11		"	1896	" "	6252
8901	8 Baker, Mary	1	dau	6wks	"	"			
	9								
	10								
	11								
	12								
	13								
	14								
	15	ENROLLMENT OF NOS. 1,2,3,4,5,6,7,8 HEREON							
	16	APPROVED BY THE SECRETARY							
	17	OF INTERIOR JAN 17 1903							

TRIBAL ENROLLMENT OF PARENTS

	Name of Father	Year	County	Name of Mother	Year	County
1	Wm Baker	Dead	Sugar Loaf	E-la-ti-ma	Dead	Miss
2	Noatimbe	1896	Miss		"	"
3	David	Dead	"	No 2		
4	No 1			No 2		
5	No 1			No 2		
6	Pasley Isaac	Dead	Sugar Loaf	Amy Isaac	Dead	Miss
7	" "	"	" "	" "	"	"
8	No1			No2		
9				No3 On 1896 roll as Besiny Baker		
10				No4 On 1896 roll as Noah Baker		
11	No1 Died November 26, 1899; proof of death filed Dec 19 1902					
12			Mary LeFlore Choctaw card #3045 is guardian of N°6 See copy of			
13			papers filed in Choctaw case #3045 Feby 3, 1903.			
14			Sidney Amos Choctaw card #3053 is guardian of N°7 See copy of			#1 to 7 inc
15	No1 died Nov 26, 1899. Enrollment cancelled by Department July 8. 1904			papers filed herein July 10, 1903		Date of Application for Enrollment.
16			For child of No3 see NB (Apr 26 '06) Card #155			6/21/99
17				No8 enrolled Dec 16/99		

Choctaw By Blood Enrollment Cards 1898-1914

RESIDENCE: Sugar Loaf COUNTY. **Choctaw Nation** Choctaw Roll CARD NO.
POST OFFICE: Le Flore I.T. (Not Including Freedmen) FIELD NO. 3038

Dawes' Roll No.	NAME		Relationship to Person	AGE	SEX	BLOOD	TRIBAL ENROLLMENT		
							Year	County	No.
8902	1 Baker Oscar	22	First Named	19	M	Full	1896	Sugar Loaf	769
	2								
	3								
	4								
	5								
	6								
	7								
	8								
	9								
	10								
	11								
	12								
	13								
	14								
	15								
	16								
	17								

ENROLLMENT
OF NOS. 1 HEREON
APPROVED BY THE SECRETARY
OF INTERIOR JAN 17 1903

TRIBAL ENROLLMENT OF PARENTS

	Name of Father	Year	County	Name of Mother	Year	County
1	Wm Baker	Dead	Sugar Loaf	Losen Jones	1896	Sugar Loaf
2						
3						
4						
5						
6	No1 is now husband of Melvina Sexton – Evidence of marriage to be supplied					
7						
8						
9						
10						
11						
12						
13						
14						
15						
16				Date of Application for Enrollment.	6/21/99	
17						

Choctaw By Blood Enrollment Cards 1898-1914

RESIDENCE: Sugar Loaf	COUNTY.	CARD NO.
POST OFFICE: Red Oak I.T.	**Choctaw Nation** Choctaw Roll (Not Including Freedmen)	FIELD NO. 3039

Dawes' Roll No.	NAME		Relationship to Person First Named	AGE	SEX	BLOOD	TRIBAL ENROLLMENT		
							Year	County	No.
8903	1 Wright Sampson	24	First Named	21	M	Full	1896	Sugar Loaf	12909
	2								
	3								
	4								
	5								
	6								
	7								
	8								
	9								
	10								
	11								
	12								
	13								
	14								
	15								
	16								
	17								

ENROLLMENT OF NOS. 1 HEREON APPROVED BY THE SECRETARY OF INTERIOR JAN 17 1903

TRIBAL ENROLLMENT OF PARENTS

Name of Father	Year	County	Name of Mother	Year	County
1 Simon Wright	Dead	Sugar Loaf	Sophy Wright	Dead	Sugar Loaf
2					
3					
4					
5		Also on 1896 roll, Page 339, No. 12924			
6		as Sampson S. Wright Sugar Loaf			
7					
8		No. 1 is now husband of Beney Harlin Choc. Card #970			
9		For child of No.1 see NB. (Apr 26, 1906) Card No. 109			
10		" " " " " (March 3,1905) " " 810			
11					
12					
13					
14					
15				Date of Application for Enrollment.	
16				6/21/99	
17					

RESIDENCE: Sugar Loaf COUNTY. **Choctaw Nation** Choctaw Roll CARD NO.
POST OFFICE: Red Oak I.T. (Not Including Freedmen) FIELD NO. 3040

Dawes' Roll No.	NAME	Relationship to Person First Named	AGE	SEX	BLOOD	TRIBAL ENROLLMENT		
						Year	County	No.
8904	1 Lewis Howard 31	First Named	28	M	1/4	1896	Sugar Loaf	7809
8905	2 " Marie 7	Dau	4	F	1/8	1896	" "	7810
	3							
	4							
	5							
	6							
	7							
	8							
	9							
	10							
	11							
	12							
	13							
	14							
	15	ENROLLMENT OF NOS. 1 and 2 HEREON						
	16	APPROVED BY THE SECRETARY OF INTERIOR JAN 17 1903						
	17							

TRIBAL ENROLLMENT OF PARENTS

	Name of Father	Year	County	Name of Mother	Year	County
1	Andrew Lewis	Dead	Non Citz	Lucinda Lewis	Dead	Atoka
2	No 1			Arie Lewis	1896	Non Citz
3						
4						
5						
6						
7			For child of No1 see NB (Mar 3-05) Card #204			
8						
9						
10						
11						
12						
13						
14						
15					Date of Application for Enrollment. 6/21/99	
16	P.O. LeFlore, I.T.					
17	PO Wynnewood I 10/05 No2 now living with Marie Arie Lazarus c/o Albert Lazarus Waldorf Astoria, N.Y.					

Choctaw By Blood Enrollment Cards 1898-1914

| RESIDENCE: Sugar Loaf | COUNTY. **Choctaw Nation** (Not Including Freedmen) | | | **Choctaw Roll** | | CARD No. | |
| POST OFFICE: Red Ok I.T. | | | | | | FIELD No. 3041 | |

Dawes' Roll No.	NAME	Relationship to Person First Named	AGE	SEX	BLOOD	TRIBAL ENROLLMENT Year	County	No.
8906	₁ Lewis William J 29	Named	26	M	1/4	1896	Sugar Loaf	7776
I.W.283	₂ " Myrtle ㉚	Wife	27	F	I.W.	1896	" "	14747
8907	₃ " Eden 6	Dau	3	F	1/8	1896	" "	7777
	₄							
	₅							
	₆							
	₇							
	₈							
	₉							
	₁₀							
	₁₁	ENROLLMENT						
	₁₂	OF NOS. 2 HEREON						
	₁₃	APPROVED BY THE SECRETARY OF INTERIOR SEP 12 1903						
	₁₄	ENROLLMENT						
	₁₅	OF NOS. 1 and 3 HEREON						
	₁₆	APPROVED BY THE SECRETARY OF INTERIOR JAN 17 1903						
	₁₇							

TRIBAL ENROLLMENT OF PARENTS

Name of Father	Year	County	Name of Mother	Year	County
₁ Andrew Lewis	Dead	Non Citz	Lucinda Lewis	Dead	Atoka
₂ Zebulon Duncan	"	" "	Mary E Duncan	1896	Non Citz
₃ No 1			No 2		
₄					
₅					
₆					
₇					
₈		No1 On 1896 roll as Wᵐ J. Lewis			
₉		No2 Evidence of marriage to be supplied. Recd 6/22/99			
₁₀					
₁₁					
₁₂					
₁₃					
₁₄					Date of Application for Enrollment
₁₅					
₁₆					6/21/99
₁₇ PO Wynnewood I T					

Choctaw By Blood Enrollment Cards 1898-1914

RESIDENCE: Sugar Loaf　COUNTY. **Choctaw Nation**　**Choctaw Roll** *(Not Including Freedmen)*　CARD No. FIELD NO. **3042**
POST OFFICE: Red Oak I.T.

Dawes' Roll No.	NAME	Relationship to Person First Named	AGE	SEX	BLOOD	TRIBAL ENROLLMENT Year	County	No.
8908	1 Sexton Melvina ³¹		28	F	3/4	1896	Wade	978
	2							
	3							
	4							
	5							
	6							
	7							
	8							
	9							
	10							
	11							
	12							
	13							
	14							
	15							
	16							
	17							

ENROLLMENT OF NOS. 1 HEREON APPROVED BY THE SECRETARY OF INTERIOR Jan 17 1903

TRIBAL ENROLLMENT OF PARENTS

Name of Father	Year	County	Name of Mother	Year	County
1 Jacob Sexton	Dead		Elsie Ann McKinney	Dead	Sans Bois
2					
3					
4					
5					
6					
7		On 1896 roll as Melvina Benton			
8					

Date of Application for Enrollment. 6/21/99

42

Choctaw By Blood Enrollment Cards 1898-1914

RESIDENCE:	Sugar Loaf	COUNTY.	**Choctaw Nation**	**Choctaw Roll**	CARD NO.
POST OFFICE:	Le Flore I.T.			(Not Including Freedmen)	FIELD NO. 3043

Dawes' Roll No.	NAME		Relationship to Person	AGE	SEX	BLOOD	TRIBAL ENROLLMENT		
							Year	County	No.
8909	1 Adams Thomas	27	First Named	24	M	Full	1896	Skullyville	38
	2								
	3								
	4								
	5								
	6								
	7								
	8								
	9								
	10								
	11								
	12								
	13								
	14								
	15								
	16								
	17								

ENROLLMENT
OF NOS. 1 HEREON
APPROVED BY THE SECRETARY
OF INTERIOR JAN 17 1903

TRIBAL ENROLLMENT OF PARENTS

Name of Father	Year	County	Name of Mother	Year	County
1 Sam Adams	Dead	Sugar Loaf	Sarah Adams	1896	Sugar Loaf
2					
3					
4					
5					
6					
7					
8	No.1 Now husband of Larinda Thomas No.2 on Choc Card #2944 12/16 '02				
9	For child of No1 see NB (March 3 1905) #1396				
10					
11					
12					
13					
14					
15					
16			Date of Application for Enrollment.	6/21/99	
17					

RESIDENCE:	Skullyville	COUNTY.	**Choctaw Nation**		**Choctaw Roll**	CARD NO.	
POST OFFICE:	Lodi I.T.				*(Not Including Freedmen)*	FIELD NO.	3044

Dawes' Roll No.	NAME		Relationship to Person	AGE	SEX	BLOOD	TRIBAL ENROLLMENT		
							Year	County	No.
8910	1 Gaines Thomas	40	First Named	37	M	Full	1896	Skullyville	4665
8911	2 DIED PRIOR TO SEPTEMBER 25 1902 Sillis		Wife	38	F	"	1896	"	4666
8912	3 " Wesley	18	Son	15	M	"	1896	"	4667
8913	4 " Israel	11	"	8	M	"	1896	"	4668
8914	5 " William	7	"	4	M	"	1896	"	4669
	6								
	7								
	8								
	9								
	10								
	11								
	12								
	13								
	14								
	15	ENROLLMENT OF NOS. 1,2,3,4,5 HEREON							
	16	APPROVED BY THE SECRETARY OF INTERIOR JAN 17 1903							
	17								

TRIBAL ENROLLMENT OF PARENTS

	Name of Father	Year	County	Name of Mother	Year	County
1	John Gaines	Dead	Skullyville	Wicey Gaines	Dead	Sans Bois
2	Chubbe	"	Sugar Loaf		"	Sugar Loaf
3	No 1			No 2		
4	No 1			No 2		
5	No 1			No 2		
6						
7						
8			No2 On 1896 roll as Sillen Gaines			
9			No2 Died January 1st 1901: Proof of death filed Dect 23rd 1902			
10						
11						
12						
13						
14						
15					Date of Application for Enrollment.	
16					6/21/99	
17						

44

Choctaw By Blood Enrollment Cards 1898-1914

RESIDENCE: Sugar Loaf	COUNTY. **Choctaw Nation**	**Choctaw Roll**	CARD No.
POST OFFICE: Le Flore I.T.		(Not Including Freedmen)	FIELD No. 3045

Dawes' Roll No.	NAME		Relationship to Person First Named	AGE	SEX	BLOOD	TRIBAL ENROLLMENT		
							Year	County	No.
8915	1 LeFlore Mary	72		69	F	Full	1896	Sugar Loaf	7802
	2								
	3								
	4								
	5								
	6								
	7								
	8								
	9								
	10								
	11								
	12								
	13								
	14								
	15	ENROLLMENT OF NOS. 1 HEREON APPROVED BY THE SECRETARY OF INTERIOR JAN 17 1903							
	16								
	17								

TRIBAL ENROLLMENT OF PARENTS

Name of Father	Year	County	Name of Mother	Year	County
1 Thomas LeFlore	Dead	Red River	Sha-ka-pa-ho-na	Dead	Sugar Loaf
2					
3					
4					
5					
6					
7					
8					
9					
10					
11					
12					
13					
14					
15					
16			Date of Application for Enrollment.	6/21/99	
17					

Nº1 is guardian of William Isaac on Choctaw card #3037 and of Selena Phillips on Choctaw card #969. See copy of papers issued by Sugar Loaf Co. Court, filed Feby 3, 1903.

Choctaw By Blood Enrollment Cards 1898-1914

RESIDENCE: Chickasaw Nation ~~COUNTY.~~ **Choctaw Nation**   Choctaw Roll   CARD NO.
POST OFFICE: Pauls Valley, I.T.   (Not Including Freedmen)   FIELD NO. 3046

Dawes' Roll No.	NAME	Relationship to Person	AGE	SEX	BLOOD	TRIBAL ENROLLMENT		
						Year	County	No.
8916	1 Riddle, Lorin A ³¹	First Named	28	M	1/2	1896	Tobucksy	10775
	2							
	3							
	4							
	5							
	6							
	7							
	8							
	9							
	10							
	11							
	12							
	13							
	14							
	15	ENROLLMENT OF NOS. 1 HEREON						
	16	APPROVED BY THE SECRETARY OF INTERIOR JAN 17 1903						
	17							

TRIBAL ENROLLMENT OF PARENTS

	Name of Father	Year	County	Name of Mother	Year	County
1	William Riddle	Dead	Chick Roll	Margaret Riddle	Dead	Gaines
2						
3						
4						
5						
6						
7						
8	On 1896 roll as Loring A Riddle					
9	For child of No.1 see NB (March 3 1905) #1362					
10						
11						
12						
13						
14					Date of Application for Enrollment.	
15						
16					6/21/99	
17						

Choctaw By Blood Enrollment Cards 1898-1914

RESIDENCE: Gaines   COUNTY. **Choctaw Nation**   Choctaw Roll   CARD NO.
POST OFFICE: Wilburton, I.T.   *(Not Including Freedmen)*   FIELD NO.   3047

Dawes' Roll No.	NAME	Relationship to Person First Named	AGE	SEX	BLOOD	TRIBAL ENROLLMENT Year	County	No.
DEAD	₁ Holson, Sampson	Named	33	M	Full	1896	Gaines	5316
I.W. 918	₂ " Texanna ㊵	Wife	37	F	I.W	1896	"	14608
8917	₃ " Charles R ⁷	Son	4	M	1/2	1896	"	5318
8918	₄ " James L ²	Son	1mo	M	1/2			
	₅							
	₆ No. 1 HEREON DISMISSED UNDER							
	₇ ORDER OF THE COMMISSION TO THE FIVE CIVILIZED TRIBES OF MARCH 31, 1905.							
	₈							
	₉ See Choctaw cards #D664, 665 and 666 for children of No 1 by marriage with Cherokee							
	₁₀ ENROLLMENT							
	₁₁ OF NOS. 2 HEREON APPROVED BY THE SECRETARY							
	₁₂ OF INTERIOR AUG 3 1904							
	₁₃							
	₁₄ ENROLLMENT OF NOS. 3 and 4 HEREON							
	₁₅ APPROVED BY THE SECRETARY OF INTERIOR JAN 17 1903							
	₁₆							
	₁₇ See Choctaw card #R135							

TRIBAL ENROLLMENT OF PARENTS

Name of Father	Year	County	Name of Mother	Year	County
Henry Holson	Dead	Sugar Leaf	Malinda Holson	Dead	Sugar Leaf
₂ C. Boling	"	Non Citz	Sarah Boling	"	Non Citz
₃ No1			No2		
₄ No.1			No.2		
₅					
₆					
₇					
₈					
₉ No1 on 1896 roll as Samson Holson					
₁₀ No2 " 1896 " " Texannah "			Certified copy of divorce proceedings		
₁₁ No3 " 1896 " " Chas R "			between Nº1 and his former wife Sallie Holson, filed Jany. 21, 1903		
₁₂ As to marriage, see testimony of No1					
₁₃ Additional testimony to be supplied:				#1 to 3	
₁₄ Recd Aug 4/99 in testimony of Louis Rockett, which see[sic]				Date of Application for Enrollment.	
₁₅ No.4 Enrolled Aug 6th, 1900				6/22/99	
₁₆ 6/23/02 No.1 died Dec. 9, 1901 See testimony of No2 this date					
₁₇					

RESIDENCE: Sans Bois   COUNTY. **Choctaw Nation**   **Choctaw Roll**   CARD NO.
POST OFFICE: Garland, I.T.   *(Not Including Freedmen)*   FIELD NO. **3048**

Dawes' Roll No.	NAME	Relationship to Person First Named	AGE	SEX	BLOOD	TRIBAL ENROLLMENT		
						Year	County	No.
1	Sanders, Arty M		65	F	1/4			
2								
3								
4								
5								
6								
7								
8								
9								
10								
11								
12								
13								
14								
15								
16								
17								

TRIBAL ENROLLMENT OF PARENTS

	Name of Father	Year	County	Name of Mother	Year	County
1	Wilson Nichols	Dead	Non Citz	Delitha Nichols	Dead	Choctaw
2						
3						
4						
5						
6						
7						
8						
9						
10						
11						
12						
13						
14						
15						
16						
17						

No1 denied in 96 Case #1418
Admitted by U.S. Court, Southern District
Dec 20/97, Case No 96, as Orty Mincy
Sanders
As to residence, see her testimony
Judgment of U.S. C[ourt] [admit]ting No1 vacated and set aside by Decree of Choctaw Chickasaw Cit Court Decr 17/02
Not now in CCC C [case] #[...]
[illegible]

NOV 29 1904

DENIED CITIZENSHIP BY THE CHOCTAW AND CHICKASAW CITIZENSHIP COURT

Date of Application for Enrollment.
6/22/99

Choctaw By Blood Enrollment Cards 1898-1914

RESIDENCE:	Skullyville	COUNTY.								
POST OFFICE:	Bokoshe, I.T.								CARD NO. FIELD NO.	3049

Choctaw Nation   **Choctaw Roll** *(Not Including Freedmen)*

Dawes' Roll No.	NAME	Relationship to Person First Named	AGE	SEX	BLOOD	TRIBAL ENROLLMENT Year	County	No.
1	Reynolds, Amanda M	Named	33	F	1/8			
2								
3								
4								
5								
6								
7								
8								
9								
10								
11								
12								
13								
14								
15								
16								
17								

NOV 29 1904

TRIBAL ENROLLMENT OF PARENTS

	Name of Father	Year	County	Name of Mother	Year	County
1	Newton Sanders	1896	Non Citz	Arty M Sanders	1896	Sans Bois
2						
3						
4						
5						
6	No1 denied in 96 Case #1418					
7	No1 now in C.C.C.C. Case #73T					
8	Admitted by U.S. Court Southern					
9	District Dec. 20/97, Case No 96 as					
10	Amanda Minerva Reynolds					
11	Came to Territory December 18, 1896					
	see her testimony					
12	Judgment No1 of U.S. Court finding not vacated and set aside by Decree of Choctaw Chickasaw Circuit Court Dec 1/98					
13	Above note as to admission is error; No1 admitted as above stated, as Amanda Minirva Sanders					
14	No1 also made separate application to Dawes Commission in 1896, as Amanda M Reynolds, Choctaw case #674; denied; no appeal					
15					Date of Application for Enrollment.	
16					6/22/99	
17						

DENIED CITIZENSHIP BY THE CHOCTAW AND CHICKASAW CITIZENSHIP COURT

49

Choctaw By Blood Enrollment Cards 1898-1914

RESIDENCE: Sugar Loaf COUNTY. **Choctaw Nation** Choctaw Roll CARD No.
POST OFFICE: Le Flore I.T. *(Not Including Freedmen)* FIELD No. 3050

Dawes' Roll No.	NAME		Relationship to Person	AGE	SEX	BLOOD	TRIBAL ENROLLMENT		
							Year	County	No.
8919	1 John, Silman	39	First Named	36	M	Full	1896	Sugar Loaf	6533
8920	2 " Ellen	30	Wife	27	F	"	1896	" "	6250
8921	3 " Sissie	19	Dau	16	F	"	1896	" "	6535
8922	4 " Fannie	16	Dau	13	F	"	PR 1893	Sugar Loaf	394
8923	5 Isaac Lewis DIED PRIOR TO SEPTEMBER 25, 1902		StepSon	5	M	"	1896	" "	6253
8924	6 Benton Elie	15	Ward	12	M	"	1896	" "	820
8925	7 John Nora	1	Dau	2mo	F	"			
	8								
	9								
	10								
	11								
	12								
	13								
	14								
	15	ENROLLMENT OF NOS. 1,2,3,4,5,6,7 HEREON							
	16	APPROVED BY THE SECRETARY							
	17	OF INTERIOR JAN 17 1903							

TRIBAL ENROLLMENT OF PARENTS

	Name of Father	Year	County	Name of Mother	Year	County
1	Riley John	Dead	Miss	Nancy John	1896	Miss
2	Willis Sockey	"	"	Martha Sockey	1896	"
3	No 1			Mealy John	Dead	"
4	No 1			" "	"	"
5	Pusley Isaac	Dead	Sugar Loaf	No 2		
6	Thomas Benton	"	" "	Lizzie Benton	"	Sugar Loaf
7	No. 1			No. 2		
8						
9						
10			No2 On 1896 roll as Ellen Isaac			
11			No5 " 1896 " " Lanay "			
			No4 " Page 39 No 394, 1893 Sugar Loaf Co. as Fannie Jimmie			
12			No6 " 1896 roll as Nellie Benton			
13			No4 Also on 1896 roll, Choctaw Nation, page 160, No 6527			
			No7 Enrolled Oct 16th 1900.			
14			N°5 Died in Feby. 1902, proof of death filed Jany 5, 1903.			
15	No5 died Feb - 1902				Date of Application for Enrollment.	
16			For child of No.3 see NB (March 3, 1905) #1433		6/22/99	
17						

Hughes or [Illegible] IT 11/1/04

50

Choctaw By Blood Enrollment Cards 1898-1914

RESIDENCE: Sugar Loaf COUNTY.		Choctaw Nation				Choctaw Roll (Not Including Freedmen)		CARD NO.	
POST OFFICE: Le Flore I.T.								FIELD NO. 3051	

Dawes' Roll No.	NAME	Relationship to Person First Named	AGE	SEX	BLOOD	TRIBAL ENROLLMENT		
						Year	County	No.
8926	1 Sexton Amos DIED PRIOR TO SEPTEMBER 25 1902		35	M	Full	1896	Sugar Loaf	65
	2							
	3							
	4							
	5							
	6							
	7							
	8							
	9							
	10							
	11							
	12							
	13							
	14							
	15	ENROLLMENT OF NOS. 1 HEREON APPROVED BY THE SECRETARY OF INTERIOR JAN 17 1903						
	16							
	17							

TRIBAL ENROLLMENT OF PARENTS

	Name of Father	Year	County	Name of Mother	Year	County
1	Amos Sexton	1896	Sugar Loaf	Nitcey Sexton	Dead	Sugar Loaf
2						
3						
4						
5						
6	No1 admitted by act of Choctaw Council of October 30, 1890					
7						
8	On 1896 roll as Sexton Amos.					
9	No1 died Feb. 18, 1900. Enrollment cancelled by Department July 8, 1904					
10						
11						
12						
13						
14						
15	See card 2939 for child of No.1. Sidney Amos says correct name				Date of Application for Enrollment.	
16	is Sexton Amos. See copy of letter of Nov. 22, 1902, filed herein.				6/22/99	
17						

51

RESIDENCE:	Sugar Loaf	COUNTY.				Choctaw Roll		CARD NO.
POST OFFICE:	Le Flore I.T.	**Choctaw Nation**				(Not Including Freedmen)		FIELD NO. 3052

Dawes' Roll No.	NAME	Relationship to Person First Named	AGE	SEX	BLOOD	TRIBAL ENROLLMENT		
						Year	County	No.
8927	1 Hickman Cornelius H [51]	Named	48	M	Full	1896	Sugar Loaf	5254
8928	2 " Eliza A [39]	Wife	36	F	"	1896	" "	5255
8929	3 " Jeff [15]	Son	12	M	"	1896	" "	5256
8930	4 " Ernest [12]	Son	9	M	"	1896	" "	5257
	5							
	6							
	7							
	8							
	9							
	10							
	11							
	12							
	13							
	14							
	15	ENROLLMENT OF NOS. 1,2,3,4 HEREON APPROVED BY THE SECRETARY OF INTERIOR JAN 17 1903						
	16							
	17							

TRIBAL ENROLLMENT OF PARENTS

Name of Father	Year	County	Name of Mother	Year	County
1 Fe-le-ma-cha-be	Dead	Miss	Fa-la-mat-e-ma	Dead	Miss
2 Mat Sockey	"	Sugar Loaf	Miney Sockey	1896	Sugar Loaf
3 No 1			No 2		
4 No 1			No 2		
5					
6					
7					
8	No1 On 1896 roll as C. H. Hickman				
9	No2 " 1896 " " Liza Ann "				
10					
11	Nos 1,2 and 3 admitted by act of Choctaw Council of April 9, 1891				
12					
13					
14				Date of Application for Enrollment.	
15					
16				6/22/99	
17					

Choctaw By Blood Enrollment Cards 1898-1914

RESIDENCE: Sugar Loaf COUNTY. **Choctaw Nation** Choctaw Roll (Not Including Freedmen)	CARD No. FIELD No. 3053

Dawes' Roll No.	NAME		Relationship to Person First Named	AGE	SEX	BLOOD	TRIBAL ENROLLMENT		
							Year	County	No.
8931	1 Amos Sidney	33		30	M	Full	P.R. 1893	Sugar Loaf	16
8932	2 DIED PRIOR TO SEPTEMBER 25 1902 " Nellie		Wife	22	F	"	1896	" "	819
8933	3 " Tecumseh	11	Son	8	M	"	P.R. 1893	" "	18
8934	4 Benton James	9	StepSon	6	M	"	1896	" "	821
8935	5 " Jacob	5	" "	2	M	"			
	6								
	7								
	8								
	9								
	10								
	11								
	12								
	13								
	14								
	15	ENROLLMENT OF NOS. 1,2,3,4,5 HEREON							
	16	APPROVED BY THE SECRETARY OF INTERIOR JAN 17 1903							
	17								

TRIBAL ENROLLMENT OF PARENTS

	Name of Father	Year	County	Name of Mother	Year	County
1	Jim Amos	1896	Sugar Loaf	Nancy Amos	Dead	Sugar Loaf
2	Columbus Jack	Dead	" "	Winnie Jack	1896	" "
3	No 1			Jinny Amos	Dead	" "
4	Thomas Benton	Dead	Sugar Loaf	No 2		
5	" "	"	" "	No 2		
6						
7						
8	No1 On page 2 No 16, 1893 P.R. Sugar Loaf Co					
9	No2 " 1896 roll as Nellie Benton					
10	No3 " Page 2 No 18, 1893 P.R. Sugar Loaf Co					
	No1 on 1896 roll, Page 160, No 6524 as Sidney James					
11	No3 " 1896 " " 160 " 6525 " Tecumseh "					
12						
13						
14	N°1 is legal guardian of Lela Isaac on Choctaw card #3037 July 10, 1903					
15	No2 died Feb 14, 1902. Enrollment cancelled by Department July 8, 1904				Date of Application for Enrollment	
16					6/22/99	
17						

Choctaw By Blood Enrollment Cards 1898-1914

RESIDENCE:	Sugar Loaf	COUNTY.	**Choctaw Nation**	Choctaw Roll	CARD NO.	
POST OFFICE:	Le Flore, I.T.			(Not Including Freedmen)	FIELD NO.	3054

Dawes' Roll No.		NAME	Relationship to Person First Named	AGE	SEX	BLOOD	TRIBAL ENROLLMENT		
							Year	County	No.
8936	1	Amos, Jimmie ~~DIED PRIOR TO SEPTEMBER 25 1902~~	First Named	61	M	Full	1896	Sugar Loaf	6526
8937	2	" Emily ²⁵	Dau	22	F	"	1893	" "	393
	3								
	4								
	5								
	6								
	7								
	8								
	9								
	10								
	11								
	12								
	13								
	14								
	15	ENROLLMENT OF NOS. 1 and 2 HEREON							
	16	APPROVED BY THE SECRETARY OF INTERIOR JAN 17 1903							
	17								

TRIBAL ENROLLMENT OF PARENTS

	Name of Father	Year	County	Name of Mother	Year	County
1	Amos	Dead	in Mississippi	Wa-ka-ya-huna	Dead	in Mississippi
2	No 1			Nancy Amos	"	Sugar Loaf
3						
4						
5						
6						
7						
8						
9	No1 on 1896 roll as Amos James					
10	No2 " 1893 Pay Roll Sugar Loaf Co, Page 39, No 393					
11	as Emily Jimmie					
12	No2 also on 1896 roll Page 21, No 814, as					
13	Emily Billy, Sugar Loaf Co					
14	~~No1 died Aug 29, 1900; Enrollment cancelled by Department July 8, 1904~~					
15	~~No2 "Died prior to September 25, 1902, not entitled to allotment." Indian Office letter of August 29, 1907 (I.T. 59759 1907)~~					
16				Date of Application for Enrollment.	6/22/99	
17						

54

| RESIDENCE: | Tobucksy | COUNTY. | | | | | | | | |
| POST OFFICE: | McAlester, I.T. | | | | | | | | | |

Choctaw Nation — Choctaw Roll *(Not Including Freedmen)*

CARD NO. FIELD NO. **3055**

Dawes' Roll No.	NAME	Relationship to Person First Named	AGE	SEX	BLOOD	TRIBAL ENROLLMENT		
						Year	County	No.
8938 ₁	Ainsworth Napoleon ⁴⁶	First Named	43	M	1/4	1896	Tobucksy	96
I.W. 825 ₂	" Nora W ⁴⁵	Wife	42	F	IW			
8939 ₃	" Ben P ¹⁸	Son	15	M	1/8	1896	Tobucksy	97
8940 ₄	" Helen ¹⁵	Dau	13	F	1/8	1896	"	98
8941 ₅	" Agnes ¹⁴	"	11	"	1/8	1896	"	99
₆								
₇								
₈								
₉								
₁₀								
₁₁	ENROLLMENT							
₁₂	OF NOS. 2 HEREON APPROVED BY THE SECRETARY							
₁₃	OF INTERIOR MAY 21 1904							
₁₄								
₁₅	ENROLLMENT OF NOS. 1, 3, 4, 5 HEREON							
₁₆	APPROVED BY THE SECRETARY							
₁₇	OF INTERIOR JAN 17 1903							

TRIBAL ENROLLMENT OF PARENTS

	Name of Father	Year	County	Name of Mother	Year	County
₁	John G. Ainsworth	Dead	Non Citz	Martha Ainsworth	Dead	Skullyville
₂	James Thompson	"	" "	Helen N.J. Thompson	"	Non Citz
₃	No1			Emily K Ainsworth	"	" " "
₄	No1			" " "	"	" " "
₅	No1			" " "	"	" " "
₆						
₇						
₈						
₉						
₁₀	No1 on 1896 roll as N. B. Ainsworth					
₁₁						
₁₂	No2 Evidence of marriage to be supplied. Recd July 27/99					
₁₃	Evidence of marriage of parents of No3,					
₁₄	4-5 to be supplied: Recd July 27/99					
₁₅					Date of Application for Enrollment.	
₁₆					6/22/99	
₁₇						

RESIDENCE: Sans Bois   COUNTY. **Choctaw Nation**   Choctaw Roll   CARD NO.
POST OFFICE: Sans Bois I.T.   *(Not Including Freedmen)*   FIELD NO. 3056

Dawes' Roll No.	NAME	Relationship to Person First Named	AGE	SEX	BLOOD	TRIBAL ENROLLMENT		
						Year	County	No.
8942	1 McCurtain David C ²⁹	Named	26	M	1/2	1896	Skullyville	9060
8943	2 " Kate N ²⁷	Wife	24	F	1/4	1896	Skullyville	9061
8944	3 " Ewart P. ³	Son	3wks	M	3/8			
8945	4 " Juanita Jeanetta ¹	Dau	1mo	F	3/8			
	5							
	6							
	7							
	8							
	9							
	10							
	11							
	12							
	13							
	14							
	15	ENROLLMENT OF NOS. 1,2,3,4 HEREON						
	16	APPROVED BY THE SECRETARY						
	17	OF INTERIOR JAN 17 1903						

TRIBAL ENROLLMENT OF PARENTS

	Name of Father	Year	County	Name of Mother	Year	County
1	Green McCurtain	1896	Sans Bois	M.A. Ainsworth	1896	Non Citz
2	Ely E. Mitchell	1896	Skullyville	S.E. Mitchell	1896	" "
3	No 1			No 2		
4	No. 1			No. 2		
5						
6						
7						
8						
9						
10	No1 On 1896 roll as D. C. McCurtain					
11	No2 " 1896 " " Kate M McCurtain As to evidence of mar-					
12	riage of father and mother see card of Ely E. Mitchell Card					
13	No 2448 As to marriage of father and mother see testimony					
14	of G. W. Dukes					
15	No.4 Enrolled Aug 29, 1901					
16	For child of Nos 1&2 see NB (Mar 3-05) Card #136			#1 to 3		
17				Date of Application for Enrollment.	6/22/99	

56

Choctaw By Blood Enrollment Cards 1898-1914

RESIDENCE: Sugar Loaf	COUNTY. **Choctaw Nation**	**Choctaw Roll** (Not Including Freedmen)	CARD NO.
POST OFFICE: Le Flore I.T.			FIELD NO. 3057

Dawes' Roll No.	NAME	Relationship to Person First Named	AGE	SEX	BLOOD	TRIBAL ENROLLMENT		
						Year	County	No.
8946	1 Lewis Sallie 64	First Named	61	F	Full	1896	Sugar Loaf	7820
	2							
	3							
	4							
	5							
	6							
	7							
	8							
	9							
	10							
	11							
	12							
	13							
	14							
	15 ENROLLMENT OF NOS. 1 HEREON							
	16 APPROVED BY THE SECRETARY							
	17 OF INTERIOR JAN 17 1903							

TRIBAL ENROLLMENT OF PARENTS

	Name of Father	Year	County	Name of Mother	Year	County
1		Dead	Miss	Is-pal-le	Dead	Sugar Loaf
2						
3						
4						
5						
6			On 1896 roll as Sully Lewis			
7						
8						
9						
10						
11						
12						
13						
14						Date of Application for Enrollment.
15						
16						6/22/99
17						

Choctaw By Blood Enrollment Cards 1898-1914

RESIDENCE: Sugar Loaf COUNTY. Choctaw Nation Choctaw Roll CARD No.
POST OFFICE: Le Flore, I.T. (Not Including Freedmen) FIELD NO. 3058

Dawes' Roll No.	NAME		Relationship to Person First Named	AGE	SEX	BLOOD	TRIBAL ENROLLMENT		
							Year	County	No.
8947	1 Joel, Henry	44	First Named	41	M	Full	1893	Sugar Loaf	356
8948	2 " Sillis	53	Wife	50	F	"	1893	" "	357
	3								
	4								
	5								
	6								
	7								
	8								
	9								
	10								
	11								
	12								
	13								
	14								
	15								
	16								
	17								

ENROLLMENT
OF NOS. 1 and 2 HEREON
APPROVED BY THE SECRETARY
OF INTERIOR JAN 17 1903

TRIBAL ENROLLMENT OF PARENTS

	Name of Father	Year	County	Name of Mother	Year	County
1	William Joel	Dead	Sugar Loaf	O-lubbee	Dead	Skullyville
2	E-thla-pa-humo	"	" "	E-ma-ho-tema	"	Sugar Loaf
3						
4						
5						
6						
7						
8						
9						
10						
11						
12						
13						
14						
15					Date of Application for Enrollment.	
16					6/22/99	
17						

58

Choctaw By Blood Enrollment Cards 1898-1914

| RESIDENCE: Sugar Loaf | COUNTY. | **Choctaw Nation** | | Choctaw Roll | CARD No. |
| POST OFFICE: Le Flore I.T. | | | (Not Including Freedmen) | | FIELD No. 3059 |

Dawes' Roll No.	NAME		Relationship to Person	AGE	SEX	BLOOD	TRIBAL ENROLLMENT		
							Year	County	No.
8949	1 Blue William	63	First Named	62	M	1/2	1896	Sugar Loaf	778
8950	2 " George	24	Son	21	M	3/4	1896	" "	779
I.W. 1318	3 " Rhoda	24	Wife of No.2	24	F	I.W.			
16206	4 Isaac, Boe		Son of No.3	5	M	1/2			
	5								
	6								
	7	ENROLLMENT OF NOS. 4 HEREON APPROVED BY THE SECRETARY OF INTERIOR MAR 4- 1907							
	8								
	9								
	10								
	11	ENROLLMENT OF NOS. 3 HEREON APPROVED BY THE SECRETARY OF INTERIOR MAR 14 1905							
	12								
	13								
	14								
	15	ENROLLMENT OF NOS. 1 and 2 HEREON APPROVED BY THE SECRETARY OF INTERIOR JAN 17 1903							
	16								
	17								

TRIBAL ENROLLMENT OF PARENTS

	Name of Father	Year	County	Name of Mother	Year	County
1		Dead	Miss	Ali-ho-ke	Dead	Bok Tuklo
2	No 1			Lucy Blue	"	Gaines
3	John Scott		non citz	Tevet Scott		non citz
4	Presley Isaac			No 3		
5						
6	No4 transferred from Choctaw NB (Act of March 3,1905) #1535 Feb 18,1907 See decision					
7	Nos. 2 and 3 were married May 3, 1900			of that date.		
8	No.3 originally opted for enrollment on Choctaw card D-952 Dec. 17, 1902:					
9	transferred to this card Jan 29, 1905. See decision of Jan. 13, 1905					
10	For child of No3 see NB (Mar 3-1905) #1535					
11						
12	No4 is son of Presley Isaac a citizen by blood of Choctaw Nation					
13	now deceased whose name appears at No. 6249					
	1896 Choctaw Census Roll, Sugar Loaf Co.					
14	No4 born Jan. 21, 1897					
15						
16				Date of Application for Enrollment.	6/22/99	
17						

59

RESIDENCE: Sugar Loaf	COUNTY.							
POST OFFICE: Le Flore I.T.		Choctaw Nation			Choctaw Roll (Not Including Freedmen)		CARD No. FIELD No. 3060	

Dawes' Roll No.	NAME	Relationship to Person	AGE	SEX	BLOOD	TRIBAL ENROLLMENT		
						Year	County	No.
8951	1 Lewis Adeline 26	First Named	23	F	3/4	1896	Sugar Loaf	5220
8952	2 Jones Frank 8	Son	5	M	7/8	1896	" "	6501
8953	3 Hudson Rosa 5	Dau	2	F	5//8		" "	
~~8954~~	~~4 DIED PRIOR TO SEPTEMBER 25, 1902 William~~	~~Son~~	~~2mo~~	~~M~~	~~5/8~~			
15048	5 Lewis, Lemon 1	Son	3mo	M	7/8			
	6							
	7							
	8							
	9							
	10							
	11	ENROLLMENT						
	12	OF NOS. ~ 5 ~ HEREON APPROVED BY THE SECRETARY						
	13	OF INTERIOR FEB 16 1904						
	14							
	15	ENROLLMENT OF NOS. 1,2,3,4 HEREON						
	16	APPROVED BY THE SECRETARY						
	17	OF INTERIOR JAN 17 1903						

TRIBAL ENROLLMENT OF PARENTS

	Name of Father	Year	County	Name of Mother	Year	County
1	William Blue	1896	Sugar Loaf	Lucy Blue	Dead	Gaines
2	Mallison Jones	1896	" "	No 1		
3	Charley Hudson	"	" "	No 1		
4	" "	"	" "	~~No. 1~~		
5	Alex. J Lewis	"	" "	No. 1		
6						
7						
8						
9	For child of No1 see NB (Apr 26-06) Card #850					
10	No1 is the wife of Alexander J Lewis on Choctaw card #2957:					
11	evidence of marriage filed Sept 15, 1902					
	~~No.5 born June 30, 1902: application made and proof of~~					
12	birth filed Sept 15, 1902: transferred to this card from					
13	Choctaw card #675, Oct. 27, 1903					
14	No 4 died Dec. 19, 1900: Enrollment cancelled by Department July 8, 1904				#1 to 3	
15	No.4 Enrolled June 25, 1900				Date of Application for Enrollment.	
	Nº4 Died Dec. 19, 1900, proof of death filed Dec 31 1902					
16	No1 Change of surname from Hudson to Lewis authorized by				6/22/99	
17	the Department November 28, 1903 (D.C. #33289-1903)					

Choctaw By Blood Enrollment Cards 1898-1914

RESIDENCE:	Sugar Loaf	COUNTY.	**Choctaw Nation**		**Choctaw Roll**	CARD NO.	
POST OFFICE:	Le Flore, I.T.				(Not Including Freedmen)	FIELD NO.	3061

Dawes' Roll No.	NAME		Relationship to Person First Named	AGE	SEX	BLOOD	TRIBAL ENROLLMENT		
							Year	County	No.
8955	Lewis, Alamus	DIED PRIOR TO SEPTEMBER 25 1902		26	M	Full	1896	Sugar Loaf	7818
8956	" Lena	22	Wife	19	F	"	1896	" "	77
3									
4									
5									
6									
7									
8									
9									
10									
11									
12									
13									
14									
15	ENROLLMENT OF NOS. 1 and 2 HEREON APPROVED BY THE SECRETARY OF INTERIOR JAN 17 1903								
16									
17									

TRIBAL ENROLLMENT OF PARENTS

	Name of Father	Year	County	Name of Mother	Year	County
1	John Lewis	Dead	Sugar Loaf	Sallie Lewis	1896	Sugar Loaf
2	Richard Anderson	"	" "	Mary A Anderson	Dead	" "
3						
4						
5						
6						
7	No1 on 1896 roll as Alimos Lewis					
8	No2 " 1896 " " Lena Anderson					
9	No1 died Feb 2, 1901; proof of death filed Dec 19 1902					
10	No1 died Feb 2, 1901. Enrollment cancelled by Department July 8, 1904					
11	For child of No2 see NB (Mar 3-1905) Card #205					
12						
13						
14						
15				Date of Application for Enrollment		
16				6/22/99		
17	P.O. Lodi, IT					

61

Choctaw By Blood Enrollment Cards 1898-1914

RESIDENCE: Sugar Loaf COUNTY. **Choctaw Nation** **Choctaw Roll** CARD NO.
POST OFFICE: Monroe, I.T. 1/30/05 (Not Including Freedmen) FIELD NO. 3062

Dawes' Roll No.	NAME		Relationship to Person	AGE	SEX	BLOOD	TRIBAL ENROLLMENT		
							Year	County	No.
15676	1 Moore, Maud	20	First Named	17	F	1/8			
	2								
	3								
	4								
	5								
	6								
	7								
	8	Take no further action in enrollment of No 1							
	9	Protest of Attys for Choctaw and Chickasaw							
	10	Nations Jan 23 '04							
	11	Protest over ruled: see Departmental letter of March 31, 1904							
	12								
	13								
	14								
	15	ENROLLMENT OF NOS. 1 HEREON							
	16	APPROVED BY THE SECRETARY							
	17	OF INTERIOR DEC -2 1904							

TRIBAL ENROLLMENT OF PARENTS

	Name of Father	Year	County	Name of Mother	Year	County
1	Henry Killen	Dead	Choctaw	Elizabeth Killen		white woman
2						
3						
4						
5						
6						
7			See decision in Choctaw jacket #5367			
8			Mother of No1 on Choctaw card #5367			
9			Admitted by Dawes Commission, Case No 999. No appeal.			
10						
11						
12						
13						
14						
15						
16	PO Comanche I.T. 3/21/06					
17	P.O. Heavener, I.T. 12/17/03					

See Choctaw 6367

62

Choctaw By Blood Enrollment Cards 1898-1914

RESIDENCE: Sugar Loaf COUNTY. **Choctaw Nation** Choctaw Roll CARD NO.
POST OFFICE: Heavener, I.T. *(Not Including Freedmen)* FIELD NO. 3063

Dawes' Roll No.	NAME	Relationship to Person	AGE	SEX	BLOOD	TRIBAL ENROLLMENT		
						Year	County	No.
15677	1 Moore, Malinda 22	First Named	19	F	1/8			
15836	2 " , Floyd S	Son	3	M	1/16			
15837	3 " , Maud Alleen	Dau	1	F	1/16			
	4							
	5							
	6							
	7							
	8							
	9							
	10							
	11							
	12							
	13							
	14							
	15							
	16							
	17							

ENROLLMENT
OF NOS. ~ 2 and 3 ~ HEREON
APPROVED BY THE SECRETARY
OF INTERIOR JUN 12 1905

ENROLLMENT
OF NOS. ~ 1 ~ HEREON
APPROVED BY THE SECRETARY
OF INTERIOR DEC -2 1904

TRIBAL ENROLLMENT OF PARENTS

Name of Father	Year	County	Name of Mother	Year	County
1 Henry Killen	Dead	Choctaw	Elizabeth Killen		white woman
2 Elzie W. Moore		Non citizen	No 1		
3 " " "		" "	No 1		
4					
5					
6 See decision in Choctaw jacket #5367					
7 Mother of No1 on Choctaw card #5367					
8 Admitted by Dawes Commission Case No 999					
9 as Malinda Killen. No appeal.					
9 No2 was born Nov. 13, 1899					
10 No3 " " Aug 30, 1901					
11 Application for enrollment of Nos 2 and 3 received and their					
names placed on this card April 18, 1905, under Act of Congress					
12 approved March 3, 1905					
13					
14					
15			Date of Application for Enrollment.		
16			6/22/99		
17					

See Choctaw 5367

63

Choctaw By Blood Enrollment Cards 1898-1914

RESIDENCE: Sugar Loaf COUNTY. **Choctaw Nation** Choctaw Roll CARD No.
POST OFFICE: Monroe, I.T. (Not Including Freedmen) FIELD No. 3064

Dawes' Roll No.	NAME	Relationship to Person	AGE	SEX	BLOOD	TRIBAL ENROLLMENT		
						Year	County	No.
15678	1 Cox, Matilda 25	First Named	22	F	1/8			
15838	2 " Ona Leo	Son	5	M	1/16			
15839	3 " Constant E	"	3	"	1/16			
	4							
	5							
	6							
	7							
	8							
	9							
	10							
	11							
	12							
	13							
	14							
	15							
	16							
	17							

ENROLLMENT OF NOS. ~ 1 ~ HEREON APPROVED BY THE SECRETARY OF INTERIOR DEC -2 1904

ENROLLMENT OF NOS. ~ 2 and 3 ~ HEREON APPROVED BY THE SECRETARY OF INTERIOR JUN 12 1905

TRIBAL ENROLLMENT OF PARENTS

Name of Father	Year	County	Name of Mother	Year	County
1 Henry Killen	Dead	Choctaw	Elizabeth Killen		white woman
2 J E Cox		noncitizen	No 1		
3 " " "		" "	No 1		
4					
5					
6					
7					
8					
9					
	See decision in Choctaw jacket #5367				
10	Mother of No.1 on Choctaw card No 5367				
11	Admitted by Dawes Commission, Case No 999. No appeal				
12	No2 born Nov 28, 1897: application made and proof of birth filed March 25, 1905				
13	No3 " March 30, 1900: " " " " " " " " " " "				
14					
15	For child of No1 see NB (Mar 3-1905) Card # 130.				
16			Date of Application for Enrollment.	#1 6/22/99	
17					

See Choctaw 5367   PO 6/20/05 Howe I.T.

Choctaw By Blood Enrollment Cards 1898-1914

RESIDENCE: Sugar Loaf COUNTY. **Choctaw Nation**   Choctaw Roll   CARD No.
POST OFFICE: Red Oak, I.T.   *(Not Including Freedmen)*   FIELD No. 3065

Dawes' Roll No.	NAME	Relationship to Person First Named	AGE	SEX	BLOOD	TRIBAL ENROLLMENT Year	County	No.
8957	1 Wright, Islin ³³	Named	30	M	Full	1896	Sugar Loaf	12903
8958	2 ~~Ann~~ DIED PRIOR TO SEPTEMBER 25, 1902	~~Wife~~	~~32~~	~~F~~	"	~~1896~~	" "	~~12904~~
8959	3 " Carrie ⁴	Dau	1	"	"			
8960	4 Lewis, Judie ¹⁷	Sister	14	"	"	1896	Sugar Loaf	7832
	5							
	6							
	7							
	8							
	9							
	10							
	11							
	12							
	13							
	14							
	15							
	16							
	17							

ENROLLMENT
OF NOS. 1,2,3,4 HEREON
APPROVED BY THE SECRETARY
OF INTERIOR JAN 17 1903

TRIBAL ENROLLMENT OF PARENTS

Name of Father	Year	County	Name of Mother	Year	County
1 Simon Wright	Dead	Sugar Loaf	Sophie Wright	Dead	Sans Bois
2 ~~Jerry White~~	"	~~Wade~~	~~Rebecca White~~	"	~~Sugar Loaf~~
3 No 1			No 2		
4 Emziah Lewis	Dead	Sugar Loaf	Sophie Wright	Dead	Sans Bois
5					
6					
7					
8		No.2 died April 1902; proof of death filed Dec 30 1902			
9		No.2 died April 1902. Enrollment cancelled by Department July 8, 1904			
10					
11					
12					
13					
14					
15					
16			Date of Application for Enrollment	6/22/99	
17					

Choctaw By Blood Enrollment Cards 1898-1914

RESIDENCE: Sugar Loaf COUNTY.	**Choctaw Nation**	Choctaw Roll (Not Including Freedmen)	CARD NO.
POST OFFICE: Red Oak, I.T.			FIELD NO. 30666

Dawes' Roll No.	NAME		Relationship to Person	AGE	SEX	BLOOD	TRIBAL ENROLLMENT		
							Year	County	No.
8961	1 Brashears, Turner	24	First Named	21	M	1/2	1896	Gaines	836
	2								
	3								
	4								
	5								
	6								
	7								
	8								
	9								
	10								
	11								
	12								
	13								
	14								
	15								
	16								
	17								

ENROLLMENT
OF NOS. 1 HEREON
APPROVED BY THE SECRETARY
OF INTERIOR JAN 17 1903

TRIBAL ENROLLMENT OF PARENTS

	Name of Father	Year	County	Name of Mother	Year	County
1	Turner Brashears	Dead	Skullyville	Kate Brashears	Dead	Non Citz
2						
3						
4						
5						
6						
7						
8						
9			For proof of marriage of parents, see			
10			enrollment of Joseph J. Moore and			
11			Mattie Moore, ne[sic] Brashears			
12						
13						
14					Date of Application for Enrollment.	
15						
16					6/22/99	
17						

Choctaw By Blood Enrollment Cards 1898-1914

RESIDENCE: Sugar Loaf COUNTY.								
POST OFFICE: Le Flore I.T. **Choctaw Nation** Choctaw Roll (Not Including Freedmen) CARD NO. FIELD NO. 3067								

Dawes' Roll No.	NAME	Relationship to Person First Named	AGE	SEX	BLOOD	TRIBAL ENROLLMENT		
						Year	County	No.
8962	1 Peter John 27	First Named	24	M	Full	1896	Sugar Loaf	10159
	2							
	3							
	4							
	5							
	6							
	7							
	8							
	9							
	10							
	11							
	12							
	13							
	14							
	15							
	16							
	17							

ENROLLMENT OF NOS. 1 HEREON APPROVED BY THE SECRETARY OF INTERIOR JAN 17 1903

TRIBAL ENROLLMENT OF PARENTS

	Name of Father	Year	County	Name of Mother	Year	County
1	Thomas Peter	Dead	Gaines	Jincy Peter	Dead	Gaines
2						
3						
4						
5						
6						
7						
8						
9						
10						
11						
12						
13						
14						
15					Date of Application for Enrollment.	
16					6/22/99	
17						

RESIDENCE: Sugar Loaf	COUNTY.	**Choctaw Nation**	**Choctaw Roll**	CARD No.
POST OFFICE: Le Flore, I.T.			*(Not Including Freedmen)*	FIELD No. 3068

Dawes' Roll No.	NAME	Relationship to Person First Named	AGE	SEX	BLOOD	TRIBAL ENROLLMENT Year	County	No.
Dead	1 Bond, George		44	M	Full	1893	Sugar Loaf	60
14789	2 Durant Amanda ²⁹	Wife	26	F	"	1893	" "	61
8963	3 Bond, Mary ¹²	Dau	9	"	"	1893	" "	54
	4							
	5					ENROLLMENT		
	6					OF NOS. 2 HEREON APPROVED BY THE SECRETARY OF INTERIOR MAY 20 190?		
	7							
	8 No. 1 HEREON DISMISSED UNDER							
	9 ORDER OF THE COMMISSIONER TO THE FIVE CIVILIZED TRIBES OF JULY 18, 1905.							
	10							
	11							
	12							
	13							
	14							
	15 ENROLLMENT OF NOS. 3 HEREON							
	16 APPROVED BY THE SECRETARY OF INTERIOR JAN 17 1903							
	17							

TRIBAL ENROLLMENT OF PARENTS

Name of Father	Year	County	Name of Mother	Year	County
1 Ma-kin-tubbee	Dead	Red River		Dead	Red River
2 Tom Yota	"	Sugar Loaf	Melvina Yota	"	Sugar Loaf
No1			Ellen Bond	"	" "
4					
5					
6					
7					
8					
9					
10 No1 on 1893 Pay Roll, Page 7, No 60, Sugar Loaf Co.					
11 No2 " 1893 " " " 7, " 61 " " "					
12 No3 " 1893 " " " 6, " 54 " " "					
No2 is now wife of Isaac Durant Choctaw card #2416; evidence of marriage filed December 20, 1902					
13 No3 is now ward of Lizzie Holson on Choctaw card #2832. Guardianship					
14 papers filed 12/19 ⁰²					
15 No1 proof of death filed Dec 20 1902 ev 7/3/05					
16			Date of Application for Enrollment.	6/22/99	
17					

68

Choctaw By Blood Enrollment Cards 1898-1914

RESIDENCE: Sugar Loaf	COUNTY:	Choctaw Nation	Choctaw Roll	CARD NO.
POST OFFICE: La Flore I.T.				FIELD NO. 3069

Dawes Roll No	NAME	Relationship to Person First Named	AGE	SEX	BLOOD	TRIBAL ENROLLMENT Year	County	No.
8964	1 Yota Adam	Named	20	M	Full	1896	Sugar Loaf	14198
	2							
	3							
	4							
	5							
	6							
	7							
	8							
	9							
	10							
	11							
	12							
	13							
	14							
	15							
	16							
	17							

ENROLLMENT
OF NOS. 1 HEREON
APPROVED BY THE SECRETARY
OF INTERIOR   JAN 17 1903

TRIBAL ENROLLMENT OF PARENTS

	Name of Father	Year	County	Name of Mother	Year	County
1	Tom Yota	Dead	Sugar Loaf	Fannie Yota	Dead	Gaines
2						
3						
4						
5						
6						
7	On 1896 roll as Adam Yotah.					
8	For child of No1 see NB (March 3 1905) #1201					
9						
10						
11						
12						
13						
14						
15					Date of Application for Enrollment	
16					6/22/99	
17						

Choctaw By Blood Enrollment Cards 1898-1914

RESIDENCE: Su___ L_____ _____Y. **Choctaw Nation** | Choctaw Roll (Not Including Freedmen) | CARD NO. FIELD NO. 3070
POST OFFICE: _____

Dawes' Roll No.	NAME		Relationship to Person	AGE	SEX	BLOOD	TRIBAL ENROLLMENT		
							Year	County	No.
8965	1 Coffman, Sarah E	26	First Named	23	F	1/2	1896	Sans Bois	2161
8966	2 " Melvin E	6	Dau	3	"	1/4			2162
8967	3 " George Dewey	4	Son	6mo	M	1/4			
8968	4 " Elizabeth P	2	Dau	2w	F	1/4			
	5								
	6								
	7								
	8								
	9								
	10 For child of No1 see NB (Apr 26-06) #519								
	11								
	12								
	13								
	14								
	15								
	16								
	17								

ENROLLMENT
OF NOS. 1,2,3,4 HEREON
APPROVED BY THE SECRETARY
OF INTERIOR JAN 17 1903

TRIBAL ENROLLMENT OF PARENTS

Name of Father	Year	County	Name of Mother	Year	County
1 Alick McCann	Dead	Sans Bois	Mary McCann	Dead	Non Citz
2 John Coffman	1896	Non Citz	No1		
3 " "	1896	" "	No1		
4 " "	1896	" "	No.1		
5					
6					
7 No1 on 1896 roll as Caufman					
8 No2 " 1896 " " Melvin Caufman					
9 As to marriage of parents of No1, see					
10 testimony of Austin McCann.					
11 No.4 Enrolled January 29, 1901					
12					
13 For child of No1 see NB (Mar 3-1905) Card #206					
14				#1 to 3 inc	
15				Date of Application for Enrollment.	
16				6/22/99	
17 PO Caddo I.T. 4/17/03					

70

Choctaw By Blood Enrollment Cards 1898-1914

RESIDENCE: Sans Bois COUNTY.							CARD NO.
POST OFFICE: Sans Bois, I.T.	**Choctaw Nation** *(Not Including Freedmen)*	**Choctaw Roll**				FIELD NO.	3071

Dawes' Roll No.	NAME		Relationship to Person First Named	AGE	SEX	BLOOD	TRIBAL ENROLLMENT Year	County	No.
8969	1 King, Leonidas	38	First Named	35	M	Full	1896	Sans Bois	7423
8970	2 " Rachael	41	Wife	38	F	"	1896	" "	7424
8971	3 " Ada	9	Dau	6	"	"	1896	" "	7426
	4								
	5								
	6								
	7								
	8								
	9								
	10								
	11								
	12								
	13								
	14								
	15	ENROLLMENT OF NOS. 1,2,3 HEREON							
	16	APPROVED BY THE SECRETARY OF INTERIOR JAN 17 1903							
	17								

TRIBAL ENROLLMENT OF PARENTS

Name of Father	Year	County	Name of Mother	Year	County
1 Tecumseh King	Dead	Sans Bois	Sarah King	Dead	Sans Bois
2 Chas McGilberry	"	" "	Annie McGilberry	"	" "
3 No 1			No 2		
4					
5					
6					
7					
8					
9					
10					
11					
12					
13					
14					
15			Date of Application for Enrollment.		
16			6/22/99		
17					

Choctaw By Blood Enrollment Cards 1898-1914

RESIDENCE: Sans Bois   COUNTY. **Choctaw Nation**   **Choctaw Roll** *(Not Including Freedmen)*   CARD NO. 3072

POST OFFICE: Sans Bois, I.T.   FIELD NO.

Dawes' Roll No.	NAME		AGE	SEX	BLOOD	TRIBAL ENROLLMENT Year	County	No.
8972	1 Coley, Sophia	48 First Named	43	F	Full	1896	Sans Bois	2064
8973	2 " Frank	19 Son	16	M	"	1896	" "	2067
8974	3 " Cicero	16 "	13	"	"	1896	" "	2068
8975	4 " Sillen	17 Dau	14	F	"	1896	" "	2069
8976	5 " Nora J	9 "	6	"	"	1896	" "	2070
	6							
	7							
	8							
	9							
	10							
	11							
	12							
	13							
	14							
	15							
	16							
	17							

ENROLLMENT
OF NOS. 1,2,3,4,5 HEREON
APPROVED BY THE SECRETARY
OF INTERIOR JAN 17 1903

TRIBAL ENROLLMENT OF PARENTS

	Name of Father	Year	County	Name of Mother	Year	County
1	Willis Cannard	Dead	Sans Bois	Liza Cannard	Dead	Sans Bois
2	Joseph Coley	"	" "	No1		
3	" "	"	" "	No1		
4	" "	"	" "	No1		
5	" "	"	" "	No1		
6						
7						
8	No5 on 1896 roll as Noel Coley					
9						
10						
11	For child of No4 see NB (Mar 3-1905) Card #207					
12						
13						
14						
15					Date of Application for Enrollment.	
16					6/22/99	
17	No4 PO Sulphur IT 3/14/05					

Choctaw By Blood Enrollment Cards 1898-1914

RESIDENCE: Sugar Loaf COUNTY. **Choctaw Nation** **Choctaw Roll** (Not Including Freedmen) CARD NO. FIELD NO. 3073
POST OFFICE: Le Flore I.T.

Dawes' Roll No.	NAME	Relationship to Person First Named	AGE	SEX	BLOOD	TRIBAL ENROLLMENT		
						Year	County	No.
8977	1 Miyabe Esias 27	First Named	24	M	Full	1896	Sugar Loaf	8515
8978	2 Ellen DIED PRIOR TO SEPTEMBER 25 26 902	Wife	23	F	"	1896	" "	8516
8979	3 " Clara 3	Dau	5mo	"	"			
	4							
	5							
	6							
	7							
	8							
	9							
	10							
	11							
	12							
	13							
	14							
	15	ENROLLMENT OF NOS. 1,2,3 HEREON						
	16	APPROVED BY THE SECRETARY OF INTERIOR JAN 17 1903						
	17							

TRIBAL ENROLLMENT OF PARENTS

Name of Father	Year	County	Name of Mother	Year	County
1 Fifus Miaybe[sic]	1896	Nashoba	Losey Miaybe	Dead	Sugar Loaf
2 Jackson Dwight	1896	Sugar Loaf	Susan Dwight	"	" "
3 No1			No2		
4					
5					
6					
7					
8		No.2 died May 30, 1902 Proof of death filed Dec 24, 1902			
9		No2 died May 30, 1902. Enrollment cancelled by Department July 8, 1904			
10					
11					
12					
13					
14					
15			Date of Application for Enrollment.	#1&2	
16				6/23/99	
17			No3 enrolled Dec 14/99		

RESIDENCE:	Sugar Loaf	COUNTY.		CARD NO.	
POST OFFICE:	Wister, I.T.	**Choctaw Nation**	Choctaw Roll *(Not Including Freedmen)*	FIELD NO.	3074

Dawes' Roll No.	NAME	Relationship to Person First Named	AGE	SEX	BLOOD	TRIBAL ENROLLMENT		
						Year	County	No.
8980	1 Page, Winnie DIED PRIOR TO SEPTEMBER 25??,1902		69	F	Full	1896	Sugar Loaf	10142
	2							
	3							
	4							
	5							
	6							
	7							
	8							
	9							
	10							
	11							
	12							
	13							
	14							
	15							
	16							
	17							

ENROLLMENT
OF NOS. 1 HEREON
APPROVED BY THE SECRETARY
OF INTERIOR   JAN 17 1903

TRIBAL ENROLLMENT OF PARENTS

Name of Father	Year	County	Name of Mother	Year	County
1 Ta le ho lubbee	Dead	Skullyville	E la pa ho yo	Dead	Skullyville
2					
3					
4					
5					
6					
7 No1 died January 4, 1901; proof of death filed Dec 19 1902					
8					
9					
10					
11					
12					
13					
14				Date of Application for Enrollment.	
15					
16				6/23/99	
17					

Choctaw By Blood Enrollment Cards 1898-1914

RESIDENCE:	Gaines	COUNTY.					CARD No.	
POST OFFICE:	Wilburton, I.T.	**Choctaw Nation**		**Choctaw Roll** (Not Including Freedmen)			FIELD No. 3075	

Dawes' Roll No.	NAME		Relationship to Person	AGE	SEX	BLOOD	TRIBAL ENROLLMENT		
							Year	County	No.
I.W. 284	1 Dunlap, James D	51	First Named	48	M	I.W.	1896	Gaines	14458
8981	2 " Susan L	26	Wife	23	F	3/4	1896	"	3274
8982	3 " Ruth	5	Dau	2	"	3/8			
8983	4 " Sibyl	3	"	3 wks	"	3/8			
	5								
	6								
	7								
	8								
	9								
	10								
	11	ENROLLMENT							
	12	OF NOS. 1 HEREON							
	13	APPROVED BY THE SECRETARY OF INTERIOR SEP 12 1903							
	14								
	15	ENROLLMENT OF NOS. 2,3,4 HEREON							
	16	APPROVED BY THE SECRETARY							
	17	OF INTERIOR JAN 17 1903							

TRIBAL ENROLLMENT OF PARENTS

	Name of Father	Year	County	Name of Mother	Year	County
1	Geo W Dunlap	Dead	Non Citz	Irena Dunlap	Dead	Non Citz
2	Samuel Dennis	"				
3	No 1			No 2		
4	No 1			No 2		
5						
6						
7	For child of [Illegible] 2 see NB (Apr 26-06) #1286					
8	" " " (Mar 3-1905) #208 Evidence of marriage to be supplied: Recd Aug 9/99					
9						
10	No 1 on 1896 roll as Jas. D. Dunlap					
11	No 2 " 1896 " " Susan "					
12						
13	Married under license presented by					
14	Judge Nelson County Judge of Gaines Co See his testimony			Date of Application for Enrollment.		
15	Nos 3-4 Affidavits of birth to be supplied: Recd Aug 9/99			Aug 1/99		
16						
17	Affidavit of No1 as to the maiden and subsequent married					

names of No2 prior to her marriage to No1 filed May 6, 1903

RESIDENCE:	Gaines	COUNTY.	**Choctaw Nation**				**Choctaw Roll**		CARD No.	
POST OFFICE:	Wilburton, I.T.						*(Not Including Freedmen)*		FIELD No.	3076

Dawes' Roll No.	NAME		Relationship to Person	AGE	SEX	BLOOD	TRIBAL ENROLLMENT		
							Year	County	No.
8984	1 Riddle George W	61	First Named	58	M	1/2	1896	Gaines	10734
I.W. 160	2 " Elvarine A	50	Wife	47	F	I.W.	1896	"	14964
15049	3 " John W	20	Son	17	M	1/4	1896	"	10736
8985	4 " Edmond K	18	"	15	"	1/4	1896	"	10737
8986	5 " Melinee	14	Dau	11	F	1/4	1896	"	10738
8987	6 " Samuel L	11	Son	8	M	1/4	1896	"	10939
8988	7 " Eureka J	8	"	5	"	1/4	1896	"	10740
8989	8 " Thomas J	5	"	1½	"	1/4			

ENROLLMENT
OF NOS. ~~ 3 ~~ HEREON
APPROVED BY THE SECRETARY
OF INTERIOR   FEB 16 1904

ENROLLMENT
OF NOS. 2 ~~~~~   HEREON
APPROVED BY THE SECRETARY
OF INTERIOR   JUN 13 1903

ENROLLMENT
OF NOS. 1,4,5,6,7,8   HEREON
APPROVED BY THE SECRETARY
OF INTERIOR   JAN 17 1903

TRIBAL ENROLLMENT OF PARENTS

	Name of Father	Year	County	Name of Mother	Year	County
1	John Riddle	Dead	Gaines	Eve Riddle	Dead	Skullyville
2	Richard Eden	"	Non Citz	Ellen Eden	"	Non Citz
3	No1			No2		
4	No1			No2		
5	No1			No2		
6	No1			No2		
7	No1			No2		
8	No1			No2		
9						
10						
11	No1 on 1896 roll as Geo W Riddle					
12	No2 " 1896 " " E. A. "			Affidavits of Green McCurtain and John		
13	No3 " 1896 " " Jno W. "			W. Riddle as to identity of No3		
	No4 " 1896 " " Edmund K "			filed Nov 18, 1903.		
14	No5 " 1896 " " Melinie "					
15	No2 admitted in 1896 as an intermarried citizen by				Date of Application for Enrollment.	Aug 1/99
16	Dawes Commission: Choctaw Card #663. No appeal.					
17						

Choctaw By Blood Enrollment Cards 1898-1914

RESIDENCE:	Skullyville	COUNTY.			

RESIDENCE: Skullyville   COUNTY. **Choctaw Nation**   **Choctaw Roll** (Not Including Freedmen)   CARD NO.
POST OFFICE: Cameron, I.T.   FIELD NO. **3077**

Dawes' Roll No.	NAME	Relationship to Person First Named	AGE	SEX	BLOOD	TRIBAL ENROLLMENT Year	County	No.
1	McComic, Lottie L		26	F	1/8			
2	" Ethel	Dau	10	"	1/16			
3	" Edgel[sic]	"	8	"	1/16			
4	" Ester	"	6	"	1/16			
5	" Pearlie M.	"	6mo	"	1/16			
6	" James Roy	Son	3mo	M	1/16			
7								

DENIED CITIZENSHIP BY THE CHOCTAW AND CHICKASAW CITIZENSHIP COURT

Nos 1 to 4 incl denied by C.C.C.C. March 21 '04

Nos 5&6 DISMISSED MAY 24 1904

TRIBAL ENROLLMENT OF PARENTS

Name of Father	Year	County	Name of Mother	Year	County
1 A B Bagwell		Non Citz	Mollie E Bagwell		Choctaw
2 Geo B. McComic		" "	No1		
3 " "		" "	No1		
4 " "		" "	No1		
5 " "		" "	No1		
6 " "		" "	No.1		

Nos 1 to 4 incl denied in 96 Case #421
Admitted by U.S. Court, Central District, Aug 26/97
Case No 27, as Mississippi Choctaws and identified as such
As to residence, see testimony of Geo. B. McComic, also as to birth of No5.
No5 Affidavit of birth to be supplied; Recd Aug 10/99
No.6 born May 30, 1901: Enrolled Oct 22d, 1901
No 1 to 4 incl denied in C.C.C.C. Case #54

Date of Application for Enrollment. Aug 1/99

P.O. Farmers, I.T.

77

RESIDENCE: Tobucksy COUNTY. **Choctaw Nation** Choctaw Roll CARD NO.
POST OFFICE: South McAlester, I.T. *(Not Including Freedmen)* FIELD NO. 3078

Dawes' Roll No.	NAME		Relationship to Person	AGE	SEX	BLOOD	TRIBAL ENROLLMENT		
							Year	County	No.
I.W. 919	1 Fry, Thomas W.	59	First Named	55	M	IW			
15437	2 " Fannie	35	Wife	32	F	1/8			
15438	3 " Daniel W	12	Son	9	M	1/16			
15439	4 " Everett	15	S.Son	12	"	1/16			
15440	5 " Henrietta	15	S.Dau	12	F	1/16			
	6								
	7								
	8								
	9	ENROLLMENT							
	10	OF NOS. 2-3-4-5 HEREON							
	11	APPROVED BY THE SECRETARY OF INTERIOR MAY 9 1904							
	12								
	13								
	14	ENROLLMENT							
	15	OF NOS. 1 HEREON							
	16	APPROVED BY THE SECRETARY OF INTERIOR AUG 3 1904							
	17								

TRIBAL ENROLLMENT OF PARENTS

	Name of Father	Year	County	Name of Mother	Year	County
1	William Fry	Dead	Non Citz	Peggy Fry	Dead	Non Citz
2	Thompson	"	" "	Sarah Thompson	"	Choctaw
3	No1			No2		
4	Jas. Harbolt		Non Citz	No2		
5	" "		" "	No2		
6						
7						
8		No1 was admitted by Dawes Com as an				
9		Intermarried Citizen, Case No 1349. No appeal.				
10		The other parties above mentioned were				
11		admitted by Dawes Com., Case No 1349, as				
12		citizens by blood. No appeal.				
13		As to residence see testimony of No1.				
14						
15					Date of Application for Enrollment.	
16						Aug 1/9
17						

RESIDENCE:	Sugar Loaf	COUNTY.						CARD NO.	
POST OFFICE:	Poteau, I.T.		**Choctaw Nation**			**Choctaw Roll** *(Not Including Freedmen)*		FIELD NO.	3079

Dawes' Roll No.	NAME	Relationship to Person First Named	AGE	SEX	BLOOD	TRIBAL ENROLLMENT		
						Year	County	No.
1	Dannon, Lula A	Named	24	F	1/8			
2	" Zoel H	Dau	1½	"	1/16			
3	" Violet Cleon	Dau	2mo	F	1/16			
4								
5								
6								
7								
8	N⁰ˢ 2&3 DISMISSED							
9	MAY 24 1904							
10								
11								
12								
13								
14	DENIED CITIZENSHIP BY THE CHOCTAW AND							
15	CHICKASAW CITIZENSHIP COURT							
16								
17								

TRIBAL ENROLLMENT OF PARENTS

	Name of Father	Year	County	Name of Mother	Year	County
1	C. M. Bagwell		Non Citz	Eliza J. Bagwell		Choctaw
2	Luther A Cannon		" "	No 1		
3	" " "		" "	No. 1		
4						
5						
6	No 1 denied by [illegible] No 1 [illegible]					
7	No 1 was admitted by U.S. Court, Central					
8	District Aug. 26/97, Case No 27, as a Missississippi Choctaw and she is therefore identified					
9	as such.					
10	As to residence and birth of No2, see testimony					
11	of Luther A. Cannon No.3 Enrolled March 6th, 1901					
12	Judgment of US Ct admitting No 1 vacated and set aside by Decree of Choctaw Chickasaw Cit Court Decr 17'02					
13	No 1 now in C.C.C.C. Case #54					
14					Date of Application for Enrollment.	
15					Aug 1/99	
16						
17						

Choctaw By Blood Enrollment Cards 1898-1914

RESIDENCE: Tobucksy   COUNTY. **Choctaw Nation**   **Choctaw Roll**   CARD NO.
POST OFFICE: Kiowa, I.T.   *(Not Including Freedmen)*   FIELD NO.   3080

Dawes' Roll No.	NAME	Relationship to Person First Named	AGE	SEX	BLOOD	TRIBAL ENROLLMENT Year	County	No.
DEAD.	1 Holt, Annie	DEAD	28	F	1/8			
15441	2 " Mary A	10 Dau	7	"	1/16			
15442	3 " John W	5 Son	2	M	1/16			
DEAD.	4 " Jerry Allen	Son	2mo	M	1/16			
	5							
	6							
	7							
	8	No. 1 and 4 HEREON DISMISSED UNDER ORDER OF THE COMMISSION TO THE FIVE CIVILIZED TRIBES OF MARCH 31, 1905.						
	9							
	10							
	11							
	12							
	13							
	14							
	15	ENROLLMENT OF NOS. 2 3 HEREON APPROVED BY THE SECRETARY OF INTERIOR MAY 9 1904						
	16							
	17							

TRIBAL ENROLLMENT OF PARENTS

	Name of Father	Year	County	Name of Mother	Year	County
1	Thompson	Dead	Non Citz	Sarah Thompson	Dead	Choctaw
2	John Holt		" "	No 1		
3	" "		" "	No 1		
4	" "		" "	No.1	Dead	
5						
6						
7						
8						
9	Nos1 & 2 Admitted by Dawes Com. as Citizens by blood					
10	Case No 1349. No appeal					
11	No2 was admitted as Mary Holt					
12	As to residence and birth of No3, see testimony of John Holt.					
13	No3 Affidavit of birth to be supplied : Recd					#1 to 3
14	Aug 9/99					Date of Application for Enrollment.
15	No.4 Enrolled May 29, 1901					Aug 1/99
16	No.1 Died April 20, 1901. Evidence of death filed May 29, 1901					
17	No.4 " July 17, 1901 " " " " Dec. 30, 1902					

RESIDENCE:	Gaines	COUNTY.	**Choctaw Nation**		**Choctaw Roll**	CARD No.	
POST OFFICE:	Demant[sic] I.T				*(Not Including Freedmen)*	FIELD No. 3081	

Dawes' Roll No.	NAME		Relationship to Person First Named	AGE	SEX	BLOOD	TRIBAL ENROLLMENT		
							Year	County	No.
DEAD.	1 Yota, Scott	51	Named	48	M	Full	1896	Gaines	14207
8990	2 " Levi	21	Son	18	"	"	1896	"	14208
DEAD.	3 " Ned	17	"	14	"	"	1896	"	14209
DEAD.	4 " Peter	16	"	13	"	"	1896	"	14210
DEAD.	5 " Duke	15	"	12	"	"	1896	"	14211
	6								
	7								
	8								
	9								
	10 No.1342-5 HEREON DISMISSED UNDER								
	11 ORDER OF THE COMMISSION TO THE FIVE								
	CIVILIZED TRIBES OF MARCH 31, 1905.								
	12								
	13								
	14								
	15 ENROLLMENT								
	OF NOS. 2 HEREON								
	16 APPROVED BY THE SECRETARY								
	OF INTERIOR FEB 3 1904								
	17								

TRIBAL ENROLLMENT OF PARENTS

	Name of Father	Year	County	Name of Mother	Year	County
1	Thos Yo-tubbee	Dead	Sugar Loaf	Liza Yo-tubbee	Dead	Jacks Fork
2	No1			Siley Yota	"	Gaines
3	No1			" "	"	"
4	No1			" "	"	"
5	No1			" "	"	"
6						
7						
8						
9						
10	No.2 is now husband of Susan Carney, Choc. Card #360.				12/28 '02	
11	No1 died December – 1901; proof of death filed Dec 15 1902					
12	No3 " December – 1901; " " " " " "			"		
13	No4 " December – 1901; " " " " " "			"		
	No5 " December – 1901; " " " " " "			"		
14					Date of Application for Enrollment.	
15					Aug 1/99	
16						
17						

RESIDENCE:	Tobucksy	COUNTY.								CARD NO.
POST OFFICE:	Kiowa, I.T.	**Choctaw Nation**				**Choctaw Roll** *(Not Including Freedmen)*			FIELD NO.	3082

Dawes' Roll No.	NAME		Relationship to Person	AGE	SEX	BLOOD	TRIBAL ENROLLMENT		
							Year	County	No.
8991	1 Gaither, Lula	28	First Named	25	F	1/8	1893	Kiamitia	21
8992	2 Barker, Julius A	12	Son	9	M	1/16	1893	"	23
8993	3 " Elizabeth A	10	Dau	7	F	1/16	1893	"	22
I.W.285	4 Gaither, Beal	29	Hus.	29	M	IW			
	5								
	6								
	7								
	8								
	9	ENROLLMENT							
	10	OF NOS. 4 HEREON APPROVED BY THE SECRETARY							
	11	OF INTERIOR SEP 12 1903							
	12	ENROLLMENT							
	13	OF NOS. 1,2, and 3 HEREON APPROVED BY THE SECRETARY							
	14	OF INTERIOR FEB 4 1903							
	15								
	16								
	17								

TRIBAL ENROLLMENT OF PARENTS

Name of Father	Year	County	Name of Mother	Year	County
1 Chas Hathaway	Dead	Non Citz	Prudence Hathaway	Dead	Tobucksy
2 Robert Barker	"	" "	No1		
3 " "	"	" "	No1		
4 Granvill Gaither	"	" "	Adaline Gaither	Dead	Non Citz
5					
6					
7					
8		No1 on 1893 Pay Roll, Page 115, No 21, Kiamitia Co. as Lula Barker			
9		No2 " 1893 " " " 115 " 23 " " " Julius "			
10		No3 " 1893 " " " 115 " 22 " " " Bettie "			
11		No1 " 1896 Roll, Page 24, No 906, Tobucksy Co as Lula Borker			
12		No2 " 1896 " " 24 " 909 " " " Julius "			
		No3 " 1896 " " 24 " 910 " " " Bessie "			
13					
14				Date of Application for Enrollment.	
15				Aug 1/99	
16					
17					

Choctaw By Blood Enrollment Cards 1898-1914

RESIDENCE:	Gaines	COUNTY.								

RESIDENCE: Gaines COUNTY.   **POST OFFICE:** Hartshorne, I.T.   **Choctaw Nation**   **Choctaw Roll** *(Not Including Freedmen)*   **CARD No.**   **FIELD No.** 3083

Dawes' Roll No.	NAME	Relationship to Person First Named	AGE	SEX	BLOOD	TRIBAL ENROLLMENT		
						Year	County	No.
8994	1 Nelson, Houston ³⁷	First Named	34	M	Full	1896	Gaines	9582
8995	2 " Rhoda ³⁵	Wife	32	F	"	1896	"	9583
8996	3 Anderson, Alice ~~DIED PRIOR TO SEPTEMBER 25, 1902~~	S.Dau	16	"	"	1896	"	82
	4							
	5							
	6							
	7							
	8							
	9							
	10							
	11							
	12							
	13							
	14							
	15	ENROLLMENT OF NOS. 1, 2 and 3 HEREON						
	16	APPROVED BY THE SECRETARY OF INTERIOR FEB 4 1903						
	17							

TRIBAL ENROLLMENT OF PARENTS

Name of Father	Year	County	Name of Mother	Year	County
1 Smallwood Nelson		Gaines	Rhoda Nelson	Dead	Gaines
2 Wilson Webster	Dead	"	Ho-ne-ta-ma	"	Jacks Fork
3 Silan Anderson	"	"	No 2		
4					
5					
6					
7					
8					
9					
10					
11	No.3 died June 1901: Proof of death filed Dec 30 1902				
12					
13					
14			Date of Application for Enrollment.		
15			Aug 1/99		
16					
17					

RESIDENCE:	Skullyville	COUNTY.					CARD NO.	
POST OFFICE:	Fort Smith, Ark.	**Choctaw Nation**			Choctaw Roll *(Not Including Freedmen)*		FIELD NO.	3084

Dawes' Roll No.	NAME	Relationship to Person First Named	AGE	SEX	BLOOD	TRIBAL ENROLLMENT		
						Year	County	No.
1	Stokes, Lula		27	F	1/16			
2								
3								
4								
5								
6								
7								
8								
9								
10								
11								
12								
13								
14								
15								
16								
17								

TRIBAL ENROLLMENT OF PARENTS

	Name of Father	Year	County	Name of Mother	Year	County
1	James Hawkins		Choctaw	Emeline Hawkins		Non Citz
2						
3						
4						
5						
6						
7						

No1 denied by C. C. C.C. March 21 '04

No1 Denied in 96 Case #421
Admitted by U.S. Court, Central Dist. Aug 26/99
Case No 27 as a Mississippi Choctaw and identi-
fied as such
As to residence see testimony of Thomas H. Stokes

Judgment of U.S. Court admitting No1 vacated and set aside by Decree of Choctaw Chickasaw Cit Court Dec 17 '02 and same annulled (Act of 7/1/02)

	Date of Application for Enrollment.
	Aug 1/99

DENIED CITIZENSHIP BY THE CHOCTAW AND CHICKASAW CITIZENSHIP COURT Mar 21 '04

Choctaw By Blood Enrollment Cards 1898-1914

RESIDENCE:	Skullyville	COUNTY.								
POST OFFICE:	Jenson, Ark.									

Choctaw Nation

Choctaw Roll *(Not Including Freedmen)*

CARD NO.
FIELD NO. 3085

Dawes' Roll No.	NAME	Relationship to Person First Named	AGE	SEX	BLOOD	TRIBAL ENROLLMENT		
						Year	County	No.
1	Woods, Hattie	First Named	24	F	1/16			
2	" James G.	Son	6mo	M	1/32			
3								
4								
5								
6	No1 DENIED CITIZENSHIP BY THE CHOCTAW AND							
7	CHICKASAW CITIZENSHIP COURT							
8								
9								
10								
11								
12								
13								
14	Nº2 DISMISSED							
15	MAY 24 1904							
16								
17								

TRIBAL ENROLLMENT OF PARENTS

	Name of Father	Year	County	Name of Mother	Year	County
1	Jas Hawkins		Choctaw	Emeline Hawkins		Non Citz
2	Columbus L Woods		Non Citz	No1		
3						
4						
5						
6	No1 denied by C.C.C.C. March 21st 04					
	No1 Denied in 96 Case #421					
7	Admitted by U.S. Court Central Dist Aug 26/97					
8	Case No 27 as a Mississippi Choctaw and is identified as such;					
9	As to residence and birth of No2, see testimony					
10	of Columbus L. Woods.					
11	No2 now in C.C.C. Case #54					
12						
13						
14					Date of Application for Enrollment.	
15					Aug 1/99	
16						
17	P.O. Wilmore I.T. 10/19/03					

Choctaw By Blood Enrollment Cards 1898-1914

RESIDENCE: Sans Bois COUNTY.		Choctaw Nation				Choctaw Roll (No...Freedmen)		CARD NO. FIELD NO. 3086	

Dawes' Roll No.	NAME		Relationship to Person	AGE	SEX	BLOOD	TRIBAL ENROLLMENT		
							Year	County	No.
9004	1 Pope, Noel	23	First Named	20	M	Full	1896	Sans Bois	10038
9005	2 " Lizzie	13	Sister	10	F	"	1896	" "	10039
	3								
	4								
	5								
	6								
	7								
	8								
	9								
	10								
	11								
	12								
	13								
	14								
	15								
	16								
	17								

ENROLLMENT
OF NOS. 1 and 2 HEREON
APPROVED BY THE SECRETARY
OF INTERIOR FEB 4 1903

TRIBAL ENROLLMENT OF PARENTS

Name of Father		Year	County	Name of Mother	Year	County
1 Tobias Pope		Dead	Sans Bois	Annie Pope	Dead	Sans Bois
2 " "		"	" "	" "	"	" " "
3						
4						
5						
6						
7						
8 No1 on 1896 roll as Noel Polk						
9 No2 " 1896 " " Lizzie "						
10 No1 is now the husband of Judy Sexton on Choctaw Card #483 Oct 10, 1901						
11						
12						
13						
14						
15				Date of Application for Enrollment.	Aug 1/99	
16						
17 P.O. Quinton, IT. 3/4/07						

RESIDENCE: Tobucksy	COUNTY.	**Choctaw Nation**	**Choctaw Roll** (Not Including Freedmen)	CARD No.
POST OFFICE: Stewart, I.T.				FIELD No. 3087

Dawes' Roll No.	NAME	Relationship to Person First Named	AGE	SEX	BLOOD	TRIBAL ENROLLMENT Year	County	No.
I.W.286	1 Elliott, Richard H ⑤⑥	First Named	52	M	I.W	1896	Sans Boia	14491
8997	2 " Amanda ³⁶	Wife	33	F	1/4	1896	" "	3678
8998	3 " Ivory ⁷	Son	4	M	1/8	1896	" "	3679
8999	4 Jenkins, Albert ¹⁸	S.Son	15	"	1/8	1896	" "	6361
9000	5 Gamm Leathia ¹⁵	S.Dau	12	F	1/8	1896	" "	6362
9001	6 Jenkins John ¹³	S.Son	10	M	1/8	1896	" "	6363
9002	7 Gamm, Lina F E ¹	Dau of No5	1mo	F	1/16			
9003	8 Elliott, Thomas ¹	Son	1wk	M	1/16			
	9							
	10							
	11							
	12	ENROLLMENT OF NOS 1 HEREON APPROVED BY THE SECRETARY OF INTERIOR SEP 12 1903						
	13							
	14							
	15	ENROLLMENT OF NOS. 2 3 4 5 6 7 8 HEREON APPROVED BY THE SECRETARY OF INTERIOR FEB 4 1903						
	16							
	17							

TRIBAL ENROLLMENT OF PARENTS

	Name of Father	Year	County	Name of Mother	Year	County
1	John Elliott	Dead	Non Citz	Mary Elliott	Dead	Non Citz
2	William Munns	"	" "	Patsy Munns	"	Gaines
3	No1			No2		
4	Tom Jenkins	Dead	Non Citz	No2		
5	" "	"	" "	No2		
6	" "	"	" "	No2		
7	William Gamm		" "	No5		
8	Nº1			Nº2		
9						
10	No.5 is now the wife of William Gamm a non-citizen; Nov. 1st, 1901					
11	No.7 born Sept 20, 1901. Enrolled Nov. 1st 1901					
12	No2 on 1896 roll as Mary Elliott					
13	Nº8 Born Aug 12, 1902, enrolled Aug. 18, 1902					
14	Evidence of divorce of No1 from his former wife, Mary J Elliott filed Dec 1, 1902					
15	For child of No5 see NB (Apr 26-06) Card #777			#1 to 6		
16	" " " Nos1&2 " " (Mar 3-05) " #209			Date of Application for Enrollment. Aug 1/99		
17	No3- "Died prior to September 25, 1902; not entitled to land or money" See Indian Office letter May 18, 1910, D.C. #705-1910.					
	P.O. Hickory, IT, 8/15/02					

Choctaw By Blood Enrollment Cards 1898-1914

RESIDENCE: Sans Bois COUNTY. **Choctaw Nation** Choctaw Roll CARD NO.
POST OFFICE: Featherstone, I.T. (Not Including Freedmen) FIELD NO. 3088

Dawes' Roll No.	NAME		Relationship to Person	AGE	SEX	BLOOD	TRIBAL ENROLLMENT		
							Year	County	No.
9006	1 Carney, Silway	27	First Named	24	F	Full	1893	Sans Bois	822
9007	2 Daniel, Mack	16	Son	13	M	"	1893	" "	823
9008	3 Carney, Wilson	3	"	1mo	"	1/2			
15977	4 Carney, Robert	22	husband	22	M	1/2	1896	Sans Bois	2100
	5								
	6								
	7								
	8	ENROLLMENT OF NOS. 1,2, & 3 HEREON APPROVED BY THE SECRETARY							
	9								
	10	OF INTERIOR FEB 4 1903							
	11								
	12	ENROLLMENT OF NOS. 4 HEREON APPROVED BY THE SECRETARY							
	13								
	14	OF INTERIOR JUN 16 1906							
	15								
	16								
	17								

TRIBAL ENROLLMENT OF PARENTS

	Name of Father	Year	County	Name of Mother	Year	County
1	Eastman Charles	Dead	Sans Bois	Ish-te-ma-la	Dead	Sans Bois
2	John Daniel	"	" "	No1		
3	Robert Carney		Freedman	No1		
4	Wilson Carney	dead		Jennie Carney	dead	
5						
6						
7						
8						
9						
10	No1 on 1893 Pay Roll, Page 79, No 822, Sans Bois Co, as Silway Tonler					
11	No2 " 1893 " " " 79 " 823 " " " " Mike Daniel					
12	Husband of No1 and father of No3, is Robert Carney on Choctaw freedman Card #1157					
13	No4 is identified upon the 1893 Leased District Payment roll, Sans Bois County as No. 131					
14	No4 transferred from Choctaw freedman card #1157 to this card					
15	February 13 1905: See decision of November 11, 1905					
16				Date of Application for Enrollment:	Aug 1/99	
17	P.O. Quinton 11/11/05					

88

Choctaw By Blood Enrollment Cards 1898-1914

RESIDENCE:	Gaines	COUNTY.							

Choctaw Nation (Not Including Freedmen)

RESIDENCE: Gaines COUNTY.
POST OFFICE: Hartshorne, I.T.

Choctaw Roll (Not Including Freedmen)

CARD NO. FIELD NO. 3089

Dawes' Roll No.	NAME	Relationship to Person First Named	AGE	SEX	BLOOD	TRIBAL ENROLLMENT		
						Year	County	No.
I.W. 287	1 Thompson, Leona	Named	37	F	I.W	1896	Sans Bois	15085
9009	2 " Zelia 13	Dau	10	"	1/4	1896	" "	11827
	3							
	4							
	5							
	6							
	7							
	8							
	9							
	10							
	11							
	12							
	13							
	14							
	15							
	16							
	17							

ENROLLMENT OF NOS. 2 HEREON APPROVED BY THE SECRETARY OF INTERIOR FEB 4 1903

ENROLLMENT OF NOS. 1 HEREON APPROVED BY THE SECRETARY OF INTERIOR SEP 12 1903

TRIBAL ENROLLMENT OF PARENTS

Name of Father	Year	County	Name of Mother	Year	County
1 Lee Martindale		Non Citz	Minerva Martindale	Dead	Non Citz
2 Babe Thompson	Dead	Gaines	No1		
3					
4					
5					
6					
7 Certified copy of of[sic] divorce proceedings between A.B. Thompson and					
8 Margaret Thompson filed April 1, 1903					
9 Affidavits of N°1 and S.M. [Illegible] relative to residence of N°1 at the					
10 time of her marriage to Babe[sic] Thompson filed May 6, 1903.					
11					
12					
13					
14					
15			Date of Application for Enrollment.	Aug 1/99	
16					
17 Enterprise 12/22/02					

Choctaw By Blood Enrollment Cards 1898-1914

RESIDENCE: Gaines COUNTY. **Choctaw Nation** Choctaw Roll CARD NO.
POST OFFICE: Hartshorne, I.T. (Not Including Freedmen) FIELD NO. 3090

Dawes' Roll No.	NAME		Relationship to Person	AGE	SEX	BLOOD	TRIBAL ENROLLMENT		
							Year	County	No.
9010	1 Willis, Moses	42	First Named	39	M	Full	1896	Gaines	12965
9011	2 " Mary	33	Wife	30	F	"	1896	"	12966
9012	3 Nelson, Josephine	10	S.Dau	7	"	"	1896	"	9596
	4								
	5								
	6								
	7	ENROLLMENT							
	8	OF NOS. 1, 2, and 3 HEREON APPROVED BY THE SECRETARY							
	9	OF INTERIOR FEB 4 1903							
	10								
	11								
	12								
	13								
	14								
	15								
	16								
	17								

TRIBAL ENROLLMENT OF PARENTS

	Name of Father	Year	County	Name of Mother	Year	County
1	Ho-pe-nubbee	Dead	Sugar Loaf	Ish-te-ma-la-key	Dead	Gaines
2	Calvin Anderson		Jacks Fork	Salema Anderson	"	Wade
3	Roberson Nelson	Dead	Gaines	No2		
4						
5						
6						
7						
8						
9			No3 on 1896 Roll as Joseph N. Nelson			
10						
11						
12						
13						
14						
15				Date of Application for Enrollment.	Aug 1/99	
16						
17						

Choctaw By Blood Enrollment Cards 1898-1914

RESIDENCE:	Gaines	COUNTY.								
POST OFFICE:	Hartshorne, I.T.									

Choctaw Nation

Choctaw Roll (Not Including Freedmen)

CARD NO. FIELD NO. **3091**

Dawes' Roll No.	NAME		Relationship to Person	AGE	SEX	BLOOD	TRIBAL ENROLLMENT		
							Year	County	No.
14938	1 Reed, Seborn	25	First Named	22	M	Full	1896	Gaines	10752
	2								
	3								
	4								
	5								
	6								
	7								
	8								
	9								
	10								
	11								
	12								
	13								
	14								
	15								
	16								
	17								

ENROLLMENT
OF NOS. ~ 1 ~~~ HEREON
APPROVED BY THE SECRETARY
OF INTERIOR   OCT 15 1903

TRIBAL ENROLLMENT OF PARENTS

	Name of Father	Year	County	Name of Mother	Year	County
1	Josiah Reed	1896	Gaines	Jinsey Reed	Dead	Gaines
2						
3						
4						
5						
6						
7						
8						
9						
10						
11						
12						
13						
14					Date of Application for Enrollment.	
15					Aug 1/99	
16						
17						

RESIDENCE: Atoka	COUNTY.	Choctaw Nation	Choctaw Roll	CARD No.
POST OFFICE: Kiowa I.T.			*(Not Including Freedmen)*	FIELD No. 3092

Dawes' Roll No.	NAME	Relationship to Person First Named	AGE	SEX	BLOOD	TRIBAL ENROLLMENT		
						Year	County	No.
I.W.737	1 Hooe, Archie F ㉗		24	M	I.W			
9013	2 " Mattie ²⁴	Wife	21	F	1/8	1896	Tobucksy	13025
9014	3 " William Jennings²	Son	6wks	M	1/16			
	4							
	5							
	6							
	7	ENROLLMENT OF NOS. 2 and 3 HEREON APPROVED BY THE SECRETARY OF INTERIOR FEB 4 1903						
	8							
	9							
	10							
	11	DECISION PREPARED						
	12							
	13	ENROLLMENT OF NOS. ~~~ 1 ~~~ HEREON APPROVED BY THE SECREMAY-7 1904TARY OF INTERIOR						
	14							
	15							
	16							
	17							

TRIBAL ENROLLMENT OF PARENTS

	Name of Father	Year	County	Name of Mother	Year	County
1	Robert Hooe		Non Citz	Sallie Hooe	Dead	Non Citz
2	Israel Watts		Tobucksy	Lizzie Watts	"	" "
3	No. 1			No. 2		
4						
5						
6						
7						
8	No1 See Decision of March 2 '04					
9	Evidence of marriage to be supplied Recd Aug 9/99					
10	" " " of parents of					
11	No2 to be supplied. See enrollment of Israel Watts					
12	No2 on 1896 roll as Mattie Watts					
13	No.3 Enrolled Dec 6th 1900					
14	See record transferred this day from Choctaw case #D590 March 24, 1903.					
15	For child of Nos 1&2 see NB (Apr 26, 1906) Card No 98			Date of Application for Enrollment.		
16				Aug 1/99		
17						

Choctaw By Blood Enrollment Cards 1898-1914

RESIDENCE: **Sans Bois** COUNTY. **Choctaw Nation** **Choctaw Roll** CARD NO.
POST OFFICE: **Featherstone, I.T.** *(Not Including Freedmen)* FIELD NO. **3093**

Dawes' Roll No.	NAME		Relationship to Person First Named	AGE	SEX	BLOOD	TRIBAL ENROLLMENT		
							Year	County	No.
9015	1 Colbert, Sim	47	First Named	44	M	Full	1896	Sans Bois	2137
Dead	2 " Louisa	DEAD.	Wife	24	F	3/4	1896	" "	2138
9016	3 " Elba	20	Dau	17	"	Full	1896	" "	2147
	4								
	5								
	6	ENROLLMENT OF NOS. 1 and 3 HEREON							
	7	APPROVED BY THE SECRETARY OF INTERIOR FEB 4 1903							
	8								
	9	No. 2 HEREON DISMISSED UNDER							
	10	ORDER OF THE COMMISSION TO THE FIVE CIVILIZED TRIBES OF MARCH 31, 1905.							
	11								
	12								
	13								
	14								
	15								
	16								
	17								

TRIBAL ENROLLMENT OF PARENTS

	Name of Father	Year	County	Name of Mother	Year	County
1	Thos. Colbert	Dead	Sans Bois	Cha-fa-hoke	Dead	Sans Bois
2	Wallace Carney	"	Freedman	Susan Carney	"	" "
3	No 1			Linney Colbert	"	" "
4						
5						
6						
7						
8			No 3 on 1896 roll as Ebbe Colbert			
9			No 2 died Oct. 8, 1899 Proof of death filed Aug 9, 1901			
10						
11						
12						
13					Date of Application for Enrollment.	
14						
15					Aug 1/99	
16						
17						

Choctaw By Blood Enrollment Cards 1898-1914

RESIDENCE: Gaines COUNTY. **Choctaw Nation** Choctaw Roll CARD No.
POST OFFICE: Wilburton, I.T. (Not Including Freedmen) FIELD No. 3094

Dawes' Roll No.	NAME	Relationship to Person First Named	AGE	SEX	BLOOD	TRIBAL ENROLLMENT		
						Year	County	No.
DEAD.	1 Brown, James	Named	45	M	1/2	1893	Gaines	32
9017	2 " Agnes ⁵⁹	Wife	56	F	Full	1893	"	33
9018	3 " Mary ¹⁸	Dau	15	"	3/4	1896	Gaines	851
9019	4 " Wesley ¹⁵	Son	12	M	3/4	1896	"	850
	5 No. 1 HEREON DISMISSED UNDER							
	6 ORDER OF THE COMMISSION TO THE FIVE CIVILIZED TRIBES OF MARCH 31, 1905.							
	7 ENROLLMENT							
	8 OF NOS. 2 3 and 4 HEREON APPROVED BY THE SECRETARY							
	9 OF INTERIOR FEB 4 1903							
	10							
	11							
	12							
	13							
	14							
	15							
	16							
	17							

TRIBAL ENROLLMENT OF PARENTS

	Name of Father	Year	County	Name of Mother	Year	County
1	George Brown	Dead	Chickasaw	Mary Lomer		Gaines
2	"	"	in Mississippi	Mollie Lewis	Dead	Sugar Loaf
3	No1			No2		
4	No1			No2		
5						
6						
7						
8						
9						
10	Nos 1-2- are not found on Choctaw Roll furnished to					
11	the Commission, but on Choctaw Roll from which it is					
12	copied. Evidently omitted in copying as their					
13	children are found on roll furnished to the Commission.					
14	The citizenship of mother of No2[sic], Mary Lomer, is				Date of Application for Enrollment	
15	questioned. If decided that she has no right, he will follow his father, George Brown,				Aug 1/99	
16	as a Chickasaw.					
17	Red Oak I.T. 11/1/04	No1 died January 13, 1901; proof of death filed Dec 19 1902				

Choctaw By Blood Enrollment Cards 1898-1914

| RESIDENCE: Gaines COUNTY. | **Choctaw Nation** | **Choctaw Roll** *(Not Including Freedmen)* | CARD No. FIELD No. 3095 |
| POST OFFICE: Hartshorne, I.T. | | | |

Dawes' Roll No.	NAME	Relationship to Person First Named	AGE	SEX	BLOOD	TRIBAL ENROLLMENT Year	County	No.
9020	1 Nelson, Smallwood 56		53	M	Full	1896	Gaines	9585
9021	2 " Sarah 57	Wife	54	F	"	1896		9586
	3							
	4							
	5							
	6							
	7	ENROLLMENT OF NOS. 1 and 2 HEREON APPROVED BY THE SECRETARY OF INTERIOR FEB 4 1903						
	8							
	9							
	10							
	11							
	12							
	13							
	14							
	15							
	16							
	17							

TRIBAL ENROLLMENT OF PARENTS

	Name of Father	Year	County	Name of Mother	Year	County
1	John Nelson	Dead	Gaines	Liza Nelson	Dead	Gaines
2	Adam Morris	"	Sugar Loaf	Hot-ba-hu-na	"	Bok Tuklo
3						
4						
5						
6						
7	No 1 on 1896 roll as Smallwood Nelson					
8						
9						
10						
11						
12						
13						
14						
15				Date of Application for Enrollment.	Aug 1/99	
16						
17						

RESIDENCE:	Gaines	COUNTY.				

Choctaw Nation

RESIDENCE: Gaines COUNTY.
POST OFFICE: Hartshorne, I.T.

Choctaw Roll (Not Including Freedmen)

CARD NO. FIELD NO. 3096

Dawes' Roll No.	NAME	Relationship to Person First Named	AGE	SEX	BLOOD	TRIBAL ENROLLMENT Year	County	No.
9022	1 Nelson, Jane	30	27	F	Full	1896	Gaines	9589
9023	2 Eden DIED PRIOR TO SEPTEMBER 25, 1902	Son	2	M	"			
	3							
	4							
	5							
	6							
	7							
	8							
	9							
	10							
	11							
	12							
	13							
	14							
	15							
	16							
	17							

ENROLLMENT OF NOS. 1 and 2 HEREON APPROVED BY THE SECRETARY OF INTERIOR FEB 4 1903

TRIBAL ENROLLMENT OF PARENTS

	Name of Father	Year	County	Name of Mother	Year	County
1	Lesmo Fry	Dead	Bok Tuklo	Sarah Nelson		Gaines
2	Jas Nelson	"	Gaines	No1		
3						
4						
5						
6						
7						
8			No2- Affidavit of birth to be supplied:			
9		Recd Oct 7/99				
10						
11						
12						
13		No.2 died in 1899: Proof of death filed Dec 30 1902			Date of Application for Enrollment.	
14						
15					Aug 1/99	
16						
17						

RESIDENCE:	Gaines	COUNTY.							

Choctaw Nation

RESIDENCE: Gaines COUNTY.
POST OFFICE: Wilburton, I.T.

Choctaw Roll (Not Including Freedmen)

CARD No. FIELD No. 3097

Dawes' Roll No.	NAME		Relationship to Person	AGE	SEX	BLOOD	TRIBAL ENROLLMENT		
							Year	County	No.
9024	1 Austin, Charles	27	First Named	24	M	Full	1896	Gaines	92
DEAD.	2 " Polina	26	Wife	23	F	"	1896	"	8537
DEAD.	3 " Jessie	2	Dau	1mo	F	"			
	4								
	5	ENROLLMENT							
	6	OF NOS. 1 HEREON APPROVED BY THE SECRETARY							
	7	OF INTERIOR FB 4 1903							
	8	No. 2 and 3 HEREON DISMISSED UNDER							
	9	ORDER OF THE COMMISSION TO THE FIVE CIVILIZED TRIBES OF MARCH 31, 1905.							
	10								
	11								
	12								
	13								
	14								
	15								
	16								
	17								

TRIBAL ENROLLMENT OF PARENTS

	Name of Father	Year	County	Name of Mother	Year	County
1	Lewis Austin	Dead	Gained	Ellen Austin	Dead	Gaines
2	Dallas Moore	"	Jacks Ford	Salina Moore		"
3	No.1			No.2		
4						
5						
6						
7		No1 on 1896 roll as Charley Austin				
8		No2 " 1896 " " Plina Moore				
9		No.3 Enrolled June 8, 1900				
10		No2 died April - 1901: proof of death filed Dec 15 1902				
11		No3 " April - 1901: " " " " " " "				
12		N°1 is husband of Minnie McCurtain, Choctaw card #2887.				
13						
14				Date of Application for Enrollment.		
15				Aug 1/99		
16						
17						

RESIDENCE:	Gaines	COUNTY.								
POST OFFICE:	Wilburton, I.T.		**Choctaw Nation**				**Choctaw Roll** *(Not Including Freedmen)*	CARD NO. FIELD NO.	3098	

Dawes' Roll No.	NAME		Relationship to Person	AGE	SEX	BLOOD	TRIBAL ENROLLMENT		
							Year	County	No.
I.W. 1212	1 Shaw, Ola M	35	First Named	31	F	IW	1896	Gaines	14687
14339	2 James, John B	12	Son	9	M	1/4	1896	"	6601
	3								
	4								
	5								
	6	ENROLLMENT OF NOS. 2 HEREON APPROVED BY THE SECRETARY							
	7	OF INTERIOR APR 11 1903							
	8								
	9								
	10								
	11	ENROLLMENT OF NOS. ~1~ HEREON							
	12	APPROVED BY THE SECRETARY OF INTERIOR DEC 13 1904							
	13								
	14								
	15								
	16								
	17								

TRIBAL ENROLLMENT OF PARENTS

Name of Father	Year	County	Name of Mother	Year	County
1 W. G. Baird		Non Citz	Mary D. Baird		Non Citz
2 John R. James	Dead	Gaines	No1		
3					
4					
5					
6					
7					
8					
9	No1 on 1896 roll as Viola James				
10	No2 " 1896 " " Jno Baird "				
11	No1 amitted[sic] as an intermarried citizen and No2 as a citizen by blood, by Dawes Commission Choctaw Case #1050. No appeal				
12	No.1 has married out: is now the wife of John G. Shawe, a United States citizen 7/2 '01				
13	No.1 originally listed on this card as Ola M James				
14	No.1 formerly wife of John R James, recognized Choctaw by blood, who died about 1890.			Date of Application for Enrollment.	
15	For child of No1 see NB (Apr 26-06) #1245			Aug 1/99	
16					
17					

Choctaw By Blood Enrollment Cards 1898-1914

RESIDENCE:	Gaines	COUNTY.								
POST OFFICE:	Wilburton, I.T.		**Choctaw Nation**				Choctaw Roll (Not Including Freedmen)		CARD NO. FIELD NO.	3099

Dawes' Roll No.	NAME		Relationship to Person	AGE	SEX	BLOOD	TRIBAL ENROLLMENT		
							Year	County	No.
9025	1 Wade, Eastman	33	First Named	30	M	Full	1896	Gaines	12938
9026	2 " Ellen	33	Wife	30	F	"	1896	"	12939
9027	3 " Ellis	10	Son	7	M	"	1896	"	12941
	4								
	5								
	6								
	7	ENROLLMENT OF NOS. 1, 2 and 3 HEREON							
	8	APPROVED BY THE SECRETARY OF INTERIOR FEB 4 1903							
	9								
	10								
	11								
	12								
	13								
	14								
	15								
	16								
	17								

TRIBAL ENROLLMENT OF PARENTS

	Name of Father	Year	County	Name of Mother	Year	County
1	Ho-pa-kin-tubbee	Dead	Gaines	Ah-thle-to-na	Dead	Gaines
2	Dallas Moore	"	Jacks Fork	Salina More		"
3	No1			No2		
4						
5						
6						
7			For child of Nos 1&2 see NB (Mar 3-1905) Card No 210			
8						
9						
10						
11						
12						
13						
14					Date of Application for Enrollment.	
15					Aug 1/99	
16						
17						

RESIDENCE:	Jacks Fork					

RESIDENCE: Jacks Fork COUNTY. **Choctaw Nation** **Choctaw Roll** (*Not Including Freedmen*) CARD NO. FIELD NO. 3100
POST OFFICE: Stringtown, I.T.

Dawes' Roll No.	NAME		Relationship to Person	AGE	SEX	BLOOD	TRIBAL ENROLLMENT		
							Year	County	No.
9028	1 Baker, John	51	First Named	48	M	Full	1896	Jacks Fork	1925
9029	2 " Sukey	54	Wife	52	F	"	1896	" "	4526
9030	3 " Jimmie	25	Son	22	M	"	1896	" "	1927
	4								
	5								
	6	ENROLLMENT							
	7	OF NOS. 1 2 and 3 HEREON APPROVED BY THE SECRETARY							
	8	OF INTERIOR FEB 4 1903							
	9								
	10								
	11								
	12								
	13								
	14								
	15								
	16								
	17								

TRIBAL ENROLLMENT OF PARENTS

	Name of Father	Year	County	Name of Mother	Year	County
1		Dead	in Mississippi	Sukey Baker		Jacks Fork
2	James Sunny	"	Kiamitia	Lucy Sunny	Dead	Red River
3	No1			Kizzie Baker	Dead	Jacks Fork
4						
5						
6						
7	No2 on 1896 roll as Sukey Frazier					
8						
9						
10	Nos 1 and 2 are divorced. No 1 is now husband of Kate Muckintubby on Chic Card #1237					
11						
12						
13						
14				Date of Application for Enrollment.	Aug 1/99	
15						
16						
17						

100

Choctaw By Blood Enrollment Cards 1898-1914

Dawes' Roll No.	NAME		Relationship to Person	AGE	SEX	BLOOD	TRIBAL ENROLLMENT		
							Year	County	No.
9031	₁ McClish, Lorden	24	First Named	21	M	Full	1896	Gaines	9177
9032	₂ " Ross	23	Bro	20	"	"	1896	"	9178
	₃								
	₄								
	₅	ENROLLMENT OF NOS. 1 and 2 HEREON APPROVED BY THE SECRETARY OF INTERIOR FEB 4 1903							
	₆								
	₇								
	₈								
	₉								
	10								
	11								
	12								
	13								
	14								
	15								
	16								
	17								

TRIBAL ENROLLMENT OF PARENTS

	Name of Father	Year	County	Name of Mother	Year	County
₁	Ansiah McClish	Dead	Gaines	Ellen James	Dead	Gaines
₂	" "	"	"	" "	"	"
₃						
₄						
₅						
₆						
₇						
₈		For child of No 1 see NB (March 3, 1905) Card #573				
₉		" " " " 2 " " " " " " #576				
10						
11						
12						
13						
14						
15				Date of Application for Enrollment.	Aug 1/99	
16						
17	Red Oak IT 10/1/04					

RESIDENCE: Tobucksy	COUNTY. Choctaw Nation			Choctaw Roll	CARD NO.	
POST OFFICE: Kiowa, I.T				(Not Including Freedmen)	FIELD NO. 3102	

Dawes' Roll No.	NAME		Relationship to Person	AGE	SEX	BLOOD	TRIBAL ENROLLMENT		
							Year	County	No.
I.W.998	1 Bohreer, John	52	First Named	49	M	I.W.			
14340	2 " Susan	46	Wife	43	F	1/16	1896	Tobucksy	860
14341	3 " Henry	26	Son	23	M	1/32	1896	"	861
14342	4 " Addison	17	"	14	"	1/32	1896	"	864
14343	5 " Alfred	11	"	8	"	1/32	1896	"	865
14344	6 " Sula	8	Dau	5	F	1/32	1896	"	866
	7								
	8 ENROLLMENT OF NOS. 2,3,4,5 and 6 HEREON								
	9 APPROVED BY THE SECRETARY OF INTERIOR APR 11 1903								
	10								
	11 No2 on 1896 roll as Susan D Bohren								
	12 No3 " 1896 " " Henry								
	13 No4 " 1896 " " Anderson								
	No5 " 1896 " " Alfred								
	14 No6 " 1896 " " Lula								
	15 ENROLLMENT								
	16 OF NOS. ~~ 1 ~~~ HEREON APPROVED BY THE SECRETARY								
	17 OF INTERIOR OCT 21 1904								

TRIBAL ENROLLMENT OF PARENTS

	Name of Father	Year	County	Name of Mother	Year	County
1	Benj. R. Bohreer	Dead	Non Citz	Margaret L Bollinger		Non Citz
2	Jno. Blackburn	"	" "	Mary Blackburn	Dead	Atoka
3	No1			No2		
4	No1			No2		
5	No1			No2		
6	No1			No2		
7						
8						
9			All were admitted by Dawes Commission Case No 617 No appeal			
10			No4 was admitted as Adison Boreer.			
11			No5 " " Alford "			
12			No6 " " " Lula "			
13			All were admitted by Dawes Commission under the name of Boreer.			
14				Date of Application for Enrollment.		
15				Aug 1/99		
16						
17						

Choctaw By Blood Enrollment Cards 1898-1914

RESIDENCE: Gaines COUNTY. **Choctaw Nation** Choctaw Roll CARD NO.
POST OFFICE: Ola, I.T. (Not Including Freedmen) FIELD NO. 3103

Dawes' Roll No.	NAME		Relationship to Person	AGE	SEX	BLOOD	TRIBAL ENROLLMENT		
							Year	County	No.
9033	1 Brown, Milton	25	First Named	22	M	Full	1896	Gaines	849
14790	2 " Belle	23	Wife	20	F	1/2	1896	Gaines	8538
14791	3 " Wesley Ann	3	Dau	4mo	"	3/4			
14792	4 " Lula May	1	Dau	3mo	F	3/4			
	5								
	6	ENROLLMENT							
	7	OF NOS. 1 HEREON APPROVED BY THE SECRETARY							
	8	OF INTERIOR FEB 4 1903							
	9								
	10								
	11								
	12	ENROLLMENT							
	13	OF NOS. 2, 3 and 4 HEREON APPROVED BY THE SECRETARY							
	14	OF INTERIOR MAY 20 1903							
	15								
	16								
	17								

TRIBAL ENROLLMENT OF PARENTS

	Name of Father	Year	County	Name of Mother	Year	County
1	Jas Brown		Gaines	Susan Brown	Dead	Gaines
2	Thos Mitchell	dead	Choctaw	Selphie Mitchell	dead	Chickasaw
3	Nº1			Nº2		
4	Nº1			Nº2		
5						
6	No1 on 1896 roll as Mitton Brown					
7						
8	Wife and child on Chickasaw Card No 1473					
9	Nº3 Affidavit as to birth received Aug 9/99					
10	Nº4 Born Oct 4 1901. Enrolled Jany 14 1902					
11	Nºs 2-3-4 originally on Chickasaw card #1473, transferred to this card Jany 8, 1902.					
12	Nº2 is also on 1896 Choctaw Census roll page 213 #8538 as Belle Mitchell.					
13						#1 to 3
14					Date of Application for Enrollment.	
15					Aug 1/99	
16						
17	P.O. Wilburton I.T. 12/16/02					

Choctaw By Blood Enrollment Cards 1898-1914

RESIDENCE:	Gaines COUNTY.	Choctaw Nation	Choctaw Roll (Not Including Freedmen)	CARD NO.
POST OFFICE:	Krebbs, I.T.			FIELD NO. 3104

Dawes' Roll No.	NAME		Relationship to Person First Named	AGE	SEX	BLOOD	TRIBAL ENROLLMENT		
							Year	County	No.
9034	1 Wilson, Jerry	55		52	M	Full	1896	Sans Bois	12698
	2								
	3								
	4	ENROLLMENT OF NOS. 1 HEREON							
	5	APPROVED BY THE SECRETARY OF INTERIOR FEB 4 1903							
	6								
	7								
	8								
	9								
	10								
	11								
	12								
	13								
	14								
	15								
	16								
	17								

TRIBAL ENROLLMENT OF PARENTS

	Name of Father	Year	County	Name of Mother	Year	County
1		Dead	Skullyville		Dead	Gaines
2						
3						
4						
5						
6						
7						
8						
9						
10						
11						
12						
13						
14				Date of Application for Enrollment.	Aug 1/99	
15						
16						
17	P.O. Vireton IT 12.22.02					

104

RESIDENCE: Sans Bois   COUNTY. **Choctaw Nation**   **Choctaw Roll**   CARD NO.
POST OFFICE: Panther, I.T.   *(Not Including Freedmen)*   FIELD NO.   3105

Dawes' Roll No.	NAME		Relationship to Person First Named	AGE	SEX	BLOOD	TRIBAL ENROLLMENT		
							Year	County	No.
DEAD.	~~Hendrickson, William~~	54	~~Named~~	~~51~~	~~M~~	~~1/4~~	~~1896~~	~~Sans Bois~~	~~5134~~
I.W. 656	" Mary E	36	Wife	32	F	I.W.	1896	" "	14595
9035	" Clara E	6	Dau	3	"	1/8	1896	" "	5135
9036	" Aleta E	5	"	2	"	1/8			
9037	" Willie T	3	"	2mo	"	1/8			
6									
7	ENROLLMENT								
8	OF NOS. 3, 4 and 5 HEREON APPROVED BY THE SECRETARY								
9	OF INTERIOR FEB 4 1903								
10	ENROLLMENT								
11	OF NOS. 2 HEREON APPROVED BY THE SECRETARY								
12	OF INTERIOR MAR 26 1904								
13	NO. 1 HEREON DISMISSED UNDER								
14	ORDER OF THE COMMISSION TO THE FIVE								
15	CIVILIZED TRIBES OF MARCH 31, 1905.								
16									
17									

TRIBAL ENROLLMENT OF PARENTS

	Name of Father	Year	County	Name of Mother	Year	County
1	~~Wm Hendrickson~~	~~Dead~~	~~Non Citz~~	~~Mary Hendrickson~~	~~Dead~~	~~Skullyville~~
2	Chase	"	" "	Mary E Chase		Non Citz
3	No1			No2		
4	No1			No2		
5	No1			No2		
6						
7						
8			No1 on 1896 roll as Wm Hendrickson			
9			No2 " 1896 " " Mariah E "			
10			No 4-5 Affidavits of birth to be supplied: Recd Aug 9/99			
11			No1 died Sept 1, 1902; proof of death filed Dec 16, 1902			
12			Evidence of divorce between Fannie and William Hendrixon[sic] filed Jany 17, 1903.			
13						
14					Date of Application for Enrollment.	
15					Aug 2/99	
16						
17	P.O. McCurtain I.T. 12/11/02					

Choctaw By Blood Enrollment Cards 1898-1914

RESIDENCE: Gaines COUNTY. **Choctaw Nation** Choctaw Roll CARD NO.
POST OFFICE: Hartshorne, I.T. (Not Including Freedmen) FIELD NO. 3106

Dawes' Roll No.	NAME	Relationship to Person First Named	AGE	SEX	BLOOD	TRIBAL ENROLLMENT		
						Year	County	No.
I.W. 738 ₁	Chastain, Jefferson D ⁴²		39	M	I.W.	1896	Gaines	14386
14793 ₂	" Lena M ³⁵	Wife	32	F	1/8	1896	"	2273
14794 ₃	" Garvin D ¹¹	Son	8	M	1/16	1896	"	2274
14795 ₄	" Rosa B ⁹	Dau	6	F	1/16	1896	"	2275
14796 ₅	" Clarence C ⁷	Son	4	M	1/16	1896	"	2276
6								
7	ENROLLMENT							
8	OF NOS. 2,3,4 and 5 HEREON APPROVED BY THE SECRETARY							
9	OF INTERIOR MAY 20 1903							
10								
11	DECISION PREPARED							
12								
13	ENROLLMENT							
14	OF NOS. ~~~~ 1 ~~~~~ HEREON							
15	APPROVED BY THE SECRETARY OF INTERIOR MAY -7 1904							
16								
17								

TRIBAL ENROLLMENT OF PARENTS

	Name of Father	Year	County	Name of Mother	Year	County
1	E. J. Chastain	Dead	Non Citz	Susan Chastain		Non Citz
2	Willian Dunn	"	" "	Salina Dunn		Atoka
3	No1			No2		
4	No1			No2		
5	No1			No2		
6						
7						
8	No1 See Decision of March 2 '04					
9	All admitted by Dawes Commission in 1896 in Choctaw case #769; no appeal. No1 admitted as an intermarried					
10	citizen: all others admitted by blood					
11	No1 on 1896 roll as J. D. Chastain					
12						
13						
14				Date of Application for Enrollment.		
15				Aug 2/99		
16						
17						

Choctaw By Blood Enrollment Cards 1898-1914

RESIDENCE: Chickasaw Natn	COUNTY.							CARD NO.	
POST OFFICE: Chickasha, I.T.	**Choctaw Nation**				**Choctaw Roll** (Not Including Freedmen)			FIELD NO. **3107**	

Dawes' Roll No.	NAME	Relationship to Person First Named	AGE	SEX	BLOOD	TRIBAL ENROLLMENT		
						Year	County	No.
1	Harris, Jonas R. ⑥③		56	M	I.W.	1896	Chick Dist	14674
9038 2	" Rosa L ³⁶	Wife	33	F	1/8	1896	" "	6216
9039 3	" Alfred M ¹⁶	Son	13	M	1/16	1896	" "	6747
4								
5								
6	ENROLLMENT OF NOS. HEREON							
7	APPROVED BY THE SECRETARY OF INTERIOR							
8								
9								
10								
11								
12								
13	No1 transferred to Choctaw card							
14	#106 October 8 1903							
15								
16								
17								

TRIBAL ENROLLMENT OF PARENTS

Name of Father	Year	County	Name of Mother	Year	County
1 Henry H Harris	Dead	Non Citz	Eliza Harris	Dead	Non Citz
2 Wᵐ M Dunn	" "		Salina Dunn		Atoka
3 No1			No2		
4					
5					
6					
7	Nos 2 and 3 are duplicates of Rosa L. Harris and Alfred M Harris				
8	on Choctaw card #106. Their enrollment is cancelled				
9	under Departmental instructions of September 26, 1903				
10	No1 on 1896 roll as J. R. Harris				
11	No2 " 1896 " " Rosie "				
12					
13					
14				Date of Application for Enrollment.	
15				Aug 2/99	
16					
17					

CANCELLED

October 21 1903

RESIDENCE: **Gaines**	COUNTY. **Choctaw Nation**	**Choctaw Roll** CARD NO.
POST OFFICE: **Vireton, I.T.**		*(Not Including Freedmen)* FIELD NO. **3108**

Dawes' Roll No.	NAME		Relationship to Person First Named	AGE	SEX	BLOOD	Year	County	No.
9040	1 Jones, Willie	45	Named	42	M	Full	1896	Gaines	6624
DEAD.	2 " ~~Wyly~~ DEAD		Wife	~~39~~	~~F~~	"	~~1896~~	"	~~6625~~
9041	3 Jones, Douglas	21	Son	18	M	"	1896	"	6626
9042	4 " Eliza	18	Dau	15	F	"	1896	"	6627
9043	5 " George	12	Son	9	M	"	1896	"	6628
I.W. 1213	6 Hamilton, Lilie	18	Wife	17	F	I.W.			
	7								
	8	ENROLLMENT OF NOS. 1,3,4 and 5 HEREON							
	9	APPROVED BY THE SECRETARY							
		OF INTERIOR FEB 4 1903							
	10								
	11	ENROLLMENT							
	12	OF NOS. ~ 6 ~ HEREON APPROVED BY THE SECRETARY							
	13	OF INTERIOR DEC 13 1904							
	14								
	15	No. 2 HEREON DISMISSED UNDER ORDER OF THE COMMISSION TO THE FIVE							
	16	CIVILIZED TRIBES OF MARCH 31, 1905							
	17								

TRIBAL ENROLLMENT OF PARENTS

	Name of Father	Year	County	Name of Mother	Year	County
1	Jimson Jones	Dead	Gaines	Sophie Jones	Dead	Jacks Fork
2	~~Harry Kincade~~	"	~~Sans Bois~~	~~Tennessee Kincade~~		~~Sans Bois~~
3	No1			No2		
4	No1			No2		
5	No1			No2		
6	John Reynolds		Non-citizen	Cythia[sic] Reynolds		Non-citizen
7						
8						
9	No.6 married to No.1 June 4th 1900 For child of No.1 see NB (Mar 3 1905) #1328					
10	No.6 originally listed on this card as Lillie Jones					
11	No2 on 1896 roll as Wylie Jones ~~No2 died November 2d 1899 & see testimony~~					
12	taken June 7, 1900 No4 is mother of Bettie Winlock on Choctaw card #4489. See					
13	copy of testimony of Rufus Winlock taken July 27, 1903. #1 to 5					
14	No.6 Enrolled June 7th 1900 ~~No.6 is now the wife of Alexander B. Hamilton on Choctaw~~				Date of Application for Enrollment.	
15	Card #4594. Evidence of divorce and remarriage filed Aug 28, 1902				Aug 2/99	
16	No.1 is now husband of No.6 on Choc. Card 2736					
17	No6 Indianola IT 5/20/14					

Choctaw By Blood Enrollment Cards 1898-1914

RESIDENCE:	Gaines	COUNTY.								CARD NO.
POST OFFICE:	Alderson, I.T.		**Choctaw Nation**			Choctaw Roll (Not Including Freedmen)				FIELD NO. 3109

Dawes' Roll No.	NAME	Relationship to Person First Named	AGE	SEX	BLOOD	TRIBAL ENROLLMENT		
						Year	County	No.
✓ ＊ 1	Stroud, Frances L	Named	49	F	1/4			
✓ ＊ 2	" John S.	Son	21	M	1/8			
✓ ＊ 3	" Isaac M	"	18	"	1/8			
4								
5								
6								
7								
8								
9								
10								
11								
12								
13								
14								
15								
16								
17								

DENIED CITIZENSHIP BY THE CHOCTAW AND CHICKASAW CITIZENSHIP COURT

TRIBAL ENROLLMENT OF PARENTS

Name of Father	Year	County	Name of Mother	Year	County
1 Andrew Butler	Dead	Choctaw	Clarinda Butler	Dead	Non Citz
2 C. A. Stroud		Non Citz	No 1		
3 " " "		" "	No 1		
4					
5	Nos 1, 2 and 3 were denied by Dawes Com Choc Cit Case #1392				
6	Admitted by U.S. Court, Central Dist. Sept 9/97				
7	Case No 90. As to residence see testimony of				
8	No 1.				
9	No 1 now wife of Charles A Stroud on Choctaw Card #D466 July 5" 1902.				
10	Nos 1,2 and 3 were denied by Choctaw-Chickasaw Citizenship Court Feb 2 1904 Csse #48				
11					
12					
13					
14				Date of Application for Enrollment.	
15				Aug 1/99	
16					
17					

109

Choctaw By Blood Enrollment Cards 1898-1914

RESIDENCE: Skullyville   COUNTY. **Choctaw Nation**   **Choctaw Roll** *(Not Including Freedmen)*   CARD NO. FIELD NO. **3110**

POST OFFICE: Cameron, I.T.

Dawes' Roll No.	NAME	Relationship to Person First Named	AGE	SEX	BLOOD	TRIBAL ENROLLMENT Year	County	No.
* 1	Greer, Nancy E		34	F	1/8			
* 2	" Arthur	Son	18	M	1/16			
* 3	" Walter	"	14	"	1/16			
* 4	" Odas	"	11	"	1/16			
* 5	" Charles	"	8	"	1/16			
* 6	" Virgil	"	5	"	1/16			
7	" Uimont	"	2	"	1/16			
8	" Noble Dering	"	8mo	M	1/16			
9	Judgment of U.S. Court C.D. admitting Nos 1 to 6 inclusive							
10	Vacated and set aside by Decree of Choctaw Chickasaw							
11	Citizenship Court Dec 17/02 Nol to 6 inclusive was denied							
12	by Choctaw Chickasaw Citizenship Court, Feb 2 1904 Case 90							
13								
14	No 7 & 8 DISMISSED							
15	MAY 24 1904							
16	No							
17								

DENIED CITIZENSHIP BY THE CHOCTAW AND
CHICKASAW CITIZENSHIP COURT   Feb 2 04

TRIBAL ENROLLMENT OF PARENTS

	Name of Father	Year	County	Name of Mother	Year	County
1	Chas Stroud		Non Citz	Frances L Stroud		Choctaw
2	J. P. Greer		" "	No 1		
3	" " "		" "	No 1		
4	" " "		" "	No 1		
5	" " "		" "	No 1		
6	" " "		" "	No 1		
7	" " "		" "	No 1		
8	" " "		" "	Nᵒ1		
9						
10	Nos 1 to 6 inclusive denied by the Dawes Com in 96 Choc Cit Case #1392					
11	* Admitted by U.S. Court, Central Dist. Sept 9/97					
12	Case No 90. As to residence and birth of No7,					
13	see her testimony, that is Nancy E Greer.					
14	No3 was admitted as Walter Greer					Date of Application for Enrollment.
15	No4 " " " Odis					Aug 2/99
16	No7 Affidavit of birth to be supplied: Recd 8/4/99					
17	Nᵒ 8 Born Aug 6, 1901, enrolled April 16, 1902.					

110

RESIDENCE: Gaines	COUNTY.	**Choctaw Nation**	**Choctaw Roll**	CARD No.
POST OFFICE: Hartshorne, I.T.			*(Not Including Freedmen)*	FIELD No. 3111

Dawes' Roll No.	NAME	Relationship to Person First Named	AGE	SEX	BLOOD	TRIBAL ENROLLMENT		
						Year	County	No.
✓ * 1	Stroud, James W	Named	30	M	1/8			
✓ * 2	" William	Son	9	"	1/16			
3								
4								
5								
6								
7								
8								
9								
10								
11								
12								
13								
14								
15								
16								
17								

TRIBAL ENROLLMENT OF PARENTS

	Name of Father	Year	County	Name of Mother	Year	County
1	Chas Stroud		Non Citz	Frances L Stroud		Choctaw
2	No 1			Ella Stroud		Non Citz
3						
4						
5						
6	Nos 1 and 2 Denied by the Dawes Com in 96 Choc Cit Case #1392					
7	Admitted by U.S. Court, Central Dist, Sept 9/97					
8	Case No 90. As to residence, see testimony of No 1					
9	No 1 Husband of Elley Stroud on Choctaw Card #D467					
	Judgment of U.S. Court admitting Nos 1&2 vacated and set aside by Decree of Choctaw Chickasaw Cir Court Dec 17 02					
10	Nos 1&2 denied by Choctaw Chickasaw Court Feb 2 '04 Case [illegible]					
11						
12						
13						
14						
15				Date of Application for Enrollment.	Aug 2/99	
16						
17						

Choctaw By Blood Enrollment Cards 1898-1914

RESIDENCE: Gaines COUNTY. **Choctaw Nation** Choctaw Roll CARD NO.
POST OFFICE: Wilburton, I.T. *(Not Including Freedmen)* FIELD NO. 3112

Dawes' Roll No.	NAME	Relationship to Person First Named	AGE	SEX	BLOOD	TRIBAL ENROLLMENT		
						Year	County	No.
I.W. 657	₁ Latimer, James S ⁴⁷		43	M	IW	1896	Gaines	14752
14345	₂ " Allie B ²⁶	Wife	23	F	1/4	1896	"	7834
14346	₃ " Winifred ⁷	Dau	4	"	1/8	1896	"	7835
14347	₄ " Alvin ⁵	Son	1½	M	1/8			
	₅							
	₆	ENROLLMENT	DECISION PREPARED					
	₇	OF NOS. 2 3 and 4 HEREON APPROVED BY THE SECRETARY						
	₈	OF INTERIOR APR 11 1903						
	₉	ENROLLMENT						
	₁₀	OF NOS. 1 HEREON APPROVED BY THE SECRETARY						
	₁₁	OF INTERIOR MAR 26 1904						
	₁₂							
	₁₃							
	₁₄							
	₁₅							
	₁₆							
	₁₇							

TRIBAL ENROLLMENT OF PARENTS

Name of Father	Year	County	Name of Mother	Year	County
₁ G. W. Latimer	Dead	Non Citz	Nancy B Latimer		Non Citz
₂ Turner Brashears	"	Skullyville	Kate Brashears	Dead	" "
₃ No1			No2		
₄ No1			No2		
₅					
₆					
₇					
₈					
₉					

₁₀ No2 on 1896 roll as Alice B Latimer
₁₁ As to marriage of parents of No2
₁₂ see enrollment of J. J. and Mattie Moore, Card No 2900
₁₃ No4 Affidavit of birth to be supplied
₁₄ Recd Oct 7/99
₁₅ No.1 admitted as an intermarried citizen and Nos 2 and 3 as
₁₆ citizens by blood in 1896. Choctaw case #1098. no appeal
₁₇ For child of Nos 1&2 see NB (Mar 3-05) Card #211

Date of Application for Enrollment.
Aug 2/99

Choctaw By Blood Enrollment Cards 1898-1914

RESIDENCE:	Jacks Fork	COUNTY.			CARD NO.	
POST OFFICE:	Stringtown, I.T	**Choctaw Nation**	**Choctaw Roll** *(Not Including Freedmen)*		FIELD NO.	3113

Dawes' Roll No.	NAME		Relationship to Person First Named	AGE	SEX	BLOOD	TRIBAL ENROLLMENT		
							Year	County	No.
9044	1 Moore, Joseph	23		20	M	Full	1896	Jacks Fork	8863
	2								
	3								
	4	ENROLLMENT OF NOS. 1							
	5	APPROVED BY THE SECRETARY HEREON							
	6	OF INTERIOR FEB 4 1903							
	7								
	8								
	9								
	10								
	11								
	12								
	13								
	14								
	15								
	16								
	17								

TRIBAL ENROLLMENT OF PARENTS

	Name of Father	Year	County	Name of Mother	Year	County
1	Joseph Moore	Dead	Jacks Fork	Susie Moore	Dead	Jacks Fork
2						
3						
4						
5						
6						
7			On 1896 roll as Joseph More			
8						
9						
10						
11						
12						
13						
14						
15				Date of Application for Enrollment.	Aug 1/99	
16						
17	PO Blanco 12/23 '02					

RESIDENCE:	Gaines	COUNTY.							
POST OFFICE:	Wilburton, I.T.								

Choctaw Nation Choctaw Roll *(Not Including Freedmen)* CARD NO. FIELD NO. **3114**

Dawes' Roll No.	NAME	Relationship to Person First Named	AGE	SEX	BLOOD	TRIBAL ENROLLMENT Year	County	No.
9045	1 Simmons, John 34		31	M	3/4	1896	Skullyville	11141
I.W. 739	2 " Mamie 25	Wife	25	F	I.W.	1896	"	15024
9046	3 " Fred 10	Son	7	M	3/8	1896	"	1142
9047	4 " Gracy 7	Dau	4	F	3/8	1896	"	11144
9048	5 " Joshua 5	Son	2	M	3/8			
	6							
	7							
	8 ENROLLMENT							
	9 OF NOS. 1-3-4 and 5 HEREON							
	10 APPROVED BY THE SECRETARY OF INTERIOR FEB 4 1903							
	11							
	12							
	13							
	14							
	15 ENROLLMENT OF NOS. 2 HEREON							
	16 APPROVED BY THE SECRETARY OF INTERIOR MAY -7 1904							
	17							

TRIBAL ENROLLMENT OF PARENTS

	Name of Father	Year	County	Name of Mother	Year	County
1	Sam Simmons	Dead	Skullyville	Wesley Ann Simmons	Dead	Skullyville
2	Stacen	"	Non Citz		"	Non Citz
3	No1			No2		
4	No1			No2		
5	No1			No2		
6						
7						
8	No2 See Decision of March 2 '04					
9	No2 on 1896 roll as Minnie Simmons					
10	Evidence of marriage to be supplied:					
11	No.5 Affidavit of birth to be supplied.					
12	Recd Oct 7/99					
13	For child of Nos 1&2 see NB (Apr 26-06) Card #590					
	" " " " " " " (Mar 3-05) " #1440					
14					Date of Application for Enrollment	
15					Aug 2/99	
16						
17	PO Guertie I.T. 3/12/03					

PO Spiro I.T. 4/14/03

114

Choctaw By Blood Enrollment Cards 1898-1914

RESIDENCE:	Gaines	COUNTY.							CARD NO.	
POST OFFICE:	Vireton, I.T.		**Choctaw Nation**				Choctaw Roll (Not Including Freedmen)		FIELD NO. 3115	

Dawes' Roll No.	NAME		Relationship to Person	AGE	SEX	BLOOD	TRIBAL ENROLLMENT		
							Year	County	No.
9049	1 Perry, Jane	26	First Named	23	F	Full	1896	Sans Bois	10041
9050	2 Mishamahtubbee, Lena	3	Dau	3mo	"	"			
9051	3 Anderson, Ola May	1	Dau	8mo	F	"			
	4								
	5								
	6								
	7	ENROLLMENT OF NOS. 1, 2, and 3 HEREON APPROVED BY THE SECRETARY OF INTERIOR FEB 4 1903							
	8								
	9								
	10								
	11								
	12								
	13								
	14								
	15								
	16								
	17								

TRIBAL ENROLLMENT OF PARENTS

	Name of Father	Year	County	Name of Mother	Year	County
1	Joe Beams	Dead	Sans Bois	Mulsey White		Gaines
2	Dave Mishamahtubbee		Gaines	No1		
3	Noel Anderson	1896	Boktuklo[sic]	No1		
4						
5						
6						
7						
8			N°3 Born Jany 23, 1902, enrolled Sept 22 1902			
9			N°3 is illegitimate			
10						
11						
12						
13						
14				#1&2		
15				Date of Application for Enrollment.	Aug 2/99	
16						
17						

Choctaw By Blood Enrollment Cards 1898-1914

RESIDENCE: Gaines		COUNTY. **Choctaw Nation**				**Choctaw Roll** *(Not Including Freedmen)*	CARD NO.	
POST OFFICE: Wilburton, I.T.							FIELD NO.	3116

Dawes' Roll No.	NAME		Relationship to Person First Named	AGE	SEX	BLOOD	TRIBAL ENROLLMENT		
							Year	County	No.
9052	1 Moore, Selina	50		47	F	Full	1896	Gaines	8536
	2								
	3								
	4	ENROLLMENT OF NOS. 1 HEREON							
	5	APPROVED BY THE SECRETARY							
	6	OF INTERIOR FEB 4 1903							
	7								
	8								
	9								
	10								
	11								
	12								
	13								
	14								
	15								
	16								
	17								

TRIBAL ENROLLMENT OF PARENTS

	Name of Father	Year	County	Name of Mother	Year	County
1	Dan'l Anderson	Dead	Gaines	Liza Anderson	Dead	Tobucksy
2						
3						
4						
5						
6						
7						
8						
9						
10						
11						
12						
13						
14				Date of Application for Enrollment.	Aug 2/99	
15						
16						
17						

116

Choctaw By Blood Enrollment Cards 1898-1914

RESIDENCE:	Gaines	COUNTY.					CARD No.	
POST OFFICE:	Hartshorne, I.T.	Choctaw Nation		Choctaw Roll (Not Including Freedmen)			FIELD No.	3117

Dawes' Roll No.	NAME	Relationship to Person First Named	AGE	SEX	BLOOD	TRIBAL ENROLLMENT		
						Year	County	No.
9053	1 Nelson, Mary A 60		57	F	Full	1896	Gaines	9584
	2							
	3							
	4 ENROLLMENT OF NOS. 1 HEREON							
	5 APPROVED BY THE SECRETARY OF INTERIOR FEB 4 1903							
	6							
	7							
	8							
	9							
	10							
	11							
	12							
	13							
	14							
	15							
	16							
	17							

TRIBAL ENROLLMENT OF PARENTS

	Name of Father	Year	County	Name of Mother	Year	County
1	Cla-lin-tubbee	Dead	Sugar Loaf	Yim-mi	Dead	in Mississippi
2						
3						
4						
5						
6						
7			On 1896 roll as Mary Ann Nelson			
8						
9						
10						
11						
12						
13						
14				Date of Application for Enrollment	Aug 2/99	
15						
16						
17						

117

Choctaw By Blood Enrollment Cards 1898-1914

Choctaw Nation

Choctaw Roll (Not Including Freedmen)

CARD NO.
FIELD NO. 3118

Dawes' Roll No.	NAME	Relationship to Person First Named	AGE	SEX	BLOOD	TRIBAL ENROLLMENT		
						Year	County	No.
9054	1 Mishamahtubbee, Davis 36	First Named	33	M	Full	1896	Gaines	8539
9055	2 " Wynie 30	Wife	27	F	"	1896	"	8540
9056	3 " Lizzie 13	Ward	10	"	"	1896	"	8541
9057	4 " Alice 11	"	8	"	"	1896	"	8542
9058	5 Smith Jackson 16	"	13	M	"	1896	"	11254
9059	6 Jones, Impson 13	"	10	"	"	1896	"	6612
	7							
	8							
	9	ENROLLMENT OF NOS. 1,2,3,4,5 and 6 HEREON						
	10	APPROVED BY THE SECRETARY OF INTERIOR FEB 4 1903						
	11							
	12							
	13							
	14							
	15							
	16							
	17							

TRIBAL ENROLLMENT OF PARENTS

	Name of Father	Year	County	Name of Mother	Year	County
1	Jno Mishamahtubbee	Dead	Tobucksy	Mary Mishamahtubbee	Dead	Tobucksy
2	Daniel Jones	"	"	Sallie Jones	"	"
3	Jesse Anderson	"	"	Elsie Anderson	"	"
4	Joseph Lockley	"	Sans Bois	Amy Lockley		Gaines
5	Abel Smith	"	Tobucksy	Munsie Smith	Dead	Tobucksy
6	Sam Jones		Gaines	Beckey Jones		Gaines
7						
8						
9	No4 on 1896 roll as Ellie Mishemahtubbe					
10	No5 " 1896 " " Jack Smith					
11	Surnames of first four appear on 1896 roll as Mishematubbe					
12	Mother of Nos 3 & 4 is believed to be Amy Nail as No2 on 7-3128					
13						
14						
15					Aug 2/99	
16						
17						

Choctaw By Blood Enrollment Cards 1898-1914

RESIDENCE: Gaines COUNTY.	POST OFFICE: Simpson, I.T.

Choctaw Nation

Choctaw Roll (Not Including Freedmen)

CARD NO. FIELD NO. 3119

Dawes' Roll No.		NAME		Relationship to Person First Named	AGE	SEX	BLOOD	TRIBAL ENROLLMENT		
								Year	County	No.
9060	1	McCann, Nealy	25		22	F	Full	1896	Tobucksy	9183
	2									
	3									
	4	ENROLLMENT OF NOS. 1 HEREON								
	5	APPROVED BY THE SECRETARY								
	6	OF INTERIOR FEB 4 1903								
	7									
	8									
	9									
	10									
	11									
	12									
	13									
	14									
	15									
	16									
	17									

TRIBAL ENROLLMENT OF PARENTS

	Name of Father	Year	County	Name of Mother	Year	County
1		Dead	Kiamitia	Phoebe McCann	Dead	Tobucksy
2						
3						
4						
5						
6						
7			On 1896 roll as Mealy McCann			
8						
9						
10						
11						
12						
13					Date of Application for Enrollment.	
14						
15					Aug 2/99	
16						
17						

	NAME		Relationship to Person	AGE	SEX	BLOOD	TRIBAL ENROLLMENT		
							Year	County	No.
1	Nelson, Eastman	25	First Named	22	M	Full	1896	Gaines	9587
61 2	" Melvina	22	Wife	19	F	1/2	1896	Sans Bois	3157
9063 3	" Isaac	4	Son	1	M	3/4			
9064 4	" Salina	1	Dau	2mo	F	3/4			
5									
6									
7									
8									
9									
10									
11									
12									
13									
14									
15									
16									
17									

Gaines COUNTY. **Choctaw Nation** **Choctaw Roll** (Not Including Freedmen) CARD NO. FIELD NO. 3120
Hartshorne, I.T.

ENROLLMENT OF NOS. 1, 2, 3 and 4 HEREON APPROVED BY THE SECRETARY OF INTERIOR FEB 4 1903

TRIBAL ENROLLMENT OF PARENTS

	Name of Father	Year	County	Name of Mother	Year	County
1	Smallwood Nelson		Gaines	Rhoda Nelson	Dead	Gaines
2	Daniel Davis	Dead	Creek	Sophie Davis	"	Sans Bois
3	No1			No2		
4	No.1			No.2		
5						
6						
7			No2 on 1896 roll as Melvina Davis			
8						
9			No3 Affidavit of birth to be supplied:			
10			Recd Oct 7/99 No4 Enrolled May 29, 1901			
11						
12						
13						
14				Date of Application for Enrollment.	Aug 1/99	
15						
16						
17	P.O. Higgins I.T. 9/22/06					

Choctaw By Blood Enrollment Cards 1898-1914

RESIDENCE: Gaines COUNTY. **Choctaw Nation** Choctaw Roll CARD NO.
POST OFFICE: Wilburton, I.T. *(Not Including Freedmen)* FIELD NO. 3121

Dawes' Roll No.	NAME		Relationship to Person	AGE	SEX	BLOOD	TRIBAL ENROLLMENT		
							Year	County	No.
9065	₁ Paxton, Philip	40	First Named	37	M	Full	1896	Gaines	10216
9066	₂ " Cholina	31	Wife	28	F	"	1896	"	10217
9067	₃ Wesley, Ickney	13	SDau	10	F	"	1893	"	451
	4								
	5								
	6								
	7	ENROLLMENT OF NOS. 1, 2 and 3 HEREON							
	8	APPROVED BY THE SECRETARY OF INTERIOR FEB 4 1903							
	9								
	10								
	11								
	12								
	13								
	14								
	15								
	16								
	17								

TRIBAL ENROLLMENT OF PARENTS

	Name of Father	Year	County	Name of Mother	Year	County
1	John Paxton	Dead	Gaines	Patsey Paxton	Dead	Gaines
2	Josiah Reed		"	Winey Reed	"	"
3	William Wesley	Dead	Jacks Fork	No2		
4						
5	5/16/38 Sex of Nº3 changed from "M" to "F" Dept Authy May 5, 1938 – D-6832-5-7-1938 JDF					
6						
7						
8		No2 on 1896 roll as Julia Paxton				
9						
10		No3 on 1893 Pay roll, Page 47, No 451, Gaines				
11		County as Agny Paxton. Also on 1896 roll Page 290 No 112521 as Edna Stonobee Gaines Co				
12						
13						
14						
15				Date of Application for Enrollment.	Aug 2/99	
16						
17						

RESIDENCE: Gaines COUNTY. **Choctaw Nation** Choctaw Roll CARD No.
POST OFFICE: Hartshorne, I.T. (*Not Including Freedmen*) FIELD No. 3122

Dawes' Roll No.	NAME	Relationship to Person First Named	AGE	SEX	BLOOD	TRIBAL ENROLLMENT		
						Year	County	No.
DEAD. 1	Baker, Robert DEAD. 23		20	M	Full	1896	Jacks Fork	1919
2								
3								
4								
5								
6								
7	No. 1 HEREON DISMISSED UNDER							
8	ORDER OF THE COMMISSION TO THE FIVE CIVILIZED TRIBES OF MARCH 31, 1905.							
9								
10								
11								
12								
13								
14								
15								
16								
17								

TRIBAL ENROLLMENT OF PARENTS

	Name of Father	Year	County	Name of Mother	Year	County
1	Solomon Baker		...nes	Sophia Baker	Dead	Jacks Fork
2						
3						
4						
5						
6						
7						
8	No.1 Died February 25, 1902: Proof of death filed Dec 24 1902					
9						
10						
11						
12						
13						
14					Date of Application for Enrollment.	
15					Aug 2/99	
16						
17						

CANCELLED

RESIDENCE: Gaines COUNTY. **Choctaw Nation** Choctaw Roll CARD NO.
POST OFFICE: Hartshorne, I.T. *(Not Including Freedmen)* FIELD NO. 3123

Dawes' Roll No.	NAME		Relationship to Person First Named	AGE	SEX	BLOOD	TRIBAL ENROLLMENT		
							Year	County	No.
9068	1 Hurt, Annie	45	First Named	42	F	1/8	1896	Gaines	9593
15917	2 Beagles, Nellie F	9	Dau	6	"	1/16	1896	"	836
9069	3 Hurt, Susan	1	Dau	1mo	F	1/16			
I.W. 1117	4 " William	57	Husband	57	M	I.W.			
	5		No. 2						
	6	ENROLLMENT							
	7	OF NOS. 1 and 3 HEREON APPROVED BY THE SECRETARY	GRANTED						
	8	OF INTERIOR FEB 4 1903	JUN 27 1905						
	9								
	10	No 1 [Illegible] IT in 1904							
	11								
	12	No 5 PO Wilburton IT 10/25/04							
	13								
	14								
	15	ENROLLMENT OF NOS. 4 HEREON	ENROLLMENT OF NOS. Two HEREON						
	16	APPROVED BY THE SECRETARY	APPROVED BY THE SECRETARY						
	17	OF INTERIOR NOV 16 1904	OF INTERIOR AUG 23 1905						

TRIBAL ENROLLMENT OF PARENTS

	Name of Father	Year	County	Name of Mother	Year	County
1	William Graham	Dead	Non Citz	Sarah Graham	Dead	Blue
2	Allen Beagles	"	"	No1		
3	William Hurt	"	"	No1		
4	Joseph Hurt	dead	non-citizen	Nancy Hurt	dead	non-citizen
5						
6						
7						
8	No.1 is now the wife of William Hurt on Choctaw card #D592					
9	No.3 Enrolled Oct 4, 1901					
	No.2 was denied by Dawes Commission in 1896, Case 11. No appeal					
10	No1 and her husband, William Hurt, have separated. 11/19/02.					
11	Nº2 Born Jany 9, 1894, proof of birth filed Aug 3, 1903					
12	No.4 transferred from Choctaw card #D-592, Oct. 31, 1904: See decision of Oct. 15, 1904					
13	Enrollment of No. [illegible] cancelled by order of Department March [illegible], 19[illegible]					
	No. [illegible] restored to roll by Departmental authority of January 10, 1909 [Illegible]					
14						
15				Date of Application for Enrollment.	Aug 2/99	
16						
17	PO Ashland IT 8/20/05					

RESIDENCE: **Gaines** COUNTY. **Choctaw Nation** **Choctaw Roll** CARD NO.
POST OFFICE: **Hartshorne, I.T.** *(Not Including Freedmen)* FIELD NO. **3124**

Dawes' Roll No.	NAME		Relationship to Person First Named	AGE	SEX	BLOOD	TRIBAL ENROLLMENT		
							Year	County	No.
9070	1 Durant, Nellie	38	First Named	35	F	Full	1896	Gaines	3271
	2								
	3								
	4								
	5								
	6								
	7								
	8								
	9								
	10								
	11								
	12								
	13								
	14								
	15								
	16								
	17								

ENROLLMENT OF NOS. 1 HEREON APPROVED BY THE SECRETARY OF INTERIOR FEB 4 1903

TRIBAL ENROLLMENT OF PARENTS

Name of Father	Year	County	Name of Mother	Year	County
1 Wᵐ Murphey	Dead	Gaines	Me-lin-te-ho-tubbey	Dead	Gaines
2					
3					
4					
5					
6					
7					
8					
9					
10					
11					
12					
13					
14				Date of Application for Enrollment.		
15				Aug 2/99		
16						
17						

Choctaw By Blood Enrollment Cards 1898-1914

RESIDENCE: Gaines COUNTY. **Choctaw Nation** Choctaw Roll CARD NO.
POST OFFICE: Wilburton, I.T. (Not Including Freedmen) FIELD NO. 3125

Dawes' Roll No.		NAME		Relationship to Person	AGE	SEX	BLOOD	TRIBAL ENROLLMENT		
								Year	County	No.
9071	1	Riddle, Richard R	24	First Named	21	M	1/16	1896	Gaines	10735
I.W. 288	2	" Florence	23	Wife	21	F	I.W.			
9072	3	" Shingo L	3	Dau	7mo	"	1/32			
9073	4	" Daisy R	1	dau	1mo	F	1/32			
	5									
	6									
	7	ENROLLMENT OF NOS. 1, 3 and 4 HEREON								
	8	APPROVED BY THE SECRETARY								
	9	OF INTERIOR FEB 4 1903								
	10	ENROLLMENT OF NOS. 2 HEREON								
	11	APPROVED BY THE SECRETARY								
	12	OF INTERIOR SEP 12 1903								
	13									
	14									
	15									
	16									
	17									

TRIBAL ENROLLMENT OF PARENTS

	Name of Father	Year	County	Name of Mother	Year	County
1	Geo Riddle		Gaines	Evaline Riddle		white woman
2	Jno D Camp	Dead	Non Citz	Jennie Camp	Dead	Non Citz
3	No 1			No 2		
4	No.1			No.2		
5						
6						
7			Evidence of marriage to be supplied:			
8			Recd Oct 7/99			
9			As to marriage of parents of No1 see enrollment of Evaline and George Riddle			
10			No.4 born Nov. 9th 1901; Enrolled Dec. 12, 1901			
11			Affidavit of N°1 as to residence at the time of his marriage filed April 24, 1903			
12			For child of Nos 1&2 see NB (Apr 26-06) Card #768			
13			" " " " " (Mar 3-05) " #212			
14				#1&2		
15				Date of Application for Enrollment. Aug 2/99		
16				No3 enrolled Oct 7/99		
17						

Choctaw By Blood Enrollment Cards 1898-1914

RESIDENCE: Gaines	COUNTY.					
POST OFFICE: Hartshorne, I.T.	Choctaw Nation	Choctaw Roll (Not Including Freedmen)	CARD NO. FIELD NO. 3126			

Dawes' Roll No.	NAME	Relationship to Person First Named	AGE	SEX	BLOOD	TRIBAL ENROLLMENT Year	County	No.
9074	1 Mullin, Morris ³¹		28	M	Full	1893	Gaines	379
	2							
	3							
	4							
	5	ENROLLMENT OF NOS. 1 HEREON APPROVED BY THE SECRETARY OF INTERIOR FEB 4 1903						
	6							
	7							
	8							
	9							
	10							
	11							
	12							
	13							
	14							
	15							
	16							
	17							

TRIBAL ENROLLMENT OF PARENTS

	Name of Father	Year	County	Name of Mother	Year	County
1	Te-tham-bee	Dead	Gaines	Hutchee	Dead	Gaines
2						
3						
4						
5						
6			On 1893 Pay roll, Page 40, No 379, Gaines			
7			Co, as Morris Mullen			
8			For child of No.1 see NB (March 3, 1905) #1498			
9						
10						
11						
12						
13						
14				Date of Application for Enrollment.	Aug 2/99	
15						
16						
17	Higgins I.T. 8/30/05					

126

Choctaw By Blood Enrollment Cards 1898-1914

RESIDENCE:	Gaines	COUNTY.					
POST OFFICE:	Hartshorne, I.T.						

Choctaw Nation — Choctaw Roll *(Not Including Freedmen)*

CARD NO. FIELD NO. 3127

Dawes' Roll No.	NAME	Relationship to Person	AGE	SEX	BLOOD	TRIBAL ENROLLMENT Year	County	No.
9075	1 Frazier, Caldwell 39	First Named	36	M	Full	1896	Gaines	3979
	2							
	3							
	4							
	5	ENROLLMENT OF NOS. 1 HEREON						
	6	APPROVED BY THE SECRETARY OF INTERIOR FEB 4 1903						
	7							
	8							
	9							
	10							
	11							
	12							
	13							
	14							
	15							
	16							
	17							

TRIBAL ENROLLMENT OF PARENTS

	Name of Father	Year	County	Name of Mother	Year	County
1	Wilson Frazier	Dead	Gaines	Kizzie Frazier	Dead	Gaines
2						
3						
4						
5						
6						
7						
8						
9						
10						
11						
12						
13						
14						
15				Date of Application for Enrollment.	Aug 2/99	
16						
17						

Choctaw By Blood Enrollment Cards 1898-1914

RESIDENCE:	Sans Bois	COUNTY.					CARD NO.	
POST OFFICE:	Featherstone, I.T	**Choctaw Nation** *(Not Including Freedmen)* Choctaw Roll					FIELD NO.	3128

Dawes' Roll No.	NAME		Relationship to Person First Named	AGE	SEX	BLOOD	TRIBAL ENROLLMENT		
							Year	County	No.
9076	1 Nail, Nicholas	29	First Named	26	M	Full	1896	Gaines	9600
9077	2 " Amy	29	Wife	26	F	"	1896	"	
9078	3 " Lucy	4	Dau	1	"	"			
	4								
	5	ENROLLMENT							
	6	OF NOS. 1, 2 and 3 HEREON							
	7	APPROVED BY THE SECRETARY OF INTERIOR FEB 4 1903							
	8								
	9								
	10								
	11								
	12								
	13								
	14								
	15								
	16								
	17								

TRIBAL ENROLLMENT OF PARENTS

	Name of Father	Year	County	Name of Mother	Year	County
1	Cephas Nail	Dead	Sans Bois	Sophie Nail	Dead	Sans Bois
2	Caldwell Cooper	"	" "		"	" "
3	No1			No2		
4						
5						
6						
7			No2 on 1896 roll as E mia Nail			
8						
9						
10						
11						
12						
13					Date of Application for Enrollment.	
14						
15					Aug 2/99	
16						
17						

Choctaw By Blood Enrollment Cards 1898-1914

RESIDENCE:	Gaines	COUNTY.	**Choctaw Nation**			Choctaw Roll	CARD No.	
POST OFFICE:	Wilburton, I.T.					*(Not Including Freedmen)*	FIELD No.	3129

Dawes' Roll No.	NAME		Relationship to Person	AGE	SEX	BLOOD	TRIBAL ENROLLMENT		
							Year	County	No.
I.W. 289	1 Rabon, James W	50	First Named	27	M	I.W.			
9079	2 " Judith M E	23	Wife	20	F	1/16	1896	Gaines	3696
9080	3 " Aline May	3	Dau	3mo	F	1/32			
9081	4 " Sudie Marie		Dau	2mo	F	1/32			
	5								
	6								
	7	ENROLLMENT OF NOS. 2-3 and 4 HEREON APPROVED BY THE SECRETARY OF INTERIOR FEB 4 1903							
	8								
	9								
	10	ENROLLMENT OF NOS. 1 HEREON APPROVED BY THE SECRETARY OF INTERIOR SEP 12 1903							
	11								
	12								
	13								
	14								
	15								
	16								
	17								

TRIBAL ENROLLMENT OF PARENTS

Name of Father	Year	County	Name of Mother	Year	County
1 Thos. Rabon		Non Citz	Mary J Rabon		Non Citz
2 R. O. Edmonds		" "	Martha Edmonds		Gaines
3 No. 1			No. 2		
4 No. 1			No. 2		
5					
6					
7					
8	No2 on 1896 roll as Judith Edmunds				
9	No3 Enrolled Dec 8th 1900				
10	No.4 born Dec. 6, 1901: Enrolled Feby 11, 1902 For children of Nos 1&2 see NB (Mar 3 '05) #489				
11					
12					
13					
14				Date of Application for Enrollment.	
15				Aug 2/99	
16					
17 Kinta I.T. 3/27/05					

Sans Bois 5/12/02

Choctaw By Blood Enrollment Cards 1898-1914

RESIDENCE: Chickasaw Natn   COUNTY. **Choctaw Nation**   **Choctaw Roll**   CARD No.
POST OFFICE: Durwood, I.T.   Hugo I.T. 12/2/02   (Not Including Freedmen)   FIELD No. 3130

Dawes' Roll No.	NAME	Relationship to Person First Named	AGE	SEX	BLOOD	TRIBAL ENROLLMENT		
						Year	County	No.
	1 Vanhorn, Oscar	Named	28	M	1/8			
	2 " Myrtle May	Dau	1½	F	1/16			
	3 " Florrie Ethel	Dau	2 wks	F	1/16			
	4							
	5							
	6							
	7							
	8							
	9							
	10							
	11							
	12							
	13							
	14							
	15							
	16							
	17							

DISMISSED

MAY 24 1904

See 7-R-612

DENIED CITIZENSHIP BY THE CHOCTAW AND
CHICKASAW CITIZENSHIP COURT

TRIBAL ENROLLMENT OF PARENTS

	Name of Father	Year	County	Name of Mother	Year	County
1	G. W. Vanhorn	Dead	Non Citz	Emma Blake		Choctaw
2	No 1			Virginia Vanhorn		Non Citz
3	No 1			" "		" "
4						
5						
6	No 1 Denied by C.t. C.t. dock 21-04 [remainder illegible] Judgment of [remainder illegible]					
7	Nos 1,2 and 3 now in C.t.C.C. Case #122					
8	No1 Denied in 96 Case #197					
9	No1 Admitted by U.S. Court, Central District					
10	Sept 9/97 Case No 92. As to residence & birth of No2, see his testimony.					
11	No.1 is the husband of Virginia Vanhorn on Choctaw Card #D310.					
12	No3 Enrolled Aug 24, 1901					
13	Nº1 is also father of children on Choctaw card #R642.					
14					Date of Application for Enrollment.	
15					Aug 2/99	
16						
17						

130

Choctaw By Blood Enrollment Cards 1898-1914

RESIDENCE:	Chickasaw Natn	COUNTY.							

RESIDENCE: Chickasaw Natn ~~COUNTY~~. **Choctaw Nation**　Choctaw Roll *(Not Including Freedmen)*　CARD No.
POST OFFICE: Dixie, I.T.　FIELD No. **3131**

Dawes' Roll No.	NAME	Relationship to Person First Named	AGE	SEX	BLOOD	TRIBAL ENROLLMENT		
						Year	County	No.
1	~~Meek, Rose~~	~~Named~~	~~17~~	~~F~~	~~1/8~~			
2	~~" Elmer~~	~~Son~~	~~6mo~~	~~M~~	~~1/16~~			
3	~~" Joseph Valter~~	~~Son~~	~~1mo~~	~~M~~	~~1/16~~			
4								
5								
6								
7								
8								
9								
10								
11								
12								
13								
14								
15								
16								
17								

DISMISSED MAY 24 1904

DENIED CITIZENSHIP BY THE CHOCTAW AND CHICKASAW CITIZENSHIP COURT

TRIBAL ENROLLMENT OF PARENTS

	Name of Father	Year	County	Name of Mother	Year	County
1	~~Hugh Perkins~~		~~Choctaw~~	~~Emma Blake~~		~~Choctaw~~
2	~~Robert Meek~~		~~Non Citz~~	~~No1~~		
3	~~" "~~		~~" "~~	~~No.1~~		
4						
5	No1 denied by C.C.C. March 21 '04.					
6	No1 Denied in 96 Case #197					
7	Judgement of U.S. Court admitting No1 vacated and set aside by Decree of Choctaw Chickasaw Cit Court Dec 17'02					
8	Admitted by the U.S. Court Central Dist Sept 9/97					
9	Case No 92. As to residence and birth of child, see					
10	her testimony.					
11	#1 Admitted as Rose Perkins					
12	No.1 was divorced from Robt. J. Meek in Feby. 1901.					
13	Robert Meek, husband of No.1 on Choctaw R.543					
14	No.3 born Oct. 29, 1901: Enrolled Nov. 19, 1901				Date of Application for Enrollment.	
15					Aug 2/99	
16						
17	For children of No1 see (Act Apr 26 '06) NB #1053					

Choctaw By Blood Enrollment Cards 1898-1914

RESIDENCE:	Chickasaw Natn	COUNTY.				CARD NO.			

RESIDENCE: Chickasaw Natn   COUNTY.   **Choctaw Nation**   Choctaw Roll   CARD NO.
POST OFFICE: Dixie, I.T.   Ardmore, I.T.   (Not Including Freedmen)   FIELD NO. **3132**

Dawes' Roll No.	NAME		Relationship to Person	AGE	SEX	BLOOD	TRIBAL ENROLLMENT		
							Year	County	No.
9082	1 McLain, William A	36	First Named	33	M	1/8	1896	Tobucksy	9189
REFUSED	2 " Susan A	28	Wife	25	F	1/8			
9083	3 " Addie	10	Dau	7	"	1/8	1896	Tobucksy	9190
9084	4 " George W	8	Son	5	M	1/8	1896	"	9191
9085	5 " Wilmer Z	1	Dau	2 wks	F	1/8			
	6 ENROLLMENT								
	7 OF NOS. 1,3,4 and 5 HEREON APPROVED BY THE SECRETARY								
	8 OF INTERIOR FEB 4 1903								
	9 No2 Denied by C.C.C.C. March 21 '04								
	10								
	No2 Denied in 96 Case #197								
	12 Judgment of U.S. Court admitting No2 vacated and set aside by Decree of Choctaw Chickasaw Cit Court Dec 17 02								
	13 No2 now in C.C.C.C Case #722								
	No2 DENIED CITIZENSHIP BY THE CHOCTAW AND								
	15 CHICKASAW CITIZENSHIP COURT								
	16								
	No2 is now separated or divorced from No1 did married to Avin Kelton an I.W. Dec 5 '04								

TRIBAL ENROLLMENT OF PARENTS

Name of Father	Year	County	Name of Mother	Year	County
1 Jas McLain	Dead	Skullyville	Liza McLain		Tobucksy
2 Hugh Wimner		Non Citz	Emma Blake		Choctaw
3 No1			No2		
4 No1			No2		
5 No1			No2		
6					
7					
8	No1 on 1896 roll as Wm A McClain				
9	No3 " 1896 " " Addie "				
10	No4 " 1896 " " Geo W " Jr.				
11					
12	No2 was admitted by the U.S. Court,			Date of Application for Enrollment.	
13	Central Dist. Sept 9/97, Case No 92.				
14	As to residence see her testimony No.5 born Nov. 26, 1901; Enrolled Dec. 7, 1901			Aug 2/99	
15					
16	No.2 transferred to Choc card #5947 May 15, 1905 See decision of April 1, 1905				
17	PO Foster IT 5/5/02				

Choctaw By Blood Enrollment Cards 1898-1914

RESIDENCE: Gaines COUNTY. **Choctaw Nation** Choctaw Roll CARD NO.
POST OFFICE: Featherstone, I.T. (Not Including Freedmen) FIELD NO. 3133

Dawes' Roll No.	NAME		Relationship to Person First Named	AGE	SEX	BLOOD	TRIBAL ENROLLMENT		
							Year	County	No.
I.W.290	1 Klugh, August	53	First Named	50	M	IW			
9086	2 " Eliza	42	Wife	39	F	Full	1896	Tobucksy	11298
9087	3 Jefferson, Lizzie	12	S.Dau	9	"	"	1896	"	11299
	4								
	5								
	6	ENROLLMENT OF NOS. 2 and 3 HEREON APPROVED BY THE SECRETARY OF INTERIOR FEB 4 1903							
	7								
	8								
	9	ENROLLMENT OF NOS. 1 HEREON APPROVED BY THE SECRETARY OF INTERIOR SEP 12 1903							
	10								
	11								
	12								
	13								
	14								
	15								
	16								
	17								

TRIBAL ENROLLMENT OF PARENTS

	Name of Father	Year	County	Name of Mother	Year	County
1	John Klugh	Dead	Non Citz	Mary Klugh	Dead	Non Citz
2	John Folister	"	Atoka	Nellie Folister	"	Atoka
3	Isom Jefferson	"	"	No2		
4						
5						
6						
7	No2 on 1896 roll as Lizzie Stanford					
8	No3 " 1896 " " " "					
9	No2 also on 1896 " " " " Page					
10	290, No 11249, Gaines Co.					
11	No1 denied by Commission in 1896 Choctaw Case No. 223 No appeal					
12	Enrollment of No.1 cancelled by order of Department March 4, 1907					
13	Not restored to roll by Departmental authority of January 19, 1909 (File 3-171)					
14						
15				Date of Application for Enrollment. Aug 2/99		
16						
17						

RESIDENCE:	Sans Bois	COUNTY.			Choctaw Roll	CARD No.	
POST OFFICE:	Bower, I.T.		**Choctaw Nation**		(Not Including Freedmen)	FIELD No.	3134

Dawes' Roll No.	NAME	Relationship to Person First Named	AGE	SEX	BLOOD	TRIBAL ENROLLMENT		
						Year	County	No.
Void 1	McNeely, Ellen		29	F	1/4	1896	Sans Bois	8990
Void 2	" Myrtle	Dau	12	"	1/8	1896	" "	8991
Void 3	" Julia F	"	7	"	1/8	1896	" "	8993
Void 4	" Edna	"	5	"	1/8	1896	" "	8992
5								
6								
7								
8								
9								
10								
11								
12								
13								
14								
15								
16								
17								

TRIBAL ENROLLMENT OF PARENTS

	Name of Father	Year	County	Name of Mother	Year	County
1	William Monds	Dead	Non Citz	Patsey Monds	Dead	Tobucksy
2	Jas McNeely		" "	No 1		
3	" "		" "	No 1		
4	" "		" "	No 1		
5						
6						
7						
8		No 1 on 1896 roll as Ellen McNealy				
9		Surnames on 1896 roll as McNealy				
10	No 1 is now the wife of James C McNeely on Choctaw Card #D.312 Dec 6, 1900.					
11						
12						
13						
14					Date of Application for Enrollment.	
15					Aug 2/99	
16						
17						

134

Choctaw By Blood Enrollment Cards 1898-1914

RESIDENCE: Gaines COUNTY.	Choctaw Nation	Choctaw Roll (Not Including Freedmen)	CARD No.
POST OFFICE: Hartshorne, I.T.			FIELD No. 3135

Dawes' Roll No.	NAME	Relationship to Person First Named	AGE	SEX	BLOOD	TRIBAL ENROLLMENT Year	County	No.
I.W. 291	1 Ludlow, Edwin 42	Named	41	M	IW	1896	Gaines	14749
9088	2 " Anna W 36	Wife	33	F	1/2	1896	"	7831
	3							
	4							
	5	ENROLLMENT						
	6	OF NOS. 2 HEREON APPROVED BY THE SECRETARY						
	7	OF INTERIOR FEB 4 1903						
	8	ENROLLMENT						
	9	OF NOS. 1 HEREON APPROVED BY THE SECRETARY						
	10	OF INTERIOR SEP 12 1903						
	11							
	12							
	13							
	14							
	15							
	16							
	17							

TRIBAL ENROLLMENT OF PARENTS

Name of Father	Year	County	Name of Mother	Year	County
1 W^m H Ludlow	Dead	Non Citz	Frances L Ludlow	Dead	Non Citz
2 Allen Wright	"	Atoka	Harriet N Wright	"	" "
3					
4					
5					
6	No1 was admitted by Dawes Com., as an				
7	Intermarried Citizen, Case No 1242				
8					
9	As to marriage of parents of No2, see				
10	testimony of Peter Maytubby				
11					
12					
13				Date of Application for Enrollment.	
14					
15				Aug 2/99	
16					
17					

Choctaw By Blood Enrollment Cards 1898-1914

RESIDENCE: Gaines COUNTY. **Choctaw Nation** **Choctaw Roll** CARD NO.
POST OFFICE: Hartshorne, I.T. *(Not Including Freedmen)* FIELD NO. 3136

Dawes' Roll No.	NAME		Relationship to Person	AGE	SEX	BLOOD	TRIBAL ENROLLMENT		
							Year	County	No.
9089	1 Wright, Kate	30	First Named	27	F	1/2	1896	Gaines	12936
	2								
	3								
	4								
	5	ENROLLMENT							
	6	OF NOS. 1 HEREON APPROVED BY THE SECRETARY							
	7	OF INTERIOR FEB 4 1903							
	8								
	9								
	10								
	11								
	12								
	13								
	14								
	15								
	16								
	17								

TRIBAL ENROLLMENT OF PARENTS

	Name of Father	Year	County	Name of Mother	Year	County
1	Allen Wright	Dead	Atoka	Harriet N Wright	Dead	Non Citz
2						
3						
4						
5						
6						
7			On 1896 roll as Catherine Wright			
8						
9			As to marriage of parents, see			
10			testimony of Peter Maytubby			
11						
12						
13						
14					Date of Application	
15					for Enrollment.	
16					Aug 2/99	
17						

136

Choctaw By Blood Enrollment Cards 1898-1914

RESIDENCE: Atoka COUNTY. **Choctaw Nation** Choctaw Roll CARD NO.
POST OFFICE: Fort Sill, Oklahoma (Not Including Freedmen) FIELD NO. 3137

Dawes' Roll No.	NAME		Relationship to Person First Named	AGE	SEX	BLOOD	TRIBAL ENROLLMENT		
							Year	County	No.
9090	1 Wright, Frank H.	42	First Named	39	M	1/2	1896	Atoka	13950
IW 658	2 " Addie L	39	Wife	36	F	I.W.			
9091	3 " Gladys	16	Dau	13	"	1/4	1896	Atoka	13952
9092	4 " Frank H, Jr	11	Son	8	M	1/4	1896	"	13951
	5	ENROLLMENT							
	6	OF NOS. 2 HEREON APPROVED BY THE SECRETARY							
	7	OF INTERIOR MAR 26 1904							
	8								
	9	In case of any communications							
	10	being sent to No1, address No 244							
	11	San Jacinto, Dallas, Texas. He being a Missionary at Fort Sill,							
	12	Okla.							
	13	ENROLLMENT							
	14	OF NOS. 1, 3 and 4 HEREON APPROVED BY THE SECRETARY							
	15	OF INTERIOR FEB 4 1903							
	16								
	17								

TRIBAL ENROLLMENT OF PARENTS

Name of Father	Year	County	Name of Mother	Year	County
1 Allen Wright	Dead	Atoka	Harriet N Wright	Dead	Non Citz
2 Myer Lilienthal	"	Non Citz	Jennie Lilienthal	" "	
3 No1			No2		
4 No1			No2		
5					
6					
7		No1 on 1896 roll as F. H. Wright			
8		As to marriage of parents of No1,			
9		see testimony of Peter Maytubby.			
10		No2 was admitted by Dawes Commission, as an Intermarried			
11		Citizen, Case No 500. No appeal.			
12		No4 on 1896 roll as F. H. Wright Jr.			
13					
14				Date of Application for Enrollment	
15				Aug 2/99	
16					
17 P.O. Dallas, I.T. Texas					

RESIDENCE:	Gaines	COUNTY.			Choctaw Roll	CARD No.	
POST OFFICE:	Damon, I.T.	**Choctaw Nation**			*(Not Including Freedmen)*	FIELD No.	3138

Choctaw Roll (Not Including Freedmen)

Dawes' Roll No.	NAME		Relationship to Person	AGE	SEX	BLOOD	TRIBAL ENROLLMENT		
							Year	County	No.
I.W. 659	1 Johnson, Ben F	42	First Named	35	M	I.W.	1896	Gaines	14689
9093	2 " Emiline	24	Wife	21	F	1/2	1896	"	6607
9094	3 " Perry F	2	Son	4m	M	1/4			
	4								
	5	ENROLLMENT							
	6	OF NOS. HEREON APPROVED BY THE SECRETARY							
	7	OF INTERIOR							
	8								
	9	DECISION PREPARED							
	10								
	11	ENROLLMENT							
	12	OF NOS. HEREON APPROVED BY THE SECRETARY							
	13	OF INTERIOR							
	14								
	15								
	16								
	17								

TRIBAL ENROLLMENT OF PARENTS

	Name of Father	Year	County	Name of Mother	Year	County
1	Richard Johnson	Dead	Non Citz	Jane Johnson	Dead	Non Citz
2	Abel Harris		Sugar Loaf	Susan Harris		" "
3	No 1			No 2		
4						
5						
6						
7						
8						
9						
10	No1 on 1896 roll as B. F. Johnson					
11						
12	As to marriage, see testimony of No1.					
13					#1&2	
14	For proof of marriage of parents				Date of Application for Enrollment.	
15	of No2, see testimony in case of Abel Harris, her father, Card No 2272.				Aug 2/99	
16	No3 Enrolled February 1, 1901					
17	For child of Nos 1&2 see NB (Mar 3, 1905) #682					

Choctaw By Blood Enrollment Cards 1898-1914

RESIDENCE: Tobucksy COUNTY. **Choctaw Nation** (Not Including Freedmen)

POST OFFICE: South McAlester, I.T.

Choctaw Roll CARD NO.

FIELD NO. 3139

Dawes' Roll No.	NAME		Relationship to Person First Named	AGE	SEX	BLOOD	TRIBAL ENROLLMENT		
							Year	County	No.
I.W.132	1 Savage, John P	30	First Named	27	M	I.W	1896	Gaines	15028
9095	2 " Ida May	25	Wife	22	F	1/8	1896	"	11241
9096	3 " Nettie P	7	Dau	4	"	1/16	1896	"	11242
9097	4 " Thelma M	5	"	2	"	1/16			
9098	5 " Claude C	3	Son	4mo	M	1/16			
9099	6 " Willie May	1	Dau	2wk	F	1/16			
	7								
	8								
	9	ENROLLMENT OF NOS. 2,3,4,5 and 6 HEREON APPROVED BY THE SECRETARY OF INTERIOR FEB 4 1903							
	10								
	11								
	12	ENROLLMENT OF NOS. 1 HEREON APPROVED BY THE SECRETARY OF INTERIOR JUN 13 1903							
	13								
	14								
	15								
	16								
	17								

TRIBAL ENROLLMENT OF PARENTS

	Name of Father	Year	County	Name of Mother	Year	County
1	Francis M. Savage		Non Citz	Catherine M Savage		Non Citz
2	Al Beagles		" "	Anna Nelson		Gaines
3	No1			No2		
4	No1			No2		
5	No1			No2		
6	No1			No2		
7						
8						
9						
10	No1 on 1896 roll as J. P. Savage					
11						
12	Nos 4-5 Affidavits of birth to be supplied: Recd Aug 9/99					
13						Date of Application for Enrollment.
14	No1 was admitted as an intermarried citizen by Dawes Commission Choctaw Case #786: No appeal.					Aug 2/99
15	No.6 Enrolled Aug 22, 1901 = Name of No.6 is Willie May Savage 12/15 02					
16						
17	PO [Illegible] IT Dec 15/02					

Choctaw By Blood Enrollment Cards 1898-1914

RESIDENCE: Gaines COUNTY.	Choctaw Nation	Choctaw Roll	CARD NO.
POST OFFICE: Hartshorne, I.T.		(Not Including Freedmen)	FIELD NO. 3140

Dawes' Roll No.	NAME	Relationship to Person First Named	AGE	SEX	BLOOD	TRIBAL ENROLLMENT Year	County	No.
DEAD	1 Jumper, Sheldon DEAD		41	M	I.W.			
15443	2 " Lester 13	Son	10	"	1/32	1896	Tobucksy	6676
	3							
	4							
	5							
	6	ENROLLMENT						
	7	OF NOS. ~~~ 2 ~~~ HEREON						
	8	APPROVED BY THE SECRETARY OF INTERIOR MAY 9 1904						
	9							
	10							
	11	No. 1 HEREON DISMISSED UNDER						
	12	ORDER OF THE COMMISSION TO THE FIVE CIVILIZED TRIBES OF MARCH 31, 1905.						
	13							
	14							
	15							
	16							
	17							

TRIBAL ENROLLMENT OF PARENTS

	Name of Father	Year	County	Name of Mother	Year	County
1	George Jumper	Dead	Non Citz	Ellen Jumper		Non Citz
2	No 1			Mattie Jumper	Dead	Tobucksy
3						
4						
5						
6			No 1 was admitted by Dawes Commission			
7			as an intermarried citizen, Case No 214.			
8			No 2 was also admitted by Dawes Commission, Case No 214: On 2896 roll			
9			as Lester Jumper – appeal dismissed.			
10			No.1 Died July 20, 1901: Proof of death filed Dec 23 1902			
11						
12						
13						
14					Date of Application for Enrollment	
15					Aug 1/99	
16						
17						

Choctaw By Blood Enrollment Cards 1898-1914

RESIDENCE: **Gaines** COUNTY. **Choctaw Nation**   **Choctaw Roll** CARD NO.
POST OFFICE: **Hartshorne, I.T.** *(Not Including Freedmen)*   FIELD NO. **3141**

Dawes' Roll No.	NAME		Relationship to Person First Named	AGE	SEX	BLOOD	TRIBAL ENROLLMENT		
							Year	County	No.
9100	1 Ott, Alfred	44	First Named	41	M	3/4	1896	Gaines	9910
9101	2 " Lizzie	32	Wife	29	F	Full	1896	"	9911
9102	3 " Sam	18	Son	15	M	7/8	1896	"	9914
9103	4 " Mitchell	15	"	12	"	7/8	1896	"	9915
9104	5 " Sallie	13	Dau	10	F	7/8	1896	"	9913
9105	6 " Solomon	10	Son	7	M	7/8	1896	"	9916
9106	7 " Winema	6	Dau	3	F	7/8	1896	"	
9107	8 " Josephine	3	"	7mo	"	7/8			
9108	9 " Emma	1	Dau	2mo	F	7/8			
	10								
	11								
	12								
	13								
	14								
	15	ENROLLMENT OF NOS. 1,2,3,4,5,6,7,8 and 9 HEREON							
	16	APPROVED BY THE SECRETARY							
	17	OF INTERIOR FEB 4 1903							

TRIBAL ENROLLMENT OF PARENTS

	Name of Father	Year	County	Name of Mother	Year	County
1	Sam Ott	Dead	Gaines	Louisa Ott	Dead	Tobucksy
2	Lesma Fry	"	Bok Tuklo	Sarah Nelson		Gaines
3	No 1			Louisa Ott	Dead	"
4	No 1			" "	"	"
5	No 1			" "	"	"
6	No 1			No 2		
7	No 1			No 2		
8	No 1			No 2		
9	No 1			No 2		
10						
11						
12	No 7 on 1896 roll as Winnema Ott					
13						#1 to 8
14	No 8 Affidavit of birth to be supplied:					Date of Application for Enrollment.
15	No 9 Enrolled July 11, 1901. For child of Nos 1 and 2 see NB (March 3 1905) #1255					Aug 2/99
16						
17						

Choctaw By Blood Enrollment Cards 1898-1914

| RESIDENCE: Gaines COUNTY. | POST OFFICE: Hartshorne, I.T. | **Choctaw Nation** | | | Choctaw Roll (Not Including Freedmen) | CARD NO. FIELD NO. 3142 |

Dawes' Roll No.	NAME	Relationship to Person	AGE	SEX	BLOOD	TRIBAL ENROLLMENT Year	County	No.
I.W. 789	1 Brennan, Thomas 76 *	First Named	73	M	I.W.			
I.W. 1252	2 " Nancy 48	Wife	45	F	I.W.			
	3							
	4							
	5							
	6							
	7							
	8	ENROLLMENT OF NOS. 1 HEREON APPROVED BY THE SECRETARY OF INTERIOR MAY 9 1904						
	9							
	10							
	11							
	12							
	13	ENROLLMENT OF NOS. ~2~ HEREON APPROVED BY THE SECRETARY OF INTERIOR DEC 30 1904						
	14							
	15							
	16							
	17							

TRIBAL ENROLLMENT OF PARENTS

Name of Father	Year	County	Name of Mother	Year	County
1 Jas. Brennan	Dead	Non Citz	Ann Brennan	Dead	Non Citz
2 Jesse Wilson	"	" "	Lizzie Wilson	"	" "

4 See testimony taken Sept 6/04 at Atoka
5 No1 was denied in 1896 Case #69
6 No1 was admitted by U.S. Court, Central Dist, No 91,
7 Sept 11/97. As to residence see his testimony
9 No2 was admitted by Dawes Commission as an
intermarried citizen Case No 69, as Mrs. Nancy
10 Bennan. No appeal.
11 * Decision of U.S. Court Central District Sept.11, 1896, vacated and set aside
12 by decree of Choctaw Chickasaw Citizenship Court Dec 17 1902
Admitted as an intermarried Choctaw by Citizenship Court January 22 1904 Case #234
13 No.2 formerly wife of Eph Frazier, a recognized Choctaw
14 by blood who died about 1877.

Date of Application for Enrollment.
Aug 2/9⁶

17 P.O. is now Gowen I.T. 9/12/04

142

Choctaw By Blood Enrollment Cards 1898-1914

RESIDENCE: Gaines COUNTY.	**Choctaw Nation**	Choctaw Roll	CARD NO.
POST OFFICE: Hartshorne, I.T.		(Not Including Freedmen)	FIELD NO. 3143

Dawes' Roll No.	NAME	Relationship to Person First Named	AGE	SEX	BLOOD	TRIBAL ENROLLMENT		
						Year	County	No.
9109	1 Thompson, Robert B 56	First Named	53	M	1/4	1896	Kiamitia	12360
	2							
	3							
	4	ENROLLMENT						
	5	OF NOS. I HEREON APPROVED BY THE SECRETARY						
	6	OF INTERIOR FEB 4 1903						
	7							
	8							
	9							
	10							
	11							
	12							
	13							
	14							
	15							
	16							
	17							

TRIBAL ENROLLMENT OF PARENTS

Name of Father	Year	County	Name of Mother	Year	County
1 William Thompson	Dead	Non Citz	Jane Thompson	Dead	Kiamitia
2					
3					
4					
5					
6					
7					
8		On 1896 roll as Robert Thompson			
9					
10					
11					
12					
13					
14					
15				Date of Application for Enrollment. Aug 2/99		
16					
17 P.O. Dowell, I.T.					

143

Choctaw By Blood Enrollment Cards 1898-1914

RESIDENCE: Gaines COUNTY. Choctaw Nation   Choctaw Roll   CARD No.
POST OFFICE: Hartshorne, I.T   (Not Including Freedmen)   FIELD No.   3144

Dawes' Roll No.	NAME		Relationship to Person First Named	AGE	SEX	BLOOD	TRIBAL ENROLLMENT		
							Year	County	No.
15444	1 Pickens, Margaret	28	First Named	25	F	1/4	1896	Sans Bois	10083
15445	2 Surratt, Irene	8	Dau	5	"	3/8	1896	" "	11109
15446	3 " Annie	4	"	8mo	"	3/8			
15578	4 Jefferson Missie	2	"	3 "	"	3/8			
	5								
	6								
	7	ENROLLMENT							
	8	OF NOS. 1 ~ 2 ~ 3 ~ HEREON APPROVED BY THE SECRETARY							
	9	OF INTERIOR MAY 9 1904							
	10								
	11								
	12	ENROLLMENT							
	13	OF NOS. ~~~ 4 ~~ HEREON APPROVED BY THE SECRETARY							
	14	OF INTERIOR SEP 22 1904							
	15								
	16								
	17								

TRIBAL ENROLLMENT OF PARENTS

	Name of Father	Year	County	Name of Mother	Year	County
1	Dave Pickens	Dead	Chickasaw	Betsey Pickens	Dead	Skullyville
2	Cooper Surratt		Sans Bois	No1		
3	" "		" "	No1		
4	Joe Jefferson			No.1		
5						
6						
7						
8						
9						
10	No2 on 1896 roll as Addie Surratt					
11						
12	Daughter of Betsey Pickens who was a					
13	sister of Jerry Ward and Mary Lomer. If shown that mother has no right she will					Date of Application for Enrollment. #1 to 3
14	be enrolled as a Chickasaw, following					
15	her father.					Aug 2/99
16	No.4 Born Sept 8, 1902. Application made Dec. 23, 1902					
17	No.4 is illegitimate. Complete proof of birth filed June 7, 1904.					

144

Choctaw By Blood Enrollment Cards 1898-1914

RESIDENCE: Gaines COUNTY. **Choctaw Nation** Choctaw Roll CARD NO.
POST OFFICE: Hartshorne, I.T. *(Not Including Freedmen)* FIELD NO. 3145

Dawes' Roll No.	NAME		Relationship to Person	AGE	SEX	BLOOD	TRIBAL ENROLLMENT		
							Year	County	No.
9110	1 Scott, Willie	43	First Named	40	M	Full	1896	Gaines	11235
9111	2 " Elizabeth	34	Wife	31	F	"	1896	"	11236
9112	3 " Isabelle	17	Dau	14	"	"	1896	"	11237
9113	4 " Mary	15	"	12	"	"	1896	"	11238
9114	5 " Dixon	10	Son	7	M	"	1896	"	11239
9115	6 " Milton DIED PRIOR TO SEPTEMBER 25 1902		"	4	"	"	1896	"	11240
9116	7 " Sissy	1	Dau	5mo	F	"			
	8								
	9								
	10								
	11								
	12								
	13								
	14								
	15								
	16								
	17								

ENROLLMENT
OF NOS. 1,2,3,4,5,6 and 7 HEREON
APPROVED BY THE SECRETARY
OF INTERIOR FEB 4 1903

TRIBAL ENROLLMENT OF PARENTS

	Name of Father	Year	County	Name of Mother	Year	County
1		Dead			Dead	Gaines
2	Barnaby Davis	Dead	Gaines	Sophie Davis	Dead	Gaines
3	No1			No2		
4	No1			No2		
5	No1			No2		
6	No1			No2		
7	No1			No2		
8						
9						
10			No7 Affidavit of birth to be supplied: Rec'd 8/3/99			
11	No.6 died June - 1900: Enrollment cancelled by Department July 8, 1904					
12			For child of Nos 1&2 see NB (March 3, 1905) #105			
13						
14					Date of Application for Enrollment.	
15					Aug 2/99	
16						
17	PO Higgins IT. 4/15/05					

RESIDENCE:	Gaines	COUNTY.						
POST OFFICE:	Wilburton, I.T.		Choctaw Nation			Choctaw Roll (Not Including Freedmen)	CARD No. FIELD No. 3146	

Dawes' Roll No.	NAME		Relationship to Person First Named	AGE	SEX	BLOOD	TRIBAL ENROLLMENT		
							Year	County	No.
9117	1 Hampton, Grant	26		23	M	Full	1896	Atoka	6009
	2								
	3								
	4								
	5								
	6	ENROLLMENT OF NOS. 1 HEREON APPROVED BY THE SECRETARY OF INTERIOR FEB 4 1903							
	7								
	8								
	9								
	10								
	11								
	12								
	13								
	14								
	15								
	16								
	17								

TRIBAL ENROLLMENT OF PARENTS

	Name of Father	Year	County	Name of Mother	Year	County
1	Forbis Hampton	Dead	Gaines	Lizzie Hampton	Dead	Gaines
2						
3						
4						
5						
6						
7	For child of No1 see Chick NB (Apr 26 '06) #62					
8	" " " " " " " (March 3, 1905) #382					
9						
10						
11						
12						
13						
14				Date of Application for Enrollment Aug 2/99		
15						
16						
17						

Choctaw By Blood Enrollment Cards 1898-1914

| RESIDENCE: Gaines | COUNTY. | | | | | | | | |
| POST OFFICE: Hartshorne, I.T. | **Choctaw Nation** | | | Choctaw Roll *(Not Including Freedmen)* | | CARD No. FIELD No. 3147 | | | |

Dawes' Roll No.	NAME		Relationship to Person First Named	AGE	SEX	BLOOD	TRIBAL ENROLLMENT		
							Year	County	No.
9118	1 Seeley, Alfred	33	First Named	30	M	1/2	1893	Gaines	502
9119	2 " Missy	36	Wife	33	F	3/4	1893	"	503
9120	3 " Lona B	10	Dau	7	"	5/8	1893	"	504
9121	4 " Ona J	7	"	4	"	5/8			
DEAD.	5 " Pliney DEAD.		"	1	"	5/8			
DEAD.	6 " Greeny DEAD.		Cousin	10	"	1/2	1893	Gaines	514
	7								
	8	ENROLLMENT OF NOS. 1-2-3 and 4 HEREON APPROVED BY THE SECRETARY OF INTERIOR FEB 4 1903							
	9								
	10								
	11								
	12	No. 5 and 6 HEREON DISMISSED UNDER ORDER OF THE COMMISSION TO THE FIVE CIVILIZED TRIBES OF MARCH 31, 1905							
	13								
	14								
	15								
	16								
	17								

TRIBAL ENROLLMENT OF PARENTS

	Name of Father	Year	County	Name of Mother	Year	County
1	John Seeley	Dead	Chickasaw	Ellen Seeley	Dead	Gaines
2	Norris Presley	"	Gaines	Betsey Presley		"
3	No1			No2		
4	No1			No2		
5	No1			No2		
6	Bond Seeley	Dead	Chickasaw	Susan Seeley	Dead	Gaines
7						
8						
9						
10						
11	No1 on 1893 Pay roll, Page 53, No 502, Gaines Co as Alfred Sealy					
12	No2 " 1893 " " " 53 " 503 " " " Missy "					
13	No3 " 1893 " " " 53 " 504 " " " Doney "					
	No6 " 1893 " " " 53 " 514 " " " Granny "					#1 to 6
14	No.5 Died in 1900: Proof of death filed Dec 23 1902				Date of Application for Enrollment.	
15	No.6 " Sept 27, 1901: " " " " 23, 1901 as "Freeny"				Aug 2/99	
16						
17						

Choctaw By Blood Enrollment Cards 1898-1914

RESIDENCE:	Gaines	COUNTY.							
POST OFFICE:	Damon, I.T.								

Choctaw Nation

Choctaw Roll *(Not Including Freedmen)*

CARD No.

FIELD No. 3148

Dawes' Roll No.		NAME		Relationship to Person First Named	AGE	SEX	BLOOD	TRIBAL ENROLLMENT		
								Year	County	No.
DEAD	1	Reed, Josiah	DEAD		54	M	Full	1896	Gaines	10749
9122	2	" Winey	29	Wife	26	F	"	1896	"	10750
VOID.	3	" George		Son	8	M	"	1896	"	10751
9123	4	" Melvina	6	Dau	3	F	"			
9124	5	" Raymond	5	Son	1½	M	"			
9125	6	" Joe	2	Son	6mo	M	"			
	7									
	8									
	9	ENROLLMENT								
	10	OF NOS. 2,4,5 and 6 HEREON								
	11	APPROVED BY THE SECRETARY OF INTERIOR FEB 4 1903								
	12	No. 1 HEREON DISMISSED UNDER								
	13	ORDER OF THE COMMISSION TO THE FIVE								
	14	CIVILIZED TRIBES OF MARCH 31, 1905.								
	15									
	16									
	17									

TRIBAL ENROLLMENT OF PARENTS

	Name of Father	Year	County	Name of Mother	Year	County
1	We-ke-tubbee	Dead	Nashoba	Oka-hon-tema	Dead	Nashoba
2	John Carr	"	Gaines	Liza Carr	"	Gaines
3	No1			Mollie Reed	"	"
4	No1			No2		
5	No1			No2		
6	No1			No2		
7						
8						
9						
10						
11	No.1 Died Sept 5, 1901; Evidence of death filed Nov. 26, 1901.					
12	No2 on 1896 roll as Winnie Reed					
13	No.3 has been transferred to Chickasaw Card No. 1474					
14	For child of No.2 see NB (March 3, 1905) #1498 #1 to 5					
15	No6 Enrolled Sept 24 1901		Date of Application for Enrollment. Aug 2/99			
16	Nos 4-5 Affidavits of birth to be					
17	supplied: Recd Dec 18/99. Irregular and returned for correction. Recd & filed Jany 17, 1900					

Choctaw By Blood Enrollment Cards 1898-1914

RESIDENCE:	Gaines	COUNTY.						CARD No.	
POST OFFICE:	Hartshorne, I.T.	**Choctaw Nation**			Choctaw Roll *(Not Including Freedmen)*			FIELD No.	3149

Dawes' Roll No.	NAME	Relationship to Person First Named	AGE	SEX	BLOOD	TRIBAL ENROLLMENT		
						Year	County	No.
DEAD	1 Perry, John W DEAD		47	M	1/2	1896	Gaines	10207
3991	2 Perry, Mildred A 35	Wife	32	F	I.W	1896	"	14927
DEAD	3 Gross, Annie DEAD	Dau	16	"	3/4	1896	"	10208
9126	4 Perry, Emiline 17	"	14	"	3/4	1896	"	10209
9127	5 Pickens, Melvina 17	Ward	14	"	3/4	1896	"	10211
	6 No. 1 and 3 HEREON DISMISSED UNDER							
	7 ORDER OF THE COMMISSION TO THE FIVE							
	8 CIVILIZED TRIBES OF MARCH 31, 1905							
	9 ENROLLMENT							
	10 OF NOS. 4 and 5 HEREON							
	APPROVED BY THE SECRETARY							
	11 OF INTERIOR FEB 4 1903							
	12 Take no further action relative to enrollment of No 1							
	13 Protest of Attys for Choctaw and Chickasaw Nation							
	14 Jan 23/04							
	15 ENROLLMENT							
	16 OF NOS. 2 HEREON							
	APPROVED BY THE SECRETARY							
	17 OF INTERIOR OCT 21 1904							

TRIBAL ENROLLMENT OF PARENTS

Name of Father	Year	County	Name of Mother	Year	County
1 William Perry	Dead	Sugar Loaf	Amy Perry	Dead	Sugar Loaf
2 W. P. Holliday		Non Citz	Mildred Holliday	"	Non Citz
3 No 1			Polina Perry	"	Gaines
4 No 1			" "	"	"
5 An-tik-ubbee	Dead	Gaines	Sukey Pickens	Dead	Gaines
6					
7 No1 on 1896 roll as Jno. W. Perry					
8 No2 " 1896 " " Annie "					
9 No5 " 1896 " " Biney Pickens					
No.1 died April 10 1900: evidence of death filed Nov 25, 1902					
10 No 3 " " 25, 1900· " " " " Dec. 24, 1902					
11					
12 For child of No5 see NB (Apr 26-06) Card #767					
13					
14					
15			Date of Application for Enrollment.	Aug 2/99	
16					
17 PO Wilburton I.T. 12/24/02					

Choctaw By Blood Enrollment Cards 1898-1914

RESIDENCE: Gaines COUNTY. **Choctaw Nation** **Choctaw Roll** CARD NO.
POST OFFICE: Hartshorne I.T. (Not Including Freedmen) FIELD NO. 3150

Dawes' Roll No.	NAME	Relationship to Person First Named	AGE	SEX	BLOOD	TRIBAL ENROLLMENT		
						Year	County	No.
* 1	Thompson Ann	First Named	56	F	1/2			
0 2								
3								
4								
5								
6								
7								
8								
9								
10								
11								
12	REFUSED FEB 16 1907							
13								
14								
15								
16								
17								

TRIBAL ENROLLMENT OF PARENTS

	Name of Father	Year	County		Name of Mother	Year	County
1	Eli Sanders	Dead	Choctaw		Nancy Campbell	Dead	Non Citz
2							
3							
4							
5							
6							
7							
8							
9	No1 Denied in 96 Case #1379						
10	Admitted by U.S. Court Case No 161 at South McAlester I.T.						
11	Aug. 30, 1896. As to residence see her testimony						
12	Not now in C.C.C., Case #11; No1 denied by C.C.C. Court March 2, 190						
13							
14							
15					Date of Application for Enrollment.		
16					8 2 99		
17	See Pet #C 135						

150

Choctaw By Blood Enrollment Cards 1898-1914

RESIDENCE:	Gaines	COUNTY.							

Choctaw Nation

RESIDENCE: Gaines COUNTY.
POST OFFICE: Hartshorne I.T.

Choctaw Roll *(Not Including Freedmen)*

CARD NO. FIELD NO. 3151

Dawes' Roll No.	NAME	Relationship to Person First Named	AGE	SEX	BLOOD	TRIBAL ENROLLMENT		
						Year	County	No.
() × 1	Crowson Susan A	Named	38	F	1/4			
2								
3								
4								
5								
6								
7								
8								
9		REFUSED FEB 16 190?						
10								
11								
12								
13								
14								
15								
16								
17								

TRIBAL ENROLLMENT OF PARENTS

	Name of Father	Year	County	Name of Mother	Year	County
1	Jno A Woolridge	Dead Non Citz		Ann Thompson	1896	Tobucksey[sic]
2						
3						
4						
5						
6						
7						
8						
9						
10						
11	No1 denied in 96 Case #1379 Admitted by U.S. Court at South McAlester, I.T.					
12	Aug. 30th 1897, Case No. 161. As to residence see her testimony.					
13	Judgment of US Court admitting No1 vacated and set aside by Decree of Choctaw Chickasaw Cit Court Dec 1702					
× 14	No1 now in C.C.C.C. Case #111					
× 15	No1 Denied by C.C.C.C. Case #11 March 9, 1904					
16	For record see 7-3150					
17	See Petition #C-135			Date of Application for Enrollment. 8-2-99		

DENIED CITIZENSHIP BY THE CHOCTAW AND CHICKASAW CITIZENSHIP COURT

Choctaw By Blood Enrollment Cards 1898-1914

RESIDENCE:	Tobucksey[sic]	COUNTY.							CARD NO.	
POST OFFICE:	Alderson I.T.		**Choctaw Nation**				**Choctaw Roll** (Not Including Freedmen)		FIELD NO.	3152

Dawes' Roll No.	NAME	Relationship to Person First Named	AGE	SEX	BLOOD	TRIBAL ENROLLMENT		
						Year	County	No.
0 *	1 Thompson Ivey	Named	27	M	1/4			
	2 " Ida	Wife	17	F	I.W.			
	3 " Leona	Dau	8mo	F	1/8			
	4							
No1	5 DENIED CITIZENSHIP BY THE CHOCTAW AND							
	6 CHICKASAW CITIZENSHIP COURT							
	7							
No.2	8 DISMISSED MAY -7 1904							
	9 Choctaw Chickasaw Citizenship Court on Feb 3 '04 in Case #1111							
	10 dismissed [illegible] for admission to citizenship of #3 forward of							
	11 [illegible] See "Order"							
	12 DISMISSED							
	13 MAY 24 1904							
	14							
#1	15 REFUSED FEB 16 1907							
	16							
No2&3	17 DISMISSED FEB 16 1907							

TRIBAL ENROLLMENT OF PARENTS

	Name of Father	Year	County	Name of Mother	Year	County
1	Frank Thompson	Dead	Non Citz	Ann Thompson	1896	Gaines
2	Wᵐ Watzke		"	Fanny A Bettes		Non Citz
3	No. 1			No. 2		
4						
5						
6						
7						
8						

No1 denied Choctaw Cit Case #1379

No.1 admitted by US Court at South McAlester I.T. Aug 30, 1896
Case #161 As to residence see his testimony, also as to
marriage and birth of child
No.2 Certificate of marriage in due form but not in shape
to be conveniently filed, exhibited, dated Feby 22, 1898.
Affidavit of birth of child to be supplied. Recd Aug 9/99
judgement[sic] of U.S. Court admitting No1 vacated and set aside by Decree of Choctaw Chickasaw Cit Court Dec 17 02
No1 now in C.C.C. Case #111
No1 denied by C.C.C.C. Case #11 March 8ᵗʰ '04 For record see 7-3150 See Pet #C-135

Date of Application for Enrollment.
8-2-99

152

Choctaw By Blood Enrollment Cards 1898-1914

RESIDENCE:	Gaines	COUNTY.								

RESIDENCE: Gaines COUNTY. **Choctaw Nation** **Choctaw Roll** CARD NO.
POST OFFICE: Hartshorne I.T. *(Not Including Freedmen)* FIELD NO. 3153

Dawes' Roll No.	NAME		Relationship to Person First Named	AGE	SEX	BLOOD	TRIBAL ENROLLMENT		
							Year	County	No.
9128	1 Carr, Dennis	37	First Named	34	M	Full	1896	Gaines	2279
9129	2 " Jane	31	Wife	28	F	"	1896	"	2280
9130	3 " Sweeney	12	Son	9	M	"	1896	"	2281
9131	4 " Ella	4	Dau	1	F	"			
9132	5 " Lena	1	Dau	1mo	F	"			
	6								
	7								
	8	ENROLLMENT							
	9	OF NOS. 1,2,3,4 and 5 HEREON APPROVED BY THE SECRETARY							
	10	OF INTERIOR FEB 4 1903							
	11								
	12								
	13								
	14								
	15								
	16								
	17								

TRIBAL ENROLLMENT OF PARENTS

Name of Father	Year	County	Name of Mother	Year	County
1 John Carr	Dead	Gaines	Eliza Carr	Dead	Gaines
2 Isom Fletcher	"	"	Witcher Fletcher	"	"
3 No 1			No. 2		
4 No 1			No. 2		
5 No.1			No.2		
6					
7					
8					
9					
10 Affidavit of birth of child to be supplied					
11 Received October 7/99					
12 No5 Enrolled July 11, 1901					
13 For child of Nos 1 and 2 see NB (Mar 3 1905) #504					
14					
15			Date of Application for Enrollment.	For Nos 1 to 4 incl.	
16				Aug 2/99	
17					

Choctaw By Blood Enrollment Cards 1898-1914

RESIDENCE:	Gaines	COUNTY.							

Choctaw Nation — Choctaw Roll (Not Including Freedmen)

RESIDENCE: Gaines COUNTY.
POST OFFICE: Hartshorne I.T.

CARD NO.
FIELD NO. 3154

Dawes' Roll No.	NAME		Relationship to Person	AGE	SEX	BLOOD	TRIBAL ENROLLMENT		
							Year	County	No.
9133	1 Pusley Jane	20	First Named	17	F	Full	1896	Gaines	10177
	2								
	3								
	4								
	5								
	6								
	7								
	8								
	9								
	10								
	11								
	12								
	13								
	14								
	15								
	16								
	17								

ENROLLMENT
OF NOS. 1 HEREON
APPROVED BY THE SECRETARY
OF INTERIOR FEB 4 1903

TRIBAL ENROLLMENT OF PARENTS

	Name of Father	Year	County	Name of Mother	Year	County
1	Albert Pusley	Dead	Gaines	Sabyl Pusley	Dead	Gaines
2						
3						
4						
5						
6						
7						
8						
9						
10						
11						
12						
13						
14						
15						
16						
17						

(See Indian Office letter September 17-1910 DC#12-17-1910)

Date of Application for Enrollment.

8-2-99

Choctaw By Blood Enrollment Cards 1898-1914

RESIDENCE:	Gaines	COUNTY.		CARD NO.	
POST OFFICE:	Gowen I.T.	Choctaw Nation	Choctaw Roll (Not Including Freedmen)	FIELD NO.	3155

Dawes' Roll No.	NAME		Relationship to Person First Named	AGE	SEX	BLOOD	TRIBAL ENROLLMENT		
							Year	County	No.
9134	1 Adams Wilburn	28		25	M	Full	1896	Gaines	95
	2								
	3								
	4								
	5								
	6								
	7								
	8								
	9								
	10								
	11								
	12								
	13								
	14								
	15								
	16								
	17								

ENROLLMENT OF NOS. 1 HEREON APPROVED BY THE SECRETARY OF INTERIOR FEB 4 1903

TRIBAL ENROLLMENT OF PARENTS

Name of Father	Year	County	Name of Mother	Year	County
1 Ishalitubbee	Dead	Gaines	Betsy Ishalitubbee	Dead	Gaines
2					
3					
4					
5					
6					
7					
8					
9					
10					
11					
12					
13					
14					
15					
16			DATE OF APPLICATION FOR ENROLLMENT	Aug 2	1899
17					

Choctaw By Blood Enrollment Cards 1898-1914

RESIDENCE: Gaines COUNTY. **Choctaw Nation** **Choctaw Roll** CARD NO.

POST OFFICE: Hartshorne I.T. *(Not Including Freedmen)* FIELD NO. 3156

Dawes' Roll No.	NAME	Relationship to Person	AGE	SEX	BLOOD	TRIBAL ENROLLMENT		
						Year	County	No.
9135	1 Thompson Philip 28	First Named	25	M	Full	1896	Gaines	11977
	2							
	3							
	4							
	5							
	6							
	7							
	8							
	9							
	10							
	11							
	12							
	13							
	14							
	15							
	16							
	17							

ENROLLMENT OF NOS. 1 APPROVED BY THE SECRETARY OF INTERIOR HEREON FEB 4 1903

TRIBAL ENROLLMENT OF PARENTS

	Name of Father	Year	County	Name of Mother	Year	County
1	Saffron Thompson	Dead	Gaines	Lutsy Thompson	Dead	Gaines
2						
3						
4						
5						
6						
7						
8		For child of No. see N.B. (Apr 26, 1906) Card No. 239				
9						
10						
11						
12						
13						
14					Date of Application for Enrollment.	
15					8-2-99	
16						
17						

Choctaw By Blood Enrollment Cards 1898-1914

RESIDENCE: Gaines COUNTY. **Choctaw Nation** Choctaw Roll CARD NO.
POST OFFICE: Hartshorne, I.T. (Not Including Freedmen) FIELD NO. 3157

Dawes' Roll No.	NAME		Relationship to Person	AGE	SEX	BLOOD	TRIBAL ENROLLMENT		
							Year	County	No.
9136	1 Bee William	49	First Named	46	M	Full	1896	Gaines	841
9137	2 Jefferson Betsy	35	Wife	32	F	"	1896	"	10199
9138	3 Bee Fannie	25	Dau	22	F	"	1896	"	843
9139	4 " Annie	10	"	7	F	"	1896	"	845
9140	5 " Bessie B	7	"	4	F	"	1896	"	846
9141	6 Pickens Eve	11	Step Dau	8	F	"	1893		
DEAD.	7 " ~~Winnie~~		"	~~3~~	~~F~~	"			
	8								
	9								
	10	~~ENROLLMENT~~ OF NOS. 1-2-3-4-5 and 6 HEREON							
	11	APPROVED BY THE SECRETARY ~~OF INTERIOR~~ FEB 4 1903							
	12								
	13	No. 7 HEREON DISMISSED UNDER ORDER OF THE COMMISSION TO THE FIVE							
	14	CIVILIZED TRIBES OF MARCH 31, 1905.							
	15	For child of No.3 see NB (Mar 3 1905) #1421							
	16	" " " No.1 " " (Mar 3 1905) #503							
	17								

TRIBAL ENROLLMENT OF PARENTS

Name of Father	Year	County	Name of Mother	Year	County
1 Ouichatubbee	Dead	Gaines	Achama	Dead	Gaines
2 Somne Colberson	"	Tobuctsey[sic]	Tennessee	"	"
3 No 1			Jane Bee	"	"
4 No. 1			Katie "	"	"
5 No 1			" "	"	"
6 John Pickens	Dead	Gaines	No 2		
7 " "	"	"	No. 2		
8					
9 No6 also on 1896 Choctaw roll as Iva Pickens					
10 For child of No.2 see NB (March 3 1905) #1213					
11 No3 on roll as Betsy Pickens					
~~No5 " " " Belle Bee~~					
12 No6 on Page 48 No. 458, 1893 Pay Roll Gaines County as Eve Picken					
13 Affidavit of birth of Winnie Pickens to be supplied. Received.					
14 No1 is now separated from No2 and is married to Nancy Camp on					
~~Chickasaw card #696. evidence of marriage filed Dec 1 1902~~					
15 No7 Died in July 1900. Proof of death filed Dec 23rd 1902		Date of Application for Enrollment		Aug 2 1899	
16 No2 is now wife of Calvin Jefferson, Choctaw Card #2491. Evidence of marriage					
17 filed Dec 26, 1902					

Choctaw By Blood Enrollment Cards 1898-1914

RESIDENCE:	Gaines	COUNTY.						CARD No.	
POST OFFICE:	Hartshorne, I.T.	**Choctaw Nation**				Choctaw Roll (Not Including Freedmen)		FIELD No.	3158

Dawes' Roll No.	NAME	Relationship to Person First Named	AGE	SEX	BLOOD	TRIBAL ENROLLMENT		
						Year	County	No.
1	White, Rosetta	Named	25	F	1/4			
2	" Hezekiah	Son	1	M	1/8			
3	" Clovy Bryant	Son	4	M	1/8			
4	" Gracie E Belle	Dau	4mo	F	1/8			
5								
6	Nos } DISMISSED							
7	2-3&4 }							
8	MAY 25 1904							
9	Choctaw Chickasaw Citizenship Court on Feb 5 '04 in Case #111 dismissed application for admission to citizenship of No2							
10								
11								
12	* No1 Denied by C.C.C.C. Case #11 March 9 04							
13	*C.C.C.C. in Case 11 decided it had no jurisdiction over No 3&4							
14								
15	No.1 DENIED CITIZENSHIP BY THE CHOCTAW AND							
16	CHICKASAW CITIZENSHIP COURT							
17								

TRIBAL ENROLLMENT OF PARENTS

	Name of Father	Year	County	Name of Mother	Year	County
1	Frank Thompson	Dead	Non Citz	Ann Thompson		Choctaw
2	Ed White		" "	No 1		
3	" "		" "	No. 1		
4	" "		" "	No 1		
5						
6						
7						
8						
9	See Choc Cit Case #1374 ('96(No1 denied in that case.					
10	Admitted by U.S. Court, Central Dist, Aug 30/97					
11	Case No 161. As to residence and birth of child,					
12	see her testimony.					
13	No.3 was born Oct 18, 1896, subsequent to date of filing of original application in this case and enrolled Aug 6, 1900					
14	Judgment of U.S. Court admitting No1 vacated and set aside by Decree of Choctaw Chickasaw Cit Court Dec 17 02					
15	See Choctaw card R.723 for children.					
16	No4 Born Feb 23rd 1902; Enrolled June 26th 1902.			Date of Application for Enrollment.		Aug 2/99
17	No1 now in C.C.C.C. Case #111					

Choctaw By Blood Enrollment Cards 1898-1914

<table>
<tr><td>RESIDENCE: Gaines</td><td colspan="2">COUNTY.</td><td colspan="3">Choctaw Nation</td><td colspan="2">Choctaw Roll
(Not Including Freedmen)</td><td>CARD No.</td></tr>
<tr><td>POST OFFICE: Hartshorne, I.T.</td><td colspan="2"></td><td colspan="3"></td><td colspan="2"></td><td>FIELD No. 3159</td></tr>
</table>

Dawes' Roll No.	NAME	Relationship to Person First Named	AGE	SEX	BLOOD	TRIBAL ENROLLMENT Year	County	No.
I.W. 1472	1 Grady, John M ⁵⁹	Named	56	M	I.W.		D	
	2 " Buena V.	Dau	16	F	IW		D	
	3 " Horace M	Son	14	M	IW		D	
	4 " Leroy	"	11	M	IW		D	
	5							
	6							
	7							
	8							
	9							
	10							
	11							
	12							
	13							
	14							
	15	No1 has an application pending on an Intermarried [remainder illegible]						
	16 See decision of June 6, 1905							
	17							

All DENIED CITIZENSHIP BY THE CHOCTAW AND CHICKASAW CITIZENSHIP COURT

ENROLLMENT OF NOS. one HEREON APPROVED BY THE SECRETARY OF INTERIOR AUG 22 1905

TRIBAL ENROLLMENT OF PARENTS

	Name of Father	Year	County	Name of Mother	Year	County
1	J. W. Grady	Dead	Non Citz	Drucilla Grady	Dead	Non Citz
2	No1			Sarah Grady	"	white woman
3	No1			" "	"	" " "
4	No1			" "	"	" " "
5						
6	Nos 1 to 4 incl. Denied in 96 Case #262					
7	Admitted by U.S. Court, Central Dist. July 1/97					
8	As to residence, see testimony of No1. Sustained by U.S. Supreme Court					
9	Judgment of U.S. Court setting Nos 1 to 4 incl. vacated and set aside by Decree of Choctaw Chickasaw Cit Court Dec 17/02. No1 to 4 incl in C.C.C.C. Case #73					
10						
11	No 1 claims also as an intermarried citizen by reason of his marriage					
12	to Fannie E. Grady, on Choctaw Card #2774, roll No 8130.					
13	Evidence of marriage between No1 and Fannie E Hendrickson filed March 17, 1903.					
14						
15					Aug 2/99	
16					Date of Application for Enrollment	
17						

RESIDENCE: Gaines   COUNTY. **Choctaw Nation**   Choctaw Roll   CARD NO.
POST OFFICE: Hartshorne, I.T.   *(Not Including Freedmen)*   FIELD NO. 3160

Dawes' Roll No.	NAME	Relationship to Person First Named	AGE	SEX	BLOOD	TRIBAL ENROLLMENT		
						Year	County	No.
DEAD 1	Beagles, George W		19	M	1/16	1896	Gaines	833
I.W. 292 2	" Bettie E 20	Wife	17	F	I.W.			
DEAD. 3	" George A DEAD	Son	1mo	M	1/32			
4								
5	No. 1 and 3 HEREON DISMISSED UNDER							
6	ORDER OF THE COMMISSION TO THE FIVE							
7	CIVILIZED TRIBES OF MARCH 31, 1905							
8								
9	ENROLLMENT							
10	OF NOS. 2 HEREON APPROVED BY THE SECRETARY							
11	OF INTERIOR SEP 12 1903							
12								
13								
14								
15								
16								
17								

TRIBAL ENROLLMENT OF PARENTS

Name of Father	Year	County	Name of Mother	Year	County
1 Al Beagles		Non Citz	Annie Nelson		Gaines
2 Charley Lewis	Dead	" "	Fannie Lewis		Non Citz
3 No.1			No.2		
4					
5					
6			No1 on 1896 roll as Geo W. Beagles		
7			No.3 Enrolled Aug 28, 1900		
8			No1 Died June 30, 1900: proof of death filed Nov 17 1902		
9			No3 Died May 6, 1901. proof of death filed Dec 1 1902		
10					
11					
12					
13					Date of Application for Enrollment.
14					
15					Aug 2/99
16					
17					

Choctaw By Blood Enrollment Cards 1898-1914

RESIDENCE: Tobucksy COUNTY.									
POST OFFICE: Dow, I.T.									

Choctaw Nation

Choctaw Roll (Not Including Freedmen)

CARD NO. FIELD NO. 3161

Dawes' Roll No.	NAME	Relationship to Person	AGE	SEX	BLOOD	TRIBAL ENROLLMENT		
						Year	County	No.
9142	1 Freeney, Henry C ²⁵	First Named	22	M	1/16	1896	Gaines	3980
I.W. 292	2 " Fannie ²⁷	Wife	24	F	I.W.			
9143	3 " Edna M ⁵	Dau	2	"	1/32			
9144	4 " Buena Vesta ²	Dau	2m	F	1/32			
	5							
	6							
	7	ENROLLMENT						
	8	OF NOS. 1, 3 and 4 HEREON APPROVED BY THE SECRETARY						
	9	OF INTERIOR FEB 4 1903						
	10	ENROLLMENT						
	11	OF NOS. 2 HEREON APPROVED BY THE SECRETARY						
	12	OF INTERIOR SEP 12 1903						
	13							
	14							
	15							
	16							
	17							

TRIBAL ENROLLMENT OF PARENTS

Name of Father	Year	County	Name of Mother	Year	County
1 Henry Freeney	Dead	Tobucksy	Sarah Freeney	Dead	Non Citz
2 Samuel Shue		Non Citz	Hannah Shue		" "
3 No 1			No 2		
4 No 1			No 2		
5					
6					
7					
8 For child of Nos 1 and 2 see NB (Apr 26, 06) No 564					
9 No 3 Affidavit of birth to be supplied: Recd Aug 9/99					
10 No.4 Enrolled February 6, 1901.					
11					
12					
13					
14				Date of Application for Enrollment.	
15				Aug 2/99	
16					
17					

Choctaw By Blood Enrollment Cards 1898-1914

RESIDENCE: Gaines COUNTY. **Choctaw Nation** Choctaw Roll CARD NO.
POST OFFICE: Hartshorne, I.T. *(Not Including Freedmen)* FIELD No. 3162

Dawes' Roll No.	NAME		Relationship to Person	AGE	SEX	BLOOD	TRIBAL ENROLLMENT		
							Year	County	No.
9145	1 Johnson, Daniel E	32	First Named	29	M	3/4	1896	Gaines	6589
9146	2 " Lillie	25	Wife	22	F	3/4	1896	"	6590
9147	3 " Belvina	13	Dau	10	"	3/4	1896	"	6591
DEAD.	4 " Albert L	10	Son	7	M	3/4	1896	"	6592
DEAD.	5 " Nelson	6	Son	3	"	3/4			
	6								
	7								
	8	ENROLLMENT							
	9	OF NOS. 1, 2 and 3 HEREON APPROVED BY THE SECRETARY							
	10	OF INTERIOR FEB 4 1903							
	11								
	12	No. 4 and 5 HEREON DISMISSED UNDER							
	13	ORDER OF THE COMMISSION TO THE FIVE							
	14	CIVILIZED TRIBES OF MARCH 31, 1905.							
	15								
	16								
	17								

TRIBAL ENROLLMENT OF PARENTS

Name of Father	Year	County	Name of Mother	Year	County
1 Lewis Johnson	Dead	Skullyville	Liza A Johnson		Gaines
2 Alfred Sexton	"	Wade	Julie Sexton	Dead	Sugar Loaf
3 No1			No2		
4 No1			No2		
5 No1			No2		
6					
7					
8					
9 No4 on 1896 roll as Albert Lee Johnson					
10 No.4 Died October 1901: Proof of death filed Dec 23, 1902					
11 No5 Affidavit of birth to be supplied: Recd 8/3/99					
11 No.5 Died August, 1901: Proof of death filed Dec 23, 1902					
12					
13				Date of Application for Enrollment	
14					
15				Aug 2/99	
16					
17 P.O. Gowen, I.T.					

162

RESIDENCE:	Tobucksy	COUNTY.	**Choctaw Nation**	**Choctaw Roll** (Not Including Freedmen)	CARD No.
POST OFFICE:	McAlester, I.T.				FIELD No. **3163**

Dawes' Roll No.	NAME	Relationship to Person First Named	AGE	SEX	BLOOD	TRIBAL ENROLLMENT		
						Year	County	No.
9148	1 Brown John J 42	First Named	39	M	1/8	1896	Tobucksy	882
9149	2 " Margaret 42	Wife	39	F	1/2	1896	"	883
9150	3 Gordon Myrtle 23	Dau	20	"	5/16	1896	"	884
9151	4 Sterrett Susan 20	"	17	"	5/16	1896	"	885
9152	5 Brown Hattie 19	"	16	"	5/16	1896	"	886
9153	6 " Tandy 16	Son	13	M	5/16	1896	"	887
9154	7 " Rector 14	"	11	"	5/16	1896	"	888
I.W. 185	8 Gordon, Reverdy J	Husband of N°3	30	M	I.W.			
I.W. 1319	9 Sterrett, Frank M Jr 22	Husband of N°4	22	M	I.W.			
	10 ENROLLMENT					ENROLLMENT		
	11 OF NOS. 1,2,3,4,5,6 and 7 HEREON APPROVED BY THE SECRETARY					OF NOS. 9 HEREON APPROVED BY THE SECRETARY		
	12 OF INTERIOR Feb 4 1903					OF INTERIOR Mar 14 1905		
	13 ENROLLMENT							
	13 OF NOS. ___8___ HEREON							
	14 APPROVED BY THE SECRETARY							
	15 OF INTERIOR Jun 13 1903					For child of No5 see NB (March 3, 1905) #1405		
	On Sept 18, 1902 No.9 was married to No.4							
	17 No.9 originally listed for enrollment on Choc card D-799 Sept 23, 1902: transferred to this card							
	Jan 28, 1905 see decision of Jan 12, 1905							

TRIBAL ENROLLMENT OF PARENTS

	Name of Father	Year	County	Name of Mother	Year	County
1	Richard Brown	Dead	Cherokee	Lucy Brown	Dead	Skullyville
2	Jas P. Willis	"	Non Citz	Eliz. Willis	"	Kiamitia
3	No1			No2		
4	No1			No2		
5	No1			No2		
6	No1			No2		
7	No1			No2		
8	W. Gordon		Non Citizen	Laura Gordon		Non Citizen
9	John A Sterrett		Non Citz	Sallie Sterrett		Non Citz
10	No1 on 1896 roll as Jno J Brown					
11	No3 " 1896 " " Mattie "					
	No6 " 1896 " " Landy "					
12	No.3 is the wife of Reverdy J Gordon on Choctaw card D.454					
13	No.4 is now the wife of Frank M Sterrett o Choctaw card #D799 Sept 23, 1902					
14	N°8 transferred from Choctaw card #D454. See decision of April 20, 1903					
15	Record as to enrollment of No.9 forwarded to Department March 14, 1906 (over)			#1 to 7		
	[On back] Record returned see opinion of Assistant Attorney General of			Date of Application for Enrollment.		
16	March 15, 1906 in case of Omer R Nicholson			Aug 2/99		
17	Nos 4 and 9 P.O. Redlands California					

Choctaw By Blood Enrollment Cards 1898-1914

RESIDENCE: Gaines COUNTY:		Choctaw Nation				Choctaw Roll		CARD NO.	
POST OFFICE: Wilburton, I.T.						(Not Including Freedmen)		FIELD NO. 3164	

Dawes' Roll No.	NAME	Relationship to Person	AGE	SEX	BLOOD	TRIBAL ENROLLMENT		
						Year	County	No.
9155	1 Hampton, Sweeney 48	First Named	45	M	Full	1896	Gaines	5287
9156	2 " Elizabeth 25	Wife	22	F	"	1896	"	5288
9157	3 " Charlotte 13	Dau	10	"	"	1896	"	5289
9158	4 " Perry 7	Son	4	M	"	1896	"	5290
9159	5 " Julius 6	"	3	"	"			
9160	6 " Dewey	"	9mo	"	"			
9161	7 " William 2	"	1yr7mo	"	"			
	8							
	9							
	10	ENROLLMENT						
	11	OF NOS. 1,2,3,4,5,6 and 7 HEREON APPROVED BY THE SECRETARY						
	12	OF INTERIOR FEB 4 1903						
	13							
	14							
	15							
	16							
	17							

TRIBAL ENROLLMENT OF PARENTS

	Name of Father	Year	County	Name of Mother	Year	County
1	Tobias Hampton	Dead	Red River	Polina Hampton	Dead	Jacks Fork
2	Roberson Harrison	"	Gaines	Siney Grayson		Gaines
3	No1			Mary Hampton	Dead	"
4	No1			No2		
5	No1			No2		
6	No1			No2		
7	No1			" 2		
8						
9	No.7 Born Novt 25th 1900: Enrolled June 17th 1902					
10						
11	For child of Nos 1&2 see NB (Apr 26-06) Card #675					
12	" " " " " " (Mar 3-05) " #213					
13						
14					Date of Application for Enrollment.	
15					Aug 2/99	
16						
17						

164

Choctaw By Blood Enrollment Cards 1898-1914

RESIDENCE:	Gaines	COUNTY.							
POST OFFICE:	Hartshorne, I.T.							CARD NO.	

Choctaw Nation — **Choctaw Roll** *(Not Including Freedmen)* — FIELD NO. **3165**

Dawes' Roll No.	NAME	Relationship to Person First Named	AGE	SEX	BLOOD	TRIBAL ENROLLMENT		
						Year	County	No.
I.W.660	1 Robinson John W 54	First Named	52	M	I.W.			
14348	2 " Jane 37	Wife	34	F	1/2	1896	Gaines	10723
14349	3 " Minnie 16	Dau	13	F	1/4	1896	"	10724
14350	4 " Josiah 13	Son	10	M	1/4	1896	"	10725
14351	5 " Teresa 10	Dau	7	F	1/4	1896	"	10726
14352	6 " Charles J 8	Son	5	M	1/4	1896	"	10727
14353	7 " Rosa A. 5	Dau	2	F	1/4			
14354	8 " Mary Esther 1	Dau	2mo	F	1/4			
	9							
	10 ENROLLMENT OF NOS. 2,3,4,5,6,7 and 8 HEREON							
	11 APPROVED BY THE SECRETARY							
	OF INTERIOR Apr 11 1903							
	12							
	13 Decision Prepared							
	14 Oct 26-03							
	15 ENROLLMENT OF NOS. 1							
	APPROVED BY THE SECRETARY HEREON							
	16 OF INTERIOR Mar 26 1904							
	17							

TRIBAL ENROLLMENT OF PARENTS

	Name of Father	Year	County	Name of Mother	Year	County
1	N.C. Robinson		Non Citz	Jane Robinson		Non Citz
2	Josiah Impson	Dead	Jacks Fork	Jane Impson	Dead	Jacks Fork
3	No.1			No.2		
4	No1			No2		
5	No1			No2		
6	No1			No2		
7	No1			No2		
8	Nº1			Nº2		
9						
10						
11	For child of Nos 1 and 2 see NB (March 3, 1905) #1239					
12	No.1 on roll John W. Robinson. Also admitted by Dawes Commission					
13	as intermarried citizen No. 1184 as J.W. Robinson			#1 to 7 inc		
	Nos 2,3,4 5 and 6 admitted by Dawes Commission Case No. 1184					
14	No.5 On 1896 roll as Ivresia Robinson			Date of Application for Enrollment:		
15	No.6 " 1896 " " Chas. Jesse Robinson			August 2, 1899		
16	Affidavit of birth of No.7 to be supplied. Filed Nov. 2/99					
	Nº8 Born March 16, 1902; enrolled May 31, 1902					
17	Evidence of marriage between Nºˢ1 and 2 filed Jany 3, 1903					

165

Choctaw By Blood Enrollment Cards 1898-1914

Choctaw Nation

POST OFFICE: Hartshorne, I.T. | (Not Including Freedmen) | Choctaw Roll | CARD NO.

FIELD NO. 3166

Dawes' Roll No.	NAME	Relationship to Person	AGE	SEX	BLOOD	TRIBAL ENROLLMENT		
						Year	County	No.
I.W. 740	1 Lewis Thomas B ㉚	First Named	27	M	I.W.	1896	Gaines	14751
14355	2 " Ruthie 24	Wife	21	F	1/8	1896	"	7832
14356	3 " Dora 2	Dau	3 wk	F	1/16			
	4							
	5	ENROLLMENT						
	6	OF NOS. 2 and 3 HEREON APPROVED BY THE SECRETARY						
	7	OF INTERIOR APR 11 1903						
	8							
	9	DECISION PREPARED						
	10							
	11	ENROLLMENT OF NOS. ~~~ 1 ~~~ HEREON APPROVED BY THE SECRETARY						
	12	OF INTERIOR MAY -7 1904						
	13							
	14							
	15							
	16							
	17							

TRIBAL ENROLLMENT OF PARENTS

	Name of Father	Year	County	Name of Mother	Year	County
1	C. W. Lewis		Non Citz	Fanny Lewis		Non Citz
2	Al Beagles		"	Annie Nelson	1896	Gaines
3	No.1			No.2		
4						
5						
6			No 1 admitted as an intermarried citizen and No 2 as			
7			a citizen by blood in Choctaw 1896 case #1235 No appeal			
8			Evidence of marriage filed with above case			
9			No 1 See Decision of March 2 '04			
10			No.3 Enrolled November 21st, 1900			
11			For child of Nos 1&2 see NB (March 3 1905) #577			
12						
13						
14						
15					Date of Application for Enrollment.	
16						
17					Aug 2/99	

Choctaw By Blood Enrollment Cards 1898-1914

RESIDENCE:	Tobucksey[sic]	COUNTY.							

RESIDENCE: Tobucksey[sic] **COUNTY.** **Choctaw Nation** **Choctaw Roll** (Not Including Freedmen) **CARD NO. FIELD NO.** 3167
POST OFFICE: McAlester, I.T.

Dawes' Roll No.	NAME	Relationship to Person First Named	AGE	SEX	BLOOD	TRIBAL ENROLLMENT		
						Year	County	No.
9162	1 Ausley William 50	First Named	47	M	1/4	1896	Tobucksy	102
I.W. 294	2 " Mattie A 47	Wife	44	F	I.W.	1896	"	14254
9163	3 " Joseph 16	Son	13	M	1/4	1896	"	104
	4							
	5							
	6							
	7	ENROLLMENT OF NOS. 1 and 3 HEREON APPROVED BY THE SECRETARY OF INTERIOR FEB 4 1903						
	8							
	9							
	10	ENROLLMENT OF NOS. 2 HEREON APPROVED BY THE SECRETARY OF INTERIOR SEP 12 1903						
	11							
	12							
	13							
	14							
	15							
	16							
	17							

TRIBAL ENROLLMENT OF PARENTS

	Name of Father	Year	County	Name of Mother	Year	County
1	Gilbert Ausley	Dead	Tobucksy	Letha A Ausley	Dead	Tobucksy
2	D.C. Oglesby	Dead	Non Citz	N. J. Oglesby	"	Non Citz
3	No 1			Antonette Ausley	"	Tobucksy
4						
5						
6						
7						
8	Certificate of marriage of Wm Ausley and Antonette Krebbs					
9	mother of Joseph Ausley, Dated May 14, 1871, in due					
10	form, exhibited but not in form to be filed con=[sic] veniently.					
11	No.2 admitted as an intermarried citizen by					
12	Dawes Commission in 1896 Choctaw Case #487 No appeal.					
13	For child of No 3 see NB (Apr 26-06) Card #741				6\1\17	
14					Date of Application for Enrollment.	
15					Aug 2/99	
16						
17						

Choctaw By Blood Enrollment Cards 1898-1914

RESIDENCE:	Sans Bois	COUNTY.						
POST OFFICE:	Whitefield, I.T.					CARD NO.		

Choctaw Nation (Not Including Freedmen)   **Choctaw Roll**   CARD NO.   FIELD NO. 3168

Dawes' Roll No. DEAD.	NAME	Relationship to Person First Named	AGE	SEX	BLOOD	TRIBAL ENROLLMENT		
						Year	County	No.
1	White Pauline		36	F	Full	1896	Sans Bois	12699
9164	2 " Edmund 18	Son	15	M	3/4	1896	"	12700
9165	3 " Sidney 13	"	10	M	3/4	1896	"	12701
9166	4 " Lizzie 9	Dau	6	F	3/4	1896	"	12702
	5							
	6							
	7	ENROLLMENT OF NOS. 2, 3 and 4 HEREON APPROVED BY THE SECRETARY OF INTERIOR FEB 4 1903						
	8							
	9							
	10	No. 1 HEREON DISMISSED UNDER ORDER OF THE COMMISSION TO THE FIVE CIVILIZED TRIBES OF MARCH 31, 1905.						
	11							
	12							
	13							
	14							
	15							
	16							
	17							

TRIBAL ENROLLMENT OF PARENTS

	Name of Father	Year	County	Name of Mother	Year	County
1	Edmond McCurtain	Dead	Skullyville	Susan McCurtain	Dead	Skullyville
2	John White	1896	Gaines	No.1		
3	"	1896	"	No 1		
4	"	1896	"	No 1		
5						
6						
7			No1 died March 10, 1902; proof of death filed Dec 12 1902			
8						
9						
10						
11						
12						
13						Date of Application for Enrollment.
14						
15						Aug 2 189
16						
17	P.O. Hartshorne, I.T.					

RESIDENCE: Gaines COUNTY. **Choctaw Nation** Choctaw Roll CARD NO.
POST OFFICE: Gowen, I.T. (Not Including Freedmen) FIELD NO. 3169

Dawes' Roll No.	NAME		Relationship to Person	AGE	SEX	BLOOD	TRIBAL ENROLLMENT		
							Year	County	No.
9167	1 Williams Amos	46	First Named	43	M	Full	1896	Gaines	12974
	2								
	3								
	4								
	5	ENROLLMENT							
	6	OF NOS. 1 HEREON APPROVED BY THE SECRETARY							
	7	OF INTERIOR FEB 4 1903							
	8								
	9								
	10								
	11								
	12								
	13								
	14								
	15								
	16								
	17								

TRIBAL ENROLLMENT OF PARENTS

	Name of Father	Year	County	Name of Mother	Year	County
1	Yakankubbee	Dead	Skullyville	Aweche	Dead	Skullyville
2						
3						
4						
5						
6						
7			On roll as Amos William			
8						
9						
10						
11						
12						
13						
14				Date of Application for Enrollment.		
15				Aug 2/99		
16						
17						

RESIDENCE:	Gaines	COUNTY.	**Choctaw Nation**	**Choctaw Roll**	CARD NO.
POST OFFICE:	Hartshorne, I.T.			*(Not Including Freedmen)*	FIELD NO. 3170

Dawes' Roll No.	NAME		Relationship to Person	AGE	SEX	BLOOD	TRIBAL ENROLLMENT		
							Year	County	No.
9168	1 Grayson, John	66	First Named	63	M	Full	1896	Gaines	4683
9169	2 " Sina	63	Wife	60	F	"	1896	"	4684
	3								
	4								
	5								
	6	ENROLLMENT							
	7	OF NOS. 1 and 2 HEREON APPROVED BY THE SECRETARY							
	8	OF INTERIOR FEB 4 1903							
	9								
	10								
	11								
	12								
	13								
	14								
	15								
	16								
	17								

TRIBAL ENROLLMENT OF PARENTS

	Name of Father	Year	County	Name of Mother	Year	County
1		Dead	Gaines		Dead	Gaines
2	John Jones	"	Skullyville	Wynie Jones	"	Skullyville
3						
4						
5						
6						
7		No2 on 1896 roll as Sana Grayson				
8						
9						
10						
11						
12						
13						
14				Date of Application for Enrollment		
15				Aug 2/99		
16						
17						

Choctaw By Blood Enrollment Cards 1898-1914

RESIDENCE: Gaines COUNTY.	Choctaw Nation	Choctaw Roll (Not Including Freedmen)	CARD NO.
POST OFFICE: Hartshorne, I.T.			FIELD NO. 3171

Dawes' Roll No.	NAME	Relationship to Person First Named	AGE	SEX	BLOOD	TRIBAL ENROLLMENT Year	County	No.
9170	1 Johnson, Eliza A. ⁶⁹	First Named	66	F	Full	1896	Gaines	6635
	2							
	3							
	4							
	5							
	6							
	7							
	8							
	9							
	10							
	11							
	12							
	13							
	14							
	15							
	16							
	17							

ENROLLMENT
OF NOS. 1 HEREON
APPROVED BY THE SECRETARY
OF INTERIOR FEB 4 1903

TRIBAL ENROLLMENT OF PARENTS

Name of Father	Year	County	Name of Mother	Year	County
1 Chas. Sexton	Dead	Tobucksy		Dead	Tobucksy
2					
3					
4					
5					
6		On 1896 roll as Liza Ann Johnson			
7					
8					
9					
10					
11					
12					
13				Date of Application for Enrollment.	
14					
15				Aug 2/99	
16					
17					

RESIDENCE: Gaines COUNTY. **Choctaw Nation** **Choctaw Roll** CARD NO.
POST OFFICE: Hartshorne, I.T. *(Not Including Freedmen)* FIELD NO. 3172

Dawes' Roll No.	NAME	Relationship to Person	AGE	SEX	BLOOD	TRIBAL ENROLLMENT		
						Year	County	No.
9171	1 Brashears, George W 38	First Named	35	M	1/2	1896	Gaines	837
I.W. 295	2 " Lida B. 31	Wife	28	F	I.W.	1896	"	14295
9172	3 " Julia F 20	Dau	17	"	1/4		"	
9173	4 " Ivey	Dau	2½ mo	F	1/4			
	5							
	6							
	7	ENROLLMENT OF NOS. 1, 3 and 4 HEREON APPROVED BY THE SECRETARY OF INTERIOR FEB 3 1903						
	8							
	9							
	10	ENROLLMENT OF NOS. 2 HEREON APPROVED BY THE SECRETARY OF INTERIOR SEP 12 1903						
	11							
	12							
	13							
	14	For child of No3 see NB (Apr 26-06) Card #374						
	15	" " " " 1 " " " " #518						
	16							
	17							

TRIBAL ENROLLMENT OF PARENTS

	Name of Father	Year	County	Name of Mother	Year	County
1	Jno. Brashears	Dead	Gaines	Julia Brashears	Dead	Gaines
2	L. S. Bridges	"	Non Citz		"	Non Citz
3	No1			Lizzie Brashears	"	" " "
4	No.1			No.2		
5						
6			No1 on 1896 roll as Geo W. Brashears.			
7			No2 " 1896 " " Lidia B. "			
8						
9			Evidence of marriage to be supplied. Recd 8/4/99			
10						
11			Evidence as to marriage of parents of No3 to be supplied. See testimony of Eastep			
12			Venson taken Aug 4/99			
13			No4 Enrolled December 22, 1900.		Date of Application for Enrollment. #1 to 3	
14						
15					Aug 2/99	
16						
17	P.O. Ada I.T.					

Choctaw By Blood Enrollment Cards 1898-1914

RESIDENCE: Gaines COUNTY. **Choctaw Nation** Choctaw Roll CARD No.
POST OFFICE: Hartshorne, I.T. *(Not Including Freedmen)* FIELD No. 3173

Dawes' Roll No.	NAME		Relationship to Person	AGE	SEX	BLOOD	TRIBAL ENROLLMENT		
							Year	County	No.
9174	1 Pusley, Simon	25	First Named	22	M	Full	1896	Gaines	10186
9175	2 " Betsy	43	Wife	40	F	"	1896	"	10187
9176	3 " Rhoda	18	S.Dau	15	"	"	1896	"	10189
9177	4 " Lillie	16	"	13	"	"	1896	"	10190
9178	5 " William	11	"	8	"	"	1896	"	10188
	6								
	7								
	8	ENROLLMENT OF NOS. 1-2-3-4 and 5 HEREON APPROVED BY THE SECRETARY OF INTERIOR FEB 4 1903							
	9								
	10								
	11								
	12								
	13								
	14								
	15								
	16								
	17								

TRIBAL ENROLLMENT OF PARENTS

	Name of Father	Year	County	Name of Mother	Year	County
1	Calvin Pusley	Dead	Gaines	Nancy Pusley		Gaines
2	Silas Bohanan	"	Wade		Dead	"
3	Norris Pusley	"	Gaines	No2		
4	" "	"	"	No2		
5	Abner Pusley		Blue	No2		
6						
7						
8						
9						
10						
11						
12						
13					Date of Application for Enrollment.	
14						
15					Aug 2/99	
16						
17	Wilburton I.T. 8/31/06					

Choctaw By Blood Enrollment Cards 1898-1914

RESIDENCE: Gaines   COUNTY. **Choctaw Nation**   **Choctaw Roll**   CARD NO.
POST OFFICE: Gordon, I.T.   *(Not Including Freedmen)*   FIELD NO.   3174

Dawes' Roll No.	NAME		Relationship to Person	AGE	SEX	BLOOD	TRIBAL ENROLLMENT		
							Year	County	No.
9179	1 Hattensty, Henson		First Named	36	M	Full	1896	Gaines	5294
9180	2 " Phoebe	39	Wife	36	F	3/4	1896	"	5295
9181	3 " Jesse	17	Son	14	M	7/8	1896	"	5296
9182	4 " Paul	15	"	12	"	7/8	1896	"	5297
9183	5 " Noga	13	Dau	10	F	7/8	1896	"	5298
9184	6 " Mary	10	"	7	"	7/8	1896	"	5299
9185	7 " Belle	6	"	3	"	7/8	1896	"	5300
9186	8 " Lela	3	"	2mo	"	7/8			
	9								
	10								
	11	ENROLLMENT							
	12	OF NOS. 1,2,3,4,5,6,7 and 8 HEREON APPROVED BY THE SECRETARY							
	13	OF INTERIOR FEB 4 1903							
	14								
	15								
	16								
	17								

DIED PRIOR TO SEPTEMBER 25, 1902

TRIBAL ENROLLMENT OF PARENTS

	Name of Father	Year	County	Name of Mother	Year	County
1	Thos. Hattensty	Dead	in Mississippi	Ellen Hattensty		in Mississippi
2	Tom Anderson	"	"	Siney Anderson		" "
3	No1			No2		
4	No1			No2		
5	No1			No2		
6	No1			No2		
7	No1			No2		
8	No1			No2		
9						
10						
11						
12						
13	Nos1 to five inclusive were admitted by Act of Council, approved April 9/91. Duly certified copy, exhibited. Admitted under name of					#1 to 8
14	Haltenstye.					Date of Application for Enrollment
15	No. 1 died April 13, 1900. Enrollment cancelled by Department July 8, 1904					Aug 2/99
16	Nos 6-7 were born since admission of parents.					No8 enrolled Nov 2/99
17						

RESIDENCE:	Gaines	COUNTY.	**Choctaw Nation**				Choctaw Roll		CARD No.	
POST OFFICE:	Hartshorne, I.T.						*(Not Including Freedmen)*		FIELD No. 3175	

Dawes' Roll No.	NAME		Relationship to Person First Named	AGE	SEX	BLOOD	TRIBAL ENROLLMENT		
							Year	County	No.
I.W. **661**	₁ Ledon, Jacob	34	Named	31	M	I.W.	1896	Sans Bois	14735
9187	₂ " Annie	24	Wife	21	F	1/4	1896	" "	7710
9188	₃ " Eudith E	1	Dau	2mo	F	1/8			
	4								
	5								
	6								
	7	ENROLLMENT							
	8	OF NOS. 2 and 3 HEREON APPROVED BY THE SECRETARY							
	9	OF INTERIOR FEB 4 1903							
	10	ENROLLMENT							
	11	OF NOS. 1 HEREON APPROVED BY THE SECRETARY							
	12	OF INTERIOR MR 26 1904							
	13								
	14								
	15								
	16								
	17								

TRIBAL ENROLLMENT OF PARENTS

Name of Father	Year	County	Name of Mother	Year	County
₁ Frank Ledon		Non Citz	Rachel Ledon	Dead	Non Citz
₂ G.D. Surratt		Sans Bois	Nancy Surratt	"	" "
₃ Nº1			Nº2		
₄					
₅					
₆ No1 on 1896 roll as Jacob Ledue					
₇ No2 " 1896 " " Anna "					
₈					
₉ As to marriage of parents of No2,					
₁₀ see testimony of S. E. Lewis					
₁₁ Nº3 Born March 26, 1902: Enrolled May 20, 1902					
Certified copy of divorce proceedings between Nº1 and former wife filed April 20, 1903.					
₁₂					
₁₃					
₁₄			Date of Application for Enrollment.		
₁₅			Aug 2/99		
₁₆					
₁₇ P.O. Haileyville I.T.					

PO Hartshorne I.T. 3/16/03

Choctaw By Blood Enrollment Cards 1898-1914

RESIDENCE:	Gaines	COUNTY.					CARD NO.	
POST OFFICE:	Ti, Ind. Ter.						FIELD NO. 3176	

Choctaw Nation — **Choctaw Roll** *(Not Including Freedmen)*

Dawes' Roll No.	NAME	Relationship to Person First Named	AGE	SEX	BLOOD	TRIBAL ENROLLMENT Year	County	No.
9189	1 Lewis, Anderson 24		21	M	1/8	1896	Gaines	7826
	2							
	3							
	4	ENROLLMENT						
	5	OF NOS. 1 HEREON APPROVED BY THE SECRETARY						
	6	OF INTERIOR FEB 4 1903						
	7							
	8							
	9							
	10							
	11							
	12							
	13							
	14							
	15							
	16							
	17							

TRIBAL ENROLLMENT OF PARENTS

	Name of Father	Year	County	Name of Mother	Year	County
1	Isom Lewis	Dead	Chickasaw	Emeline Lewis		Gaines
2						
3						
4						
5						
6						
7						
8	For child of No1 see NB (April 26-06) Card # 679					
9	" " " " " " (March 3-05) " #1312					
10						
11						
12						
13						
14					Date of Application for Enrollment.	
15					Aug 2/99	
16						
17						

RESIDENCE:	Gaines	COUNTY.							CARD NO.	
POST OFFICE:	Wilburton, I.T.	**Choctaw Nation**			Choctaw Roll *(Not Including Freedmen)*				FIELD NO.	3177

Dawes' Roll No.	NAME		Relationship to Person	AGE	SEX	BLOOD	TRIBAL ENROLLMENT		
							Year	County	No.
I.W. 133	₁ Battles, Henry F	46	First Named	43	M	I.W.			14397
9190	₂ " Susan	43	Wife	40	F	1/4	1896	Gaines	825
9191	₃ " Finis M	23	Son	20	M	1/8	1896	"	827
9192	₄ " John	20	"	17	"	1/8	1896	"	828
9193	₅ " George W	15	"	12	"	1/8	1896	"	829
9194	₆ " Ermer E. L	12	Dau	9	F	1/8	1896	"	830
9195	₇ " Jimmie	9	Son	6	M	1/8	1896	"	831
9196	₈ " Lester	6	"	3	"	1/8	1896	"	831
9197	₉ " Pearlie	1	G.Dau	6mo	F	1/8			
I.W. 1320	₁₀ " Clementine	26	Wife of No.4	26	F	I.W.			
	₁₁ No5 on 1896 roll as Geo W Battles								
	₁₂ No6 " 1896 " " E.E. L. "								
	₁₃ No8 " 1896 " " Lessie "								
	No.9 Born May 25, 1902:Enrolled Dec 24, 1902								
	₁₄ No4 now husband of Clementine Battles who made								
	₁₅ original application Dec. 24, 1902 See 7D 975				ENROLLMENT				
	₁₆ ENROLLMENT				OF NOS. 1 ~~~~~~~~ HEREON APPROVED BY THE SECRETARY				
	₁₇ OF NOS. 2,3,4,5,6,7,8 and 9 HEREON APPROVED BY THE SECRETARY				OF INTERIOR JUN 13 1903				
	OF INTERIOR FEB 4 1903								

TRIBAL ENROLLMENT OF PARENTS

	Name of Father	Year	County	Name of Mother	Year	County
₁	G. W. Battles		Non Citz	Susan Battles	Dead	Non Citz
₂	F. M. Monks		" "	Susan Monks	"	Skullyville
₃	No1			No2		
₄	No1			No2		
₅	No1		ENROLLMENT	No2		
₆	No1		OF NOS 10 HEREON APPROVED BY THE SECRETARY	No2		
₇	No1		OF INTERIOR MAR 14 1905	No2		
₈	No1			No2		
₉	No.4			Clementine Battles		
₁₀	James Patrick		non citz	Margaret Patrick		non citizen
₁₁	Nos 1-7-8 were admitted by Dawes Com. Case No 613					
₁₂	No1 was admitted as an Intermarried Citizen					
₁₃	No7 " " " James Battles / No8 " " " Lessie "					
₁₄	No3 on 1896 roll as Finis M Battles					
₁₅	No4 " 1896 " " Jno M. "			Date of Application for Enrollment. 1 to 8 Aug 2/99		
₁₆	No1 on 96 Roll H F Battle } No4 and 10 were married Dec 6, 1900. Were not all the children admitted in case 613: See original application?					
₁₇	No10 originally listed for enrollment on Choctaw card D-975 Dec 24, 1902: transferred to this					

card Jan 29, 1905. See decision of Jan. 13, 1905.

Choctaw By Blood Enrollment Cards 1898-1914

RESIDENCE: Gaines COUNTY. **Choctaw Nation** Choctaw Roll CARD NO.
POST OFFICE: Hartshorne, I.T. *(Not Including Freedmen)* FIELD NO. 3178

Dawes' Roll No.	NAME	Relationship to Person First Named	AGE	SEX	BLOOD	TRIBAL ENROLLMENT		
						Year	County	No.
9198	1 Pusley, Joshua 21	First Named	18	M	Full	1896	Gaines	10176
	2							
	3							
	4	ENROLLMENT OF NOS. 1 HEREON						
	5	APPROVED BY THE SECRETARY						
	6	OF INTERIOR FEB 4 1903						
	7							
	8							
	9							
	10							
	11							
	12							
	13							
	14							
	15							
	16							
	17							

TRIBAL ENROLLMENT OF PARENTS

	Name of Father	Year	County	Name of Mother	Year	County
1	Calvin Pusley	Dead	Gaines	Nancy Pusley		Gaines
2						
3						
4						
5						
6						
7						
8						
9						
10						
11						
12						
13					Date of Application for Enrollment.	
14						
15					Aug 2/99	
16						
17						

Choctaw By Blood Enrollment Cards 1898-1914

RESIDENCE: Gaines COUNTY.	Choctaw Nation	Choctaw Roll (Not Including Freedmen)	CARD NO.
POST OFFICE: Hartshorne, I.T.			FIELD NO. 3179

Dawes' Roll No.	NAME		Relationship to Person First Named	AGE	SEX	BLOOD	TRIBAL ENROLLMENT		
							Year	County	No.
9199	1 Carr, Osborn	24	First Named	21	M	Full	1896	Gaines	2285
	2								
	3								
	4								
	5								
	6	ENROLLMENT OF NOS. 1 HEREON							
	7	APPROVED BY THE SECRETARY OF INTERIOR FEB 4 1903							
	8								
	9								
	10								
	11								
	12								
	13								
	14								
	15								
	16								
	17								

TRIBAL ENROLLMENT OF PARENTS

	Name of Father	Year	County	Name of Mother	Year	County
1	John Carr	Dead	Gaines	Louisa Carr	Dead	Gaines
2						
3						
4						
5	For child of No. 1 see N.B. (Apr. 26, 1906) Card No. 179					
6	" " " " " " (March 3, 1905) " " 1441					
7						
8						
9						
10						
11						
12						
13				Date of Application for Enrollment.		
14						
15				Aug 2/99		
16						
17						

179

RESIDENCE:	Gaines	COUNTY.						CARD NO.	
POST OFFICE:	Wilburton, I.T.	**Choctaw Nation**				**Choctaw Roll** *(Not Including Freedmen)*		FIELD NO.	3180

Dawes' Roll No.	NAME		Relationship to Person	AGE	SEX	BLOOD	TRIBAL ENROLLMENT		
							Year	County	No.
9200	1 James, Jackson	51	First Named	48	M	Full	1896	Gaines	6609
9201	2 " Wysie	31	Wife	28	F	"	1896	"	6610
9202	3 " Joshua	19	Son	16	M	"	1896	"	6611
9203	4 " Sissy	17	Dau	14	F	"	1896	"	6577
9204	5 " Anna	4	"	9mo	"	"			
9205	6 McKinney, Alexander	19	Ward	16	M	"	1896	Gaines	9170
9206	7 " Baxter	17	"	14	"	"	1896	"	9171
9207	8 " Louisa	13	"	10	F	"	1896	"	9173
9208	9 James, Isaac	1	Son	13mo	M	"			
	10								
	11								
	12	ENROLLMENT OF NOS. 1,2,3,4,5,6,7,8 and 9 HEREON							
	13	APPROVED BY THE SECRETARY							
	14	OF INTERIOR FEB 4 1903							
	15								
	16								
	17								

TRIBAL ENROLLMENT OF PARENTS

	Name of Father	Year	County	Name of Mother	Year	County
1	Joshua James	Dead	Skullyville	Amy James	Dead	Skullyville
2	Lesma Fry	"	Bok Tuklo	Sarah Nelson		Gaines
3	No1			Isbalen James	Dead	"
4	No1			" "	"	"
5	No1			No2		
6	Thompson McKinney	Dead	Gaines	Lizzie McKinney	Dead	Gaines
7	" "	"	"	" "	"	"
8	" "	"	"	" "	"	"
9	No1			No2		
10						
11	No.9 Born Nov. 10, 1901. Proof of birth received and filed Dec. 24, 1902					
12						
13	For child of No4 see NB (Mar 3-1905) Card #573					
14	" " " Nos 1&2 " " " " " #1116				#1 to 8	
15				Date of Application for Enrollment.		Aug 2/99
16						
17						

Choctaw By Blood Enrollment Cards 1898-1914

RESIDENCE: Gaines COUNTY.
POST OFFICE: Hartshorne I.T.

Choctaw Nation

Choctaw Roll
(Not Including Freedmen)

CARD NO.
FIELD NO. 3181

Dawes' Roll No.	NAME		Relationship to Person	AGE	SEX	BLOOD	TRIBAL ENROLLMENT		
							Year	County	No.
9209	1 Frazier, Ned	42	First Named	38	M	Full	1896	Gaines	3981
9210	2 DIED PRIOR TO SEPTEMBER 25 1902 Rhoda		Wife	28	F	"	1896	"	3982
9211	3 " David	9	Son	6	M	"	1896	"	3983
9212	4 " Martha	6	Dau	3	F	"	1896	"	3984
9213	5 DIED PRIOR TO SEPTEMBER 25 1902 Asa		Son	1/2	M	"			
	6								
	7								
	8	ENROLLMENT OF NOS. 1,2,3,4 and 5 HEREON APPROVED BY THE SECRETARY OF INTERIOR FEB 3 1903							
	9								
	10								
	11								
	12								
	13								
	14								
	15								
	16								
	17								

TRIBAL ENROLLMENT OF PARENTS

	Name of Father	Year	County	Name of Mother	Year	County
1	Wilson Frazier	Dead	Gaines	Casey Frazier	Dead	Gaines
2	Newabe	"	Tobucksy	Inlahoma	"	Tobucksy
3	No 1			No 2		
4	No 1			No 2		
5	No 1			No 2		
6						
7						
8						
9	Affidavit of birth of No.5 to be supplied. Recd Aug 4/99.					
10	No.2 died June 26 1901; No.5 died Oct - 1900; Enrollment cancelled by Department July 8. 1904					
11						
12						
13						
14						
15						
16					Date of Application for Enrollment.	
17					Aug 2 – 99	

Choctaw By Blood Enrollment Cards 1898-1914

| RESIDENCE: | Gaines | COUNTY. | **Choctaw Nation** | **Choctaw Roll** | CARD NO. | |
| POST OFFICE: | Wilburton, I.T. | | | *(Not Including Freedmen)* | FIELD NO. | 3182 |

Dawes' Roll No.	NAME		Relationship to Person	AGE	SEX	BLOOD	TRIBAL ENROLLMENT		
							Year	County	No.
9214	1 Williams Agnes	28	First Named	25	F	Full	1896	Gaines	12934
	2								
	3								
	4								
	5	ENROLLMENT OF NOS. 1 HEREON							
	6	APPROVED BY THE SECRETARY							
	7	OF INTERIOR FEB 4 1903							
	8								
	9								
	10								
	11								
	12								
	13								
	14								
	15								
	16								
	17								

TRIBAL ENROLLMENT OF PARENTS

	Name of Father	Year	County	Name of Mother	Year	County
1	Kanallitubbe	Dead	Gaines	Towa	Dead	Gaines
2						
3						
4						
5						
6	On roll as Agnie William					
7						
8						
9						
10						
11						
12						
13						
14						
15					Date of Application for Enrollment.	
16						
17					8 – 2 – 99	

Choctaw By Blood Enrollment Cards 1898-1914

RESIDENCE: Gaines COUNTY.					Choctaw Nation				CARD No.	

RESIDENCE: **Gaines** COUNTY. **Choctaw Nation**   **Choctaw Roll**   CARD No.
POST OFFICE: **Wilburton** I.T.   *(Not Including Freedmen)*   FIELD No. **3183**

Dawes' Roll No.	NAME		Relationship to Person	AGE	SEX	BLOOD	TRIBAL ENROLLMENT		
							Year	County	No.
9215 9215	1 James Lylus	36	First Named	33	M	Full	1896	Gaines	6575
9216 9216	" Jensie	43	Wife	40	F	"	1896	Gaines	6576
	3								
	4								
	5	ENROLLMENT							
	6	OF NOS. 1 and 2 HEREON APPROVED BY THE SECRETARY							
	7	OF INTERIOR FEB 4 1903							
	8								
	9								
	10								
	11								
	12								
	13								
	14								
	15								
	16								
	17								

TRIBAL ENROLLMENT OF PARENTS

	Name of Father	Year	County	Name of Mother	Year	County
1	Noseka	Dead	Tobucksy	Suka Colbert	Dead	Gaines
2	Mitchell Harris	"	~~~	Elahima	"	Towson
3						
4						
5						
6						
7						
8						
9						
10						
11						
12						
13					7/22 18	
14					Date of Application for Enrollment	
15					8 – 2 – 1899	
16						
17						

Choctaw By Blood Enrollment Cards 1898-1914

RESIDENCE: **Gaines** COUNTY. **Choctaw Nation** **Choctaw Roll** CARD NO.
POST OFFICE: **Wilburton, I.T.** *(Not Including Freedmen)* FIELD NO. **3184**

Dawes' Roll No.	NAME	Relationship to Person First Named	AGE	SEX	BLOOD	TRIBAL ENROLLMENT		
						Year	County	No.
9217	1 Thompson, Ellen ⁶⁹		66	F	Full	1896	Gaines	11992
	2							
	3							
	4							
	5	ENROLLMENT						
	6	OF NOS. 1 HEREON APPROVED BY THE SECRETARY						
	7	OF INTERIOR FEB 4 1903						
	8							
	9							
	10							
	11							
	12							
	13							
	14							
	15							
	16							
	17							

TRIBAL ENROLLMENT OF PARENTS

	Name of Father	Year	County	Name of Mother	Year	County
1		Dead	Gaines	Co-yo-ke	Dead	Gaines
2						
3						
4						
5						
6						
7						
8						
9						
10						
11						
12						
13						
14						
15				Date of Application for Enrollment. Aug 2/99		
16						
17						

Choctaw By Blood Enrollment Cards 1898-1914

		RESIDENCE: Gaines COUNTY.							CARD NO.	

RESIDENCE: Gaines **COUNTY.** **Choctaw Nation** **Choctaw Roll** (Not Including Freedmen) **CARD NO.**
POST OFFICE: Wilburton, I.T. **FIELD NO.** 3185

Dawes' Roll No.	NAME	Relationship to Person First Named	AGE	SEX	BLOOD	TRIBAL ENROLLMENT		
						Year	County	No.
9218	1 Winship, Sampson 29	First Named	26	M	Full	1896	Gaines	12977
9219	2 " Seyon 20	Wife	17	F	"	1896	"	12976
15447	3 " Cornelius 2	Son	2½	M	"			
	4							
	5							
	6	ENROLLMENT						
	7	OF NOS. 1 and 2 HEREON APPROVED BY THE SECRETARY						
	8	OF INTERIOR FEB 4 1903						
	9							
	10	ENROLLMENT						
	11	OF NOS. ~~~ 3 ~~~ HEREON APPROVED BY THE SECRETARY						
	12	OF INTERIOR MAY 9 1904						
	13							
	14							
	15							
	16							
	17							

TRIBAL ENROLLMENT OF PARENTS

	Name of Father	Year	County	Name of Mother	Year	County
1	Impson Winship	Dead	Red River	Betsy Winship	Dead	Red River
2	Noahubbee	Dead	Tobucksy	Ca-ne-o-tema	"	Tobucksy
3	Nº1			Nº2		
4						
5						
6						
7						
8	No2 on 1896 roll as Seyon Walker					
9	Nº3 Born Jany 1, 1901, application made at Wister I.T. Dec 18, 1902, at which time					
10	affidavit of the father was submitted. Nº3 enrolled Dec 4, 1903.					
	For child of Nos 1 and 2 see NB (March 3, 1905) #1228					
11						
12						
13						
14				#1 & 2		
15				Date of Application for Enrollment. Aug 2/99		
16						
17						

RESIDENCE:	Gaines	COUNTY.	**Choctaw Nation**		**Choctaw Roll**	CARD No.	
POST OFFICE:	Wilburton I.T.				(Not Including Freedmen)	FIELD No.	3186

Dawes' Roll No.	NAME	Relationship to Person First Named	AGE	SEX	BLOOD	TRIBAL ENROLLMENT		
						Year	County	No.
DEAD	1 Calvin Amos 31	Named	28	M	Full	1896	Gaines	2290
	2							
	3							
	4							
	5							
	6							
	7 No. 1 HEREON DISMISSED UNDER ORDER OF THE COMMISSION TO THE FIVE CIVILIZED TRIBES OF MARCH 31, 1905.							
	8							
	9							
	10							
	11							
	12							
	13							
	14							
	15							
	16							
	17							

TRIBAL ENROLLMENT OF PARENTS

	Name of Father	Year	County		Name of Mother	Year	County
1	Joshua Calvin	1896	Jacks Fork		Nancy Calvin	Dead	Sugar Loaf
2							
3							
4							
5							
6							
7							
8							
9							
10	No 1 died May 15, 1900; proof of death filed Dec 15 1902						
11							
12							
13							
14							Date of Application for Enrollment.
15							
16							8 - 2 - 99
17							

Choctaw By Blood Enrollment Cards 1898-1914

		RESIDENCE:	Gaines	COUNTY.	**Choctaw Nation**	**Choctaw Roll**	CARD NO.	
		POST OFFICE:	Damon I.T.			*(Not Including Freedmen)*	FIELD NO.	3187

Dawes' Roll No.	NAME			Relationship to Person	AGE	SEX	BLOOD	TRIBAL ENROLLMENT		
								Year	County	No.
9220	1	Pusley Silas	28	First Named	25	M	Full	1896	Gaines	10160
	2									
	3									
	4									
	5	ENROLLMENT								
	6	OF NOS. 1	HEREON							
		APPROVED BY THE SECRETARY								
	7	OF INTERIOR FEB 4 1903								
	8									
	9									
	10									
	11									
	12									
	13									
	14									
	15									
	16									
	17									

TRIBAL ENROLLMENT OF PARENTS

	Name of Father	Year	County	Name of Mother	Year	County
1	Calvin Pusley	Dead	Gaines	Nancy Pusley	1896	Gaines
2						
3						
4						
5						
6						
7						
8						
9						
10						
11						
12						
13						
14						
15				Date of Application		
16				for Enrollment.		
17				8 – 2 – 99		

Choctaw By Blood Enrollment Cards 1898-1914

RESIDENCE: Gaines COUNTY. **Choctaw Nation** **Choctaw Roll** CARD NO.
POST OFFICE: Damon I.T. *(Not Including Freedmen)* FIELD NO. 3188

Dawes' Roll No.	NAME		Relationship to Person First Named	AGE	SEX	BLOOD	TRIBAL ENROLLMENT		
							Year	County	No.
9221	1 Pusley Nancy	53	First Named	50	F	Full	1896	Gaines	10161
9222	2 " Anna	17	Dau	14	F	"	1896	"	10162
9223	3 " Dora	10	G. Dau	7	F	"	1896	"	10196
	4								
	5								
	6								
	7	ENROLLMENT OF NOS. 1, 2 and 3 HEREON APPROVED BY THE SECRETARY OF INTERIOR FEB 4 1903							
	8								
	9								
	10								
	11								
	12								
	13								
	14								
	15								
	16								
	17								

TRIBAL ENROLLMENT OF PARENTS

	Name of Father	Year	County	Name of Mother	Year	County
1	James Morris	Dead	Gaines	Atubuhona	Dead	Gaines
2	Calvin Pursley[sic]	"	"	No 1		
3	Adam Pursley[sic]	1896	Gaines	Silly Pusley	Dead	Gaines
4						
5						
6						
7						
8						
9						
10						
11						
12						
13						
14						
15						
16					Date of Application for Enrollment. 8-2-99	
17						

RESIDENCE:	Gaines	COUNTY.	**Choctaw Nation**				**Choctaw Roll**		CARD NO.	
POST OFFICE:	Wilburton, I.T.						*(Not Including Freedmen)*		FIELD NO.	3189

Dawes' Roll No.	NAME		Relationship to Person	AGE	SEX	BLOOD	TRIBAL ENROLLMENT		
							Year	County	No.
9224	1 Anderson, Noel	24	First Named	21	M	1/2	1896	Gaines	89
I.W. 1321	2 " Mary	22	Wife	22	F	I.W.			
	3								
	4								
	5	ENROLLMENT							
	6	OF NOS. 1 HEREON							
	7	APPROVED BY THE SECRETARY OF INTERIOR FEB 4 1903							
	8								
	9								
	10								
	11	ENROLLMENT OF NOS. 2 HEREON							
	12	APPROVED BY THE SECRETARY OF INTERIOR MAR 14 1905							
	13								
	14								
	15								
	16								
	17								

TRIBAL ENROLLMENT OF PARENTS

	Name of Father	Year	County	Name of Mother	Year	County
1	Roberson Anderson	Dead	Jacks Fork	Sina Grayson		Gaines
2	William Hurt		non citz	Mahala Hurt	dead	non citz
3						
4						
5						
6						
7	Nº1 is husband of Mary Anderson on Choctaw card #D984					
8	Nos 1 and 2 were married June 17, 1901					
9	No.2 originally listed for enrollment on Choctaw card D-984 Dec. 24, 1902 transferred to this card Jan. 29, 1905. See decision of Jan 13, 1905					
10	For child of Nos 1&2 see NB (Apr 26-06) Card #738					
11	" " " " " " " (Mar 3-05) " #463					
12						
13						
14				#1		
15				Date of Application for Enrollment.	Aug 2/99	
16						
17						

RESIDENCE:	Gaines	COUNTY.							CARD No.	
POST OFFICE:	Damon, I.T.		**Choctaw Nation**				**Choctaw Roll** *(Not Including Freedmen)*		FIELD No. 3190	

Dawes Roll No. DEAD.		NAME		Relationship to Person First Named	AGE	SEX	BLOOD	TRIBAL ENROLLMENT		
								Year	County	No.
	1	Foster, William	43		40	M	Full	1896	Gaines	3988
9225	2	" Betsy	40	Wife	37	F	"	1896	"	3989
9226	3	" Addie B	7	Dau	4	"	"	1896	"	3990
DEAD.	4	" Irena J	4	"	4mo	"	"			
9227	5	Scott, Alexander	15	S. Son	12	M	"	1896	Gaines	11250
9228	6	Foster Billy	2	Son	2	M	"			
	7									
	8									
	9	ENROLLMENT OF NOS. 2,3,5 and 6 HEREON								
	10	APPROVED BY THE SECRETARY OF INTERIOR FEB 4 1903								
	11									
	12	No. 1 and 4 HEREON DISMISSED UNDER								
	13	ORDER OF THE COMMISSION TO THE FIVE CIVILIZED TRIBES OF MARCH 31, 1905.								
	14									
	15									
	16									
	17									

TRIBAL ENROLLMENT OF PARENTS

	Name of Father	Year	County	Name of Mother	Year	County
1	A-dap-a-hu-na	Dead	Sugar Loaf	Liley	Dead	Sugar Loaf
2	Ya-ho-nubbee	"	Gaines		"	Gaines
3	No1			No2		
4	No1			No2		
5	Dave Scott	Dead	Gaines	No2		
6	No1			No2		
7						
8						
9	No3 on 1896 roll as Addie Foster.					
10						
11	No6 born May 21, 1900: enrolled December 15, 1902 No1 died in 1900; proof of death filed Dec 17, 1902.					
12	No4 " Aug - 1899: " " " " " " "					
13						#1 to 5
14						Date of Application for Enrollment.
15						Aug 2/99
16						
17						

Choctaw By Blood Enrollment Cards 1898-1914

RESIDENCE:	Gaines	COUNTY.						CARD NO.	
POST OFFICE:	Damon I.T.	**Choctaw Nation**			**Choctaw Roll** *(Not Including Freedmen)*			FIELD NO.	3191

Dawes' Roll No.		NAME		Relationship to Person	AGE	SEX	BLOOD	TRIBAL ENROLLMENT		
								Year	County	No.
9229	1	Taylor Wilburn	31	First Named	28	M	Full	1893	Gaines	544
	2									
	3									
	4									
	5									
	6	ENROLLMENT								
	7	OF NOS. 1 HEREON								
	8	APPROVED BY THE SECRETARY OF INTERIOR FEB 4 1903								
	9									
	10									
	11									
	12									
	13									
	14									
	15									
	16									
	17									

TRIBAL ENROLLMENT OF PARENTS

	Name of Father	Year	County	Name of Mother	Year	County
1	Thomas Taylor	1896	Gaines	Tennessee Taylor	1896	Gaines
2						
3						
4						
5						
6						
7			See Card #3221-3230			
8						
9						
10			No.1 On Page 58, No 544, 1893 Pay Roll Gaines Co.			
11						
12						
13						
14						
15					Date of Application for Enrollment.	
16					8 – 2 – 99	
17						

Choctaw By Blood Enrollment Cards 1898-1914

RESIDENCE:	Gaines	COUNTY.	Choctaw Nation	Choctaw Roll	CARD No.
POST OFFICE:	Hartshorne, I.T.			(Not Including Freedmen)	FIELD No. 3192

Dawes' Roll No.	NAME		Relationship to Person First Named	AGE	SEX	BLOOD	TRIBAL ENROLLMENT		
							Year	County	No.
9230	1 Pulcher, John	41	First Named	38	M	1/4	1896	Gaines	10212
	2								
	3								
	4								
	5								
	6	ENROLLMENT							
	7	OF NOS. 1 HEREON APPROVED BY THE SECRETARY							
	8	OF INTERIOR FEB 4 1903							
	9								
	10								
	11								
	12								
	13								
	14								
	15								
	16								
	17								

TRIBAL ENROLLMENT OF PARENTS

	Name of Father	Year	County	Name of Mother	Year	County
1	Albert H Pulcher	Dead	Non Citz	Phoebe Pulcher	Dead	Gaines
2						
3						
4						
5						
6						
7						
8						
9						
10						
11						
12				Date of Application for Enrollment.		
13						
14						
15				Aug 3/99		
16						
17						

RESIDENCE:	Gaines	COUNTY.							
POST OFFICE:	Wilburton, I.T.								CARD No. FIELD No. 3193

Choctaw Nation — Choctaw Roll (Not Including Freedmen)

Dawes' Roll No.	NAME		Relationship to Person	AGE	SEX	BLOOD	TRIBAL ENROLLMENT		
							Year	County	No.
9231	1 Hicker, Edmund	30	First Named	27	M	Full	1893	Gaines	214
9232	2 " Ellen	43	Wife	40	F	"	1896	"	9158
9233	3 " Benny	4	Son	6mo	M	"			
9234	4 McClish, Buddie	21	S.Son	18	"	"	1896	Gaines	9159
9235	5 " Rena	19	S.Dau	16	F	"	1896	"	9160
9236	6 " Phelin	17	S.Son	14	M	"	1896	"	
9237	7 " Susan	15	S.Dau	12	F	"	1896	"	9162
9238	8 " Walton	13	S.Son	10	M	"	1896	"	9163
	9								
	10								
	11	ENROLLMENT							
	12	OF NOS. 1,2,3,4,5,6,7 and 8 HEREON APPROVED BY THE SECRETARY OF INTERIOR Feb 4 1903							
	13								
	14								
	15	Nos 1, 3 & 4 – "Died prior to Sept 25, 1902: Not entitled to land or money."							
	16	(See Indian Office letter of Aug 28, 1911, No. 1399-1911).							
	17								

TRIBAL ENROLLMENT OF PARENTS

	Name of Father	Year	County	Name of Mother	Year	County
1	Simon Hicker	Dead	Gaines	Lucinda Hicker		Sugar Loaf
2	Simon Hancock	"	"	Liza Hancock	Dead	Gaines
3	No 1			No 2		
4	Isaac McClish	Dead	Gaines	No 2		
5	" "	"	"	No 2		
6	" "	"	"	No 2		
7	" "	"	"	No 2		
8	" "	"	"	No 2		
9						
10		No1 on 1893 Pay Roll, Page 23, No 214, Gaines				
11		Co, as Edmund Heka.				
12		No2 on 1896 roll as Ellen McClish				
13						
14		No6 is a Male, change made under Departmental			Date of Application for Enrollment.	
15		instructions' of April 9, 1904 (DC #11663-1904)			Aug 3/99	
16		For child of No5 see NB (March 3, 1905) #1224				
17	P.O. #7 Blanco, Okla. 1/15/12					

Choctaw By Blood Enrollment Cards 1898-1914

RESIDENCE: Gaines   COUNTY. **Choctaw Nation**   Choctaw Roll   CARD NO.
POST OFFICE: Ti, I.T.   *(Not Including Freedmen)*   FIELD NO. **3194**

Dawes' Roll No.	NAME	Relationship to Person	AGE	SEX	BLOOD	TRIBAL ENROLLMENT		
						Year	County	No.
9239	1 Lewis, Overton A ²⁹	First Named	26	M	1/4	1896	Gaines	9824
I.W. 296	2 " Cynthia ³³	Wife	28	F	I.W.	1896	"	14750
	3							
	4							
	5							
	6							
	7	ENROLLMENT OF NOS. 1 HEREON APPROVED BY THE SECRETARY OF INTERIOR Feb 4 1903						
	8							
	9							
	10	ENROLLMENT OF NOS. 2 HEREON APPROVED BY THE SECRETARY OF INTERIOR Sep 12 1903						
	11							
	12							
	13							
	14							
	15							
	16							
	17							

TRIBAL ENROLLMENT OF PARENTS

Name of Father	Year	County	Name of Mother	Year	County
1 Isom Lewis	Dead	Chickasaw	Emeline Lewis		Gaines
2 Francis M Jestice		Non Citz	Louisa Jestice	Dead	Non Citz
3					
4					
5					
6					
7					
8					
9					
10					
11					
12					
13					
14				Date of Application for Enrollment.	
15				Aug 3/99	
16					
17					

194

RESIDENCE:	Gaines	COUNTY.							

Choctaw Nation

POST OFFICE: Ti, I.T.

Choctaw Roll CARD No.
(Not Including Freedmen) FIELD NO. 3195

Dawes' Roll No.	NAME	Relationship to Person First Named	AGE	SEX	BLOOD	TRIBAL ENROLLMENT		
						Year	County	No.
I.W. 297	1 Snider, Samuel T 42	First Named	40	M	IW	1896	Gaines	15029
DEAD.	2 " Emiline DEAD	Wife	43	F	1/4	1896	"	11243
9240	3 " Nettie 6	Dau	3	"	1/8			
DEAD	4 " Eugene DEAD.	Son	1	M	1/8			
9241	5 Sparks Cornelia May 26	S.Dau	23	F	1/8	1896	Gaines	7825
9242	6 Barnhill Emma 21	"	18	"	1/8	1896	"	7827
9243	7 Lewis Frank 17	S.Son	14	M	1/8	1896	"	7828
9244	8 " Sullivan 15	"	12	"	1/8	1896	"	7829
9245	9 " Loren 12	"	9	"	1/8	1896	"	7830
9246	10 Snider Beulah 2	Dau	1mo	F	1/8	No. 2 and 4 HEREON DISMISSED UNDER		
9247	11 Barnhill Gladice 1	Dau of Nº6	1mo	F	1/16	ORDER OF THE COMMISSION TO THE FIVE		
9248	12 Sparks Wilford 1	Son of Nº5	5mo	M	1/16	CIVILIZED TRIBES OF MARCH 31, 1905.		
	Nº4 died Aug 26 1899 Proof of death filed Dec 20 1902							
	Nº6 is now the wife of Jasper Barnhill non-citizen evidence							
	of marriage requested Sept 27, 1902. Rec'd and filed Oct. 14, 1902							
	Nº11 Born Aug 20 1902, enrolled Sept 27, 1902							
	Nº12 Born May 7, 1902, enrolled Oct. 11, 1902							
	Sept 11/99 #1 Admitted by Dawes Com as Sam Snider #1380							

TRIBAL ENROLLMENT OF PARENTS

	Name of Father	Year	County	Name of Mother	Year	County
1	Henry Snider		Non Citz	Ester Snider	Dead	Non Citz
2	Henry Pulcher	Dead	" "	Phoebe Pulcher	"	Gaines
3	No1			No2		
4	No1			No2		
5	Isom Lewis	Dead	Chickasaw	No2		ENROLLMENT
6	" "	"	"	No2		OF NOS 3-5-6-7-8-9-10-11 and 12 HEREON
7	" "	"	"	No2		APPROVED BY THE SECRETARY OF INTERIOR FEB 4 1903
8	" "	"	"	No2		ENROLLMENT
9	" "	"	"	No2		OF NOS. HEREON APPROVED BY THE SECRETARY
10	No.1			No2		OF INTERIOR SEP 12 1903
11	Jasper Barnhill		non-citizen	Nº6		Father of Nº12 is John Sparks non-citz Mother of Nº12 is Nº5
12	No1 on 1896 roll as Sam T. Snider			No10 Enrolled May 6, 1901.		
13	No9 " 1896 " " Lorin Lewis			Nº5 is now wife of John Sparks non-citizen evidence of		
14	As to marriage, see testimony of No1 Evidence of marriage to be supplied. Reed 8/3/99			of marriage requested Oct. 11,1902. Filed Jany 6,1903.		#1 to 9
15	Nos 3-4. Affidavits of birth to be supplied.			Affidavits of birth		Date of Application for Enrollment. Aug 3/99
16	of No3 filed Oct. 7/99			For child f No5 see NB (March 3-1905) Card No 214.		
17	No2 Died June 4, 1902. Proof of death filed Dec 20 1902 received and filed Dec 24, 1902					

RESIDENCE:	Tobucksy	COUNTY.			

RESIDENCE: Tobucksy **COUNTY.** **Choctaw Nation** **Choctaw Roll** (Not Including Freedmen) **CARD NO.** **FIELD NO.** 3196
POST OFFICE: Kiowa, I.T.

Dawes' Roll No.	NAME	Relationship to Person First Named	AGE	SEX	BLOOD	TRIBAL ENROLLMENT		
						Year	County	No.
9249	1 Kemp, Warren 27	First Named	24	M	Full	1896	Tobucksy	7642
9250	2 " Melsey DIED PRIOR TO SEPTEMBER 25, 1902	Wife	23	F	"	1896	"	807
9251	3 " Ansie 11	Sister	8	"	"	1896	"	7490
9252	4 " Stebbin 2	Son	6wk	M	"			
	5							
	6							
	7	ENROLLMENT OF NOS. 1,2,3 and 4 HEREON						
	8	APPROVED BY THE SECRETARY						
	9	OF INTERIOR Feb 4, 1903						
	10							
	11							
	12							
	13							
	14							
	15							
	16							
	17							

TRIBAL ENROLLMENT OF PARENTS

	Name of Father	Year	County	Name of Mother	Year	County
1	James Kemp	Dead	Tobucksy	Selina Kemp	Dead	Tobucksy
2	Robin Leurs		Sugar Loaf		"	Sugar Loaf
3	Thompson King	Dead	Gaines	Selina King	"	Tobucksy
4	No.1			No.2		
5						
6						
7	No2 on 1896 roll as Milsie Brown					
8	No3 " 1896 " " Lizzie King					
9	No.4 Enrolled Oct. 16th, 1900					
10	No 2 died July 7, 1901· Enrollment cancelled by Department July 8, 1904					
11						
12	For child of No1 see NB (Mar 3-1905) Card No 216					
13						
14				Date of Application for Enrollment.		
15				Aug 3/99		
16						
17	No1. P.O. So. McAlester 11/1/04					

Choctaw By Blood Enrollment Cards 1898-1914

RESIDENCE:	Sans Bois	COUNTY.	**Choctaw Nation**	**Choctaw Roll**	CARD NO.	
POST OFFICE:	Whitefield, I.T.			*(Not Including Freedmen)*	FIELD NO.	3197

Dawes' Roll No.	NAME		Relationship to Person	AGE	SEX	BLOOD	TRIBAL ENROLLMENT		
							Year	County	No.
9253	1 Cooper, Stephen	29	First Named	26	M	Full	1896	Sans Bois	2108
	2								
	3								
	4								
	5								
	6	ENROLLMENT							
	7	OF NOS. 1 HEREON							
	8	APPROVED BY THE SECRETARY OF INTERIOR FEB 4 1903							
	9								
	10								
	11								
	12								
	13								
	14								
	15								
	16								
	17								

TRIBAL ENROLLMENT OF PARENTS

Name of Father	Year	County	Name of Mother	Year	County
1 Alick Cooper	Dead	Sans Bois	Elsie Cooper	Dead	Sans Bois
2					
3					
4					
5					
6		For child of No1 see NB (Mar 3/05) Card #669			
7		" " " " 1 " " (Apr 26-06) Card 472			
8					
9					
10					
11					
12					
13					
14				Date of Application for Enrollment.	
15				Aug 3/99	
16					
17 PO Hartshorne IT 4/3/05					

Choctaw By Blood Enrollment Cards 1898-1914

RESIDENCE:	Sans Bois	COUNTY.						
POST OFFICE:	Stigler, I.T.							

Choctaw Nation — Choctaw Roll (Not Including Freedmen) CARD NO. FIELD NO. 3198

Dawes' Roll No.	NAME		Relationship to Person	AGE	SEX	BLOOD	TRIBAL ENROLLMENT		
							Year	County	No.
9254	1 Perry, Daniel	26	First Named	23	M	1/2	1896	Sans Bois	10057
9255	2 " Jane	25	Wife	22	F	Full	1896	" "	2109
	3								
	4								
	5								
	6	ENROLLMENT							
	7	OF NOS. 1 and 2 HEREON							
	8	APPROVED BY THE SECRETARY OF INTERIOR Feb 4 1903							
	9								
	10								
	11								
	12								
	13								
	14								
	15								
	16								
	17								

TRIBAL ENROLLMENT OF PARENTS

	Name of Father	Year	County	Name of Mother	Year	County
1	Lyman Perry	Dead	Sans Bois		Dead	Sans Bois
2	Alick Cooper	"	" " "	Elsie Cooper	"	" " "
3						
4						
5						
6						
7		No2 on 1896 roll as Jane Cooper				
8		No1 is now guardian of Jennie Perry on Choctaw card #2814				
9		For child of No1 see NB (March 3 1905) #1055				
10						
11						
12						
13						
14						
15				Date of Application for Enrollment.	Aug 3/99	
16						
17						

198

RESIDENCE:	Gaines	COUNTY.				
POST OFFICE:	Gowen, I.T.				CARD NO.	

Choctaw Nation **Choctaw Roll** *(Not Including Freedmen)* FIELD NO. **3199**

Dawes' Roll No.	NAME	Relationship to Person First Named	AGE	SEX	BLOOD	TRIBAL ENROLLMENT		
						Year	County	No.
I.W.**298**	1 Blalock, Joseph W 33	First Named	30	M	I.W.	1896	Gaines	14298
DEAD.	2 " Mattie E ~~DEAD~~ 27	Wife	F	F	1/8	1896	"	852
9256	3 " Ida B 7	Dau	"	"	1/16	1896	"	853
9257	4 " Sallie J 6	"	"	"	1/16	1896	"	859
	5							
	6							
	7 ENROLLMENT OF NOS. 3 and 4 HEREON							
	8 APPROVED BY THE SECRETARY OF INTERIOR FEB 4 1903							
	9 ENROLLMENT							
	10 OF NOS. 1 HEREON							
	11 APPROVED BY THE SECRETARY OF INTERIOR SEP 12 1903							
	12							
	13							
	14 No. 2 HEREON DISMISSED UNDER ORDER OF THE COMMISSION TO THE FIVE							
	15 CIVILIZED TRIBES OF MARCH 31, 1905.							
	16							
	17							

TRIBAL ENROLLMENT OF PARENTS

	Name of Father	Year	County	Name of Mother	Year	County
1	John Blalack[sic]		Non Citz	Sallie Blalack		Non Citz
2	~~John Denton~~	~~Dead~~	" "	~~Johnnie Denton~~	~~Dead~~	~~Gaines~~
3	No1			No2		
4	No1			No2		
5						
6						
7	No2 on 1896 roll as Mattie Blalack					
8	No3 " 1896 " " Ida "					
9	Evidence of marriage to be supplied: Recd 8/3/99					
10						
11	No2 Died April 13, 1900. Proof of death received and filed Dec 24, 1902					
12	For child of No1 see NB Apr 26 '06) #1083					
13						
14						
15				Date of Application for Enrollment.	Aug 3/99	
16						
17	P.O. Archibald, I.T. 10/22/02					

Choctaw By Blood Enrollment Cards 1898-1914

RESIDENCE: Gaines COUNTY.	**Choctaw Nation**	**Choctaw Roll** (Not Including Freedmen)	CARD NO.
POST OFFICE: Gowen, I.T.			FIELD NO. 3200

Dawes' Roll No.	NAME	Relationship to Person First Named	AGE	SEX	BLOOD	TRIBAL ENROLLMENT Year	County	No.
I.W 1253	1 Strickland, Phoebe ²⁶		22	F	I.W			
	2							
	3							
	4							
	5							
	6							
	7							
	8							
	9							
	10							
	11							
	12							
	13	ENROLLMENT OF NOS. ~1~ HEREON APPROVED BY THE SECRETARY OF INTERIOR DEC 30 1904						
	14							
	15							
	16							
	17							

TRIBAL ENROLLMENT OF PARENTS

	Name of Father	Year	County	Name of Mother	Year	County
1	Richard Bullard	dead	Non Citz	Clementine Bullard	Dead	Non Citz
2						
3						
4						
5						
6		No.1 formerly wife of Stone McAlvane, 1893 Sugar Loaf, No. 567,				
7		and who died about the year 1901.				
8		No.1 originally listed on this card as Phoebe McAlvane.				
		For children of No1 see NB (Apr 26 '06) #1219				
9						
10						
11						
12						
13					Date of Application for Enrollment,	
14						
15					Aug 3/99	
16						
17						

RESIDENCE: Gaines COUNTY.	POST OFFICE: Hartshorne, I.T.	**Choctaw Nation**	Choctaw Roll (Not Including Freedmen)	CARD No. FIELD No. **3201**

Dawes' Roll No.	NAME	Relationship to Person First Named	AGE	SEX	BLOOD	TRIBAL ENROLLMENT Year	County	No.
9258	1 Pebworth[sic], Henry 29	Named	26	M	1/4	1896	Gaines	10167
9259	2 " Dora E 27	Wife	24	F	3/4	1896	"	10168
9260	3 " Elum N 8	Son	5	M	1/2	1896	"	10169
9261	4 " Lela M 6	Dau	3	F	1/2	1896	"	10170
9262	5 " Etta 5	"	2	"	1/2			
9263	6 " Preston 4	Son	1	M	1/2			
9264	7 " Thomas J 2	Son	3mo	M	1/2			
	8							
	9	ENROLLMENT OF NOS. 1,2,3,4,5,6,7 HEREON						
	10	APPROVED BY THE SECRETARY OF INTERIOR Feb 4 1903						
	11							
	12	Petition filed by No1 asking for restoration to the roll May 23-1907						
	13	" " " " " " " " " forwarded Dept. June 28-07						
	14	" granted by Dept. Aug. 20-07						
	15							
	16	For child of Nos 1&2 see NB (Apr 26-06) Card #318						
	17	" " " " " " " (Mar 3-05) " #1313						

TRIBAL ENROLLMENT OF PARENTS

Name of Father	Year	County	Name of Mother	Year	County
1 John Pebsworth	Dead	Towson	Mary Pebsworth	Dead	Towson
2 Wade Hampton	"	Gaines	Nancy Hampton		Gaines
3 No1			No2		
4 No1			No2		
5 No1			No2		
6 No1			No2		
7 No.1			No.2		
8 No4 on 1896 roll as Cella M Pebsworth					
9 Enrollment of No.1 cancelled by order of Department March 4,1907			"Error of identity		
10 Nos 5-6: Affidavits of birth to be supplied"- Recd Aug 9/99			not cancelled" see Departmental letter		
11			Aug 20, 1907 (D-397)		
12 Dec 8/99 See Dawes Commission					
13 record 1896. Case 1376. Denied no appeal					
No7 Enrolled June 19, 1901					
14 Full given name of No.7 is Thomas Jefferson. See letter of No1 on file in this case. July 6, 1901					
15			#1 to 6		
16			Date of Application for Enrollment.		
17 PO Coalgate Ok 1/15/08			Aug 3/99		

Choctaw By Blood Enrollment Cards 1898-1914

RESIDENCE: Tobucksy COUNTY. **Choctaw Nation** **Choctaw Roll** CARD NO.
POST OFFICE: Krebbs, I.T. *(Not Including Freedmen)* FIELD NO. **3202**

Dawes' Roll No.	NAME	Relationship to Person First Named	AGE	SEX	BLOOD	TRIBAL ENROLLMENT Year	County	No.
I.W. 1254	1 Stewart, James W 57	First Named	52	M	IW	1896	Tobucksy	15050
9265	2 " Nancy E 41	Wife	38	F	5/16	1896	"	11277
	3							
	4							
	5							
	6							
	7							
	8	ENROLLMENT						
	9	OF NOS. 2 HEREON APPROVED BY THE SECRETARY						
	10	OF INTERIOR Feb 4, 1903						
	11							
	12							
	13							
	14	ENROLLMENT						
	15	OF NOS. ~ 1 ~ HEREON APPROVED BY THE SECRETARY						
	16	OF INTERIOR Dec 30 1904						
	17							

TRIBAL ENROLLMENT OF PARENTS

Name of Father	Year	County	Name of Mother	Year	County
1 Jos O Stewart	Dead	Non Citz	Anna Stewart	Dead	Non Citz
2 Wiley Stewart	"	" "	Nancy F Stewart		Blue
3					
4					
5					
6					
7					
8					
9	No1 on 1896 roll as Jas. W. Stewart was				
10	also admitted by Dawes Commission as an				
11	intermarried citizen. Case No 814. No appeal				
12	No2 on 1896 roll as Nancy E. Steward				
13	No2 daughter of Nancy Stewart who was admitted by U.S. Indian Agent				
14	Oct. 12, 1889			Date of Application for Enrollment.	
15	No's 1 and 2 are divorced				
16				Aug 3/99	
17	No2 Wynnewood 11/11/04				

202

Choctaw By Blood Enrollment Cards 1898-1914

RESIDENCE: Gaines COUNTY. **Choctaw Nation** Choctaw Roll CARD NO.
POST OFFICE: Hartshorne, I.T. *(Not Including Freedmen)* FIELD NO. 3203

Dawes' Roll No.	NAME		Relationship to Person	AGE	SEX	BLOOD	TRIBAL ENROLLMENT		
							Year	County	No.
9266	1 Ott, Stephen	26	First Named	23	M	Full	1896	Gaines	9912
	2								
	3								
	4								
	5								
	6								
	7								
	8								
	9								
	10	ENROLLMENT							
	11	OF NOS. 1 HEREON APPROVED BY THE SECRETARY							
	12	OF INTERIOR FEB 4 1903							
	13								
	14								
	15								
	16								
	17								

TRIBAL ENROLLMENT OF PARENTS

	Name of Father	Year	County	Name of Mother	Year	County
1	Alfred Ott		Gaines	Marey	Dead	Gaines
2						
3						
4						
5						
6						
7						
8						
9						
10						
11						
12						
13						
14						
15				Date of Application for Enrollment. Aug 3/99		
16						
17						

Choctaw By Blood Enrollment Cards 1898-1914

Dawes' Roll No.	NAME		Relationship to Person	AGE	SEX	BLOOD	TRIBAL ENROLLMENT		
							Year	County	No.
9267	1 Harris, Ramsey	16	First Named	13	M	Full	1893	Tobucksy	396
	2								
	3								
	4								
	5								
	6								
	7								
	8								
	9								
	10								
	11								
	12								
	13								
	14								
	15								
	16								
	17								

ENROLLMENT
OF NOS. 1 HEREON
APPROVED BY THE SECRETARY
OF INTERIOR FEB 4 1903

TRIBAL ENROLLMENT OF PARENTS

	Name of Father	Year	County	Name of Mother	Year	County
1	Simpson Harris		Tobucksy	Narcissa Harris	Dead	Tobucksy
2						
3						
4						
5						
6	On 1893 Pay Roll, Page 43, No 396 Tobucksy Co					
7						
8						
9	No.1 on 1896 census roll, as Harris Ramsey					
10	page 275: #10755			May 16, 1900		
11						
12						
13					Date of Application for Enrollment.	
14						
15					Aug 3/99	
16						
17						

Choctaw By Blood Enrollment Cards 1898-1914

RESIDENCE: Gaines COUNTY. **Choctaw Nation** Choctaw Roll CARD No.
POST OFFICE: Hartshorne, I.T. *(Not Including Freedmen)* FIELD No. 3205

Dawes' Roll No.	NAME		Relationship to Person	AGE	SEX	BLOOD	TRIBAL ENROLLMENT		
							Year	County	No.
9268	₁ White, John W	38	First Named	35	M	1/16	1896	Gaines	12968
I.W.299	₂ " Dora	30	Wife	27	F	I.W	1896	"	15157
9269	₃ Winlock, Cora	14	S.Dau	11	"	1/2	1896	"	12969
	4								
	5								
	6								
	7								
	8								
	9								
	10								
	11	ENROLLMENT OF NOS. 1 & 3 HEREON APPROVED BY THE SECRETARY OF INTERIOR FEB 4 1903							
	12								
	13	ENROLLMENT OF NOS. 2 HEREON APPROVED BY THE SECRETARY OF INTERIOR SEP 12 1903							
	14								
	15								
	16								
	17								

TRIBAL ENROLLMENT OF PARENTS

Name of Father	Year	County	Name of Mother	Year	County
₁ Jno W White	Dead	Non Citz	Martha Riddle		Gaines
₂ Frank L Kelton	"	"	Emma Kelton		Non Citz
₃ Rufus Winlock		Tobucksy	No2		
4					
5					
6					
7 No1 on 1896 roll as Jno W White					
8					
9 As to marriage of parents of No3, see testimony of Abel McGilberry					
10 See testimony of Nº2 as to her former marriage and divorce, also					
11 the previous marriage of Nº1 and his divorce from his first wife, Dec 23, 1902					
12 Evidence of divorce between Nº1 and Pauline White filed Feby 18, 1903					
13 Evidence of divorce between Nº2 and Rufus Winlock filed Feby 18, 1903					
For child of No3 see NB (Apr 26-06) Card #614					
14				Date of Application for Enrollment.	
15				Aug 3/99	
16					
17					

205

Choctaw By Blood Enrollment Cards 1898-1914

RESIDENCE:	Gaines	COUNTY.				CARD No.
POST OFFICE:	Wilburton, I.T.	**Choctaw Nation**	Choctaw Roll (Not Including Freedmen)			FIELD No. 3206

Dawes' Roll No.	NAME	Relationship to Person First Named	AGE	SEX	BLOOD	TRIBAL ENROLLMENT Year	County	No.
I.W. 741 ₁	Vawter, James W ㉜	First Named	29	M	IW	1896	Gaines	15134
9270 ₂	" Martha A ²⁸	Wife	25	F	3/4	1896	"	12595
9271 ₃	" Eula J ⁷	Dau	4	"	3/8	1896	"	12596
9272 ₄	" Eunice E ⁵	"	2	"	3/8			
9273 ₅	" Ethel M ³	"	1 wk	"	3/8			
₆								
₇								
₈								
₉								
₁₀	ENROLLMENT OF NOS. 2,3,4 & 5 HEREON APPROVED BY THE SECRETARY OF INTERIOR FEB 4 1903							
₁₁								
₁₂								
₁₃	ENROLLMENT OF NOS. ~~~ 1 ~~~ HEREON APPROVED BY THE SECRETARY OF INTERIOR MAY 7 1904							
₁₄								
₁₅								
₁₆								
₁₇								

TRIBAL ENROLLMENT OF PARENTS

	Name of Father	Year	County	Name of Mother	Year	County
₁	W J Vawter		Non Citz	Ellen J Vawter		Non Citz
₂	S H McCasson		Sugar Loaf	Eliza McCasson		Sugar Loaf
₃	No1			No2		
₄	No1			No2		
₅	No1			No2		
₆						
₇	No 1 See Decision of March 2 '04					
₈	Certificate of M.L. Butler and affidavit of Ben Hotubbee C.C. Mathies and					
₉	EW Benton as to authority of William Watson to solemnize[sic] marriage ceremony filed					
	No3 on 1896 roll as Ella J Vawter					
₁₀						
₁₁	Nos 4-5 Affidavits of birth to be					
₁₂	supplied: Recd Oct 7/99					
₁₃	No.1 admitted as an intermarried citizen and No.3 as a citizen by					
	blood by Dawes Commission in 1896: Choctaw case #85: no appeal.					
₁₄	Surname on 1896 docket given as Vaults.				Date of Application for Enrollment.	
₁₅	For child of Nos 1&2 see NB (Apr 26 '06) Card #161				Aug 3/99	
	" " " " " " (March 3 '03) " #1137					
₁₆						
₁₇	PO Erin Springs IT 3/18/05					

RESIDENCE: Gaines COUNTY.	**Choctaw Nation**				**Choctaw Roll**	CARD NO.	
POST OFFICE: Hartshorne, I.T.					(Not Including Freedmen)	FIELD NO. **3207**	

Dawes' Roll No.	NAME	Relationship to Person First Named	AGE	SEX	BLOOD	TRIBAL ENROLLMENT		
						Year	County	No.
9274	1 McMurtry John W ³⁴	Named	31	M	1/8	1896	Gaines	9146
I.W. 1407	2 " Lucy ³⁶	Wife	33	F	I.W	1896	"	14862
15448	3 " Nettie P ⁸	Dau	5	"	1/16	1896	"	9147
15449	4 " Martha E ⁶	"	3	"	1/16	1896	"	9148
9275	5 " Jessie ⁵	"	1½	"	1/16			
9276	6 James, Frank ¹⁶	S.Son	13	M	1/8	1896	Gaines	6569
9277	7 " Rufus ¹⁴	"	11	"	1/8	1896	"	6570
9278	8 " Jesse ¹⁷	Ward	14	"	1/8	1896	"	6571
9279	9 " Willie D ¹³	"	10	"	1/8	1896	"	6572
9280	10 McMurtry, Thelma ¹	Dau	2mo	F	1/16			
	11 Enrollment of No.2 cancelled by order of Department Mch 4,1907							
	12 No5 Affidavit of birth to					Dec 8/99-See if Nos 1-2 were		
	13 be supplied:- Filed Dec 14/99					denied by Dawes Commiss-		
	As to marriage of Nos 1-2					ion in 1896		
	14 see testimony of Mary M.							
	15 James							
	16	ENROLLMENT OF NOS. 1,5,6,7,8,9,10 HEREON APPROVED BY THE SECRETARY						
	17	OF INTERIOR Feb 4 1903						

(left margin, vertical) No2 restored to roll by Dept mental authority of January 19, 1909 (File 5-51)

TRIBAL ENROLLMENT OF PARENTS						
Name of Father	Year	County		Name of Mother	Year	County
1 Thos. H. McMurtry	Dead	Non Citz		Martha McMurtry		Gaines
2 W. J. Bruton	" "			Mary Bruton		Non Citz
3 No1		ENROLLMENT		No2		
4 No1		OF NOS. ~3~4~ HEREON APPROVED BY THE SECRETARY		No2		
5 No1		OF INTERIOR May 9 1904		No2		ENROLLMENT
6 Robinson James	Dead	Gaines		No2		OF NOS. ~2~ HEREON APPROVED BY THE SECRETARY
7 " "	"	"		No2		OF INTERIOR Jun 12 1900
8 Simon James	"	Tobucksy		Florence James	Dead	Non Citz
9 " "	"	"		" "	"	" "
10 No1				No2		
11 No1 on 1896 roll as Jno. Wallace McMurtry						
12 No3 " 1896 " " Nellie P. "						
13 No8 " 1896 " " Jessie James "			Certificate of marriage between Nⁱ 1 and 2 filed Jany 3,1903			
As to marriage of parents of Nos 8-9 see	For child of Nos1 and 2 see NB (Apr26 '06) No552					
14 testimony of William Anderson	{ " " " " " " " " " " " (Mar 3 '05) "1214					
15 As to marriage of parents of Nos 6-7 see			Date of Application for Enrollment. Aug 3/99			
16 testimony of William Anderson			No10 enrolled Dec 14/99			
17 No2 was rejected by Dawes Commission in 1896 in Choctaw case #1324: No appeal: See original						

application: same was made for Nos 2,3 and 4 claiming their right through No.1

Choctaw By Blood Enrollment Cards 1898-1914

RESIDENCE: Gaines COUNTY.
POST OFFICE: Hartshorne, I.T.

Choctaw Nation

Choctaw Roll
(Not Including Freedmen)

CARD NO.
FIELD NO. 3208

Dawes' Roll No.	NAME	Relationship to Person First Named	AGE	SEX	BLOOD	TRIBAL ENROLLMENT		
						Year	County	No.
I.W. 300	1 Collins, Henry A ²⁵	First Named	22	M	I.W.			
9281	2 " Louisa ²²	Wife	19	F	1/2			
9282	3 " Nona M ¹	Dau	8mo	"	1/4			
	4							
	5							
	6							
	7							
	8							
	9							
	10							
	11							
	12							
	13							
	14							
	15							
	16							
	17							

ENROLLMENT
OF NOS. 2, 3 HEREON
APPROVED BY THE SECRETARY
OF INTERIOR FEB 4 1903

ENROLLMENT
OF NOS. 1 HEREON
APPROVED BY THE SECRETARY
OF INTERIOR SEP 12 1903

TRIBAL ENROLLMENT OF PARENTS

	Name of Father	Year	County	Name of Mother	Year	County
1	Hade Collins		Non Citz	Lucy Collins	Dead	Non Citz
2	Chas Stewart	Dead	" "	Lottie Stewart	"	Jacks Fork
3	No1			No2		
4						
5						
6						
7			No2 on 1896 roll as Louisa Stewart			
8						
9			No3 Affidavit of birth to be supplied.-Recd Aug 9/99			
10						
11			See testimony of S. E. Cole			
12						
13						
14						
15				Date of Application for Enrollment	Aug 3/99	
16						
17						

RESIDENCE: Gaines COUNTY.								
POST OFFICE: Hartshorne, I.T.								

Choctaw Nation — Choctaw Roll *(Not Including Freedmen)*

CARD NO. FIELD NO. 3209

Dawes' Roll No.	NAME		Relationship to Person	AGE	SEX	BLOOD	TRIBAL ENROLLMENT		
							Year	County	No.
9283	1 Stewart, Mary	20	First Named	17	F	1/2	1896	Gaines	11246
9284	2 Cowen Susan	16	Sister	13	"	1/2	1896	"	11248
9285	3 Cowen, Joseph Lee	1	Son of No.2	2mo	M	1/4			
	4								
	5								
	6								
	7								
	8								
	9								
	10								
	11								
	12								
	13								
	14								
	15								
	16								
	17								

ENROLLMENT OF NOS. 1, 2, 3 APPROVED BY THE SECRETARY OF INTERIOR FEB 4 1903

TRIBAL ENROLLMENT OF PARENTS

	Name of Father	Year	County	Name of Mother	Year	County
1	Chas Stewart	Dead	Non Citz	Lottie Stewart	Dead	Jacks Fork
2	" "	"	" "	" "	"	" "
3	Bates Cowen		" "	No2		
4						
5						
6						
7	No2 is now wife of Bates Cowen, Non Citizen. Evidence of marriage requested Oct. 28/02.					
8	No3 born Sept 1, 1901; enrolled Oct. 28, 1902					
9	For child of No.2 see NB (March 3, 1905) #1287					
10						
11						
12						
13						
14				#1&2		
15				Date of Application for Enrollment	Aug 3/99	
16						
17						

Choctaw By Blood Enrollment Cards 1898-1914

RESIDENCE: Gaines   COUNTY. **Choctaw Nation**   **Choctaw Roll**   CARD NO.
POST OFFICE: Hartshorne, I.T.   *(Not Including Freedmen)*   FIELD NO. 3210

Dawes' Roll No.	NAME	Relationship to Person First Named	AGE	SEX	BLOOD	TRIBAL ENROLLMENT Year	County	No.
I.W. 1408	1 Bowling Mary M 45	First Named	42	F	IW	1896	Gaines	14686
15450	2 James, Alice E 15	Dau	12	F	3/8	1896	"	6584
15451	3 " Maggie M 14	"	11	"	3/8	1896	"	6585
15452	4 " Ellis E 11	Son	8	M	3/8	1896	"	65866
15453	5 " Analaurie 9	Dau	6	F	3/8	1896		6587
15454	6 " Evalena 8	"	5	"	3/8	1896		6588
	7 Nos 1,2,3,4,5 and 6 restored to roll by Departmental authority of January 19, 1909 (File 5-51)							
	8 Enrollment of Nos 1 to 6 cancelled by order of Department March 9, 1904							
	9							
	10 ENROLLMENT							
	11 OF NOS. 2-3-4-5-6 HEREON APPROVED BY THE SECRETARY							
	12 OF INTERIOR MAY 9 1904							
	13							
	14 ENROLLMENT							
	15 OF NOS. ××× 1 ××× HEREON APPROVED BY THE SECRETARY							
	16 OF INTERIOR JUN 12 1905							
	17							

TRIBAL ENROLLMENT OF PARENTS

	Name of Father	Year	County	Name of Mother	Year	County
1	Milton Breedlove	Dead	Non Citz	Margaret A Breedlove	Dead	Non Citz
2	Emerson James	"	Gaines	No 1		
3	" "	"	"	No 1		
4	" "	"	"	No 1		
5	" "	"	"	No 1		
6	" "	"	"	No 1		
7						
8	No.1 formerly wife of Emerson James, 1893 Gaines, No 294					
9	and who died in 1896					
10	No1 on 1896 roll as Morilla M James					
11	No5 " 1896 " " Anna L "					
	No6 " 1896 " " Evelena "					
12	No.1,2,3,4,5&6 were denied in 1896 by Dawes Commission in					
13	Choctaw Case #1031: No appeal					
	No.1 is now wife of Bowlins[sic], a non-citizen 12/2 '02				Date of Application for Enrollment.	
14						
15					Aug 3/99	
16						
17						

Choctaw By Blood Enrollment Cards 1898-1914

RESIDENCE: Gaines COUNTY. **Choctaw Nation** Choctaw Roll *(Not Including Freedmen)* CARD NO.
POST OFFICE: Hartshorne, I.T. FIELD NO. 3211

Dawes' Roll No.	NAME		Relationship to Person	AGE	SEX	BLOOD	TRIBAL ENROLLMENT		
							Year	County	No.
9286	1 Anderson, Joel	38	First Named	35	M	Full	1896	Gaines	84
9287	2 " Susan	31	Wife	28	F	"	1896	"	10182
9288	3 " Edward	15	Son	12	M	"	1896	"	85
9289	4 Pusley, Jane	16	S.Dau	13	F	"	1896	"	10183
9290	5 " Mary	14	"	11	"	"	1896	"	10184
	6								
	7								
	8								
	9								
	10								
	11								
	12								
	13								
	14								
	15								
	16								
	17								

ENROLLMENT
OF NOS. 1,2,3,4,5 HEREON
APPROVED BY THE SECRETARY
OF INTERIOR Feb 4 1903

TRIBAL ENROLLMENT OF PARENTS

	Name of Father	Year	County	Name of Mother	Year	County
1	Roberson Anderson	Dead	Gaines	Siney Anderson		Gaines
2	Jackson Compalubbee	"	Tobucksy		Dead	Tobucksy
3	No1			Elsie Anderson	"	Gaines
4	Gabel Pusley	Dead	Tobucksy	No2		
5	" "	"	"	No2		
6						
7						
8						
9	No2 on 1896 roll as Susan Pusley					
10						
11						
12						
13						
14						
15				Date of Application for Enrollment.	Aug 3/99	
16						
17	No1 P.O. Gowen 11/11/04					

Choctaw By Blood Enrollment Cards 1898-1914

RESIDENCE: Gaines COUNTY. **Choctaw Nation** Choctaw Roll CARD NO.
POST OFFICE: Vireton, I.T. *(Not Including Freedmen)* FIELD NO. 3212

Dawes' Roll No.	NAME		Relationship to Person	AGE	SEX	BLOOD	TRIBAL ENROLLMENT		
							Year	County	No.
9291	₁ King, Isaac	33	First Named	30	M	Full	1896	Sans Bois	7427
9292	₂ " Ida	7	Dau	4	F	7/8	1896	" "	7428
	3								
	4								
	5	ENROLLMENT							
	6	OF NOS. 1 and 2 HEREON							
	7	APPROVED BY THE SECRETARY OF INTERIOR FEB 4 1903							
	8								
	9								
	10								
	11								
	12								
	13								
	14								
	15								
	16								
	17								

TRIBAL ENROLLMENT OF PARENTS

	Name of Father	Year	County	Name of Mother	Year	County
₁	Tecumseh King	Dead	Sans Bois	Silvey King	Dead	Sans Bois
₂	No1			Mary King	"	Gaines
3						
4						
5						
6						
7			No 1 is in Ft Leavenworth Kansas Penitentiary Jany 28, 1903			
8			See papers relative to the adoption of No2 filed herein Jan 6, 1903			
9						
10						
11						
12						
13						
14						
15				Date of Application for Enrollment.	Aug 3/99	
16						
17						

Choctaw By Blood Enrollment Cards 1898-1914

RESIDENCE:	Gaines	COUNTY.	**Choctaw Nation**	**Choctaw Roll** *(Not Including Freedmen)*	CARD NO.
POST OFFICE:	Damon, I.T.				FIELD NO. 3213

Dawes' Roll No.	NAME		Relationship to Person First Named	AGE	SEX	BLOOD	TRIBAL ENROLLMENT		
							Year	County	No.
9293	1 Pusley, Edward	27	First Named	24	M	Full	1896	Gaines	10185
	2								
	3								
	4	ENROLLMENT							
	5	OF NOS. 1 HEREON APPROVED BY THE SECRETARY							
	6	OF INTERIOR FEB 4 1903							
	7								
	8								
	9								
	10								
	11								
	12								
	13								
	14								
	15								
	16								
	17								

TRIBAL ENROLLMENT OF PARENTS

	Name of Father	Year	County	Name of Mother	Year	County
1	Calvin Pusley	Dead	Gaines	Nancy Pusley		Gaines
2						
3						
4						
5						
6						
7						
8						
9						
10						
11						
12						
13						
14						
15				Date of Application for Enrollment.	Aug 3/99	
16						
17						

RESIDENCE:	Blue	COUNTY.						CARD NO.	
POST OFFICE:	Durant, I.T.		Choctaw Nation			Choctaw Roll (Not Including Freedmen)		FIELD NO.	3214

Dawes' Roll No.	NAME	Relationship to Person First Named	AGE	SEX	BLOOD	TRIBAL ENROLLMENT		
						Year	County	No.
DEAD. 1	Folsom, Tandy W	Named	40	M	3/4	1896	Bl	4390
2								
3								
4								
5								
6								
7	No. 1 HEREON DISMISSED UNDER							
8	ORDER OF THE COMMISSION TO THE FIVE							
9	CIVILIZED TRIBES OF MARCH 31, 1905.							
10								
11								
12								
13								
14								
15								
16								
17								

CANCELLED

Applicant died prior to ratification of Choctaw-Chickasaw agreement Sept 25, 1902

TRIBAL ENROLLMENT OF PARENTS

	Name of Father	Year	County		Name of Mother	Year	County
1	Jack Folsom	Dead	Blue		Basic J. Folsom		Blue
2							
3							
4							
5							
6							
7							
8	On 1896 roll as Tandy W. Fulsom						
9							
10	Wife and children are Chickasaws. See Chickasaw card #1236 also see						
11	No 1 Died March 7, 1900, proof of death filed Oct. 23, 1902					Choctaw #4382	
12							
13							
14							
15					Date of Application for Enrollment.		Aug 3/99
16							
17							

Choctaw By Blood Enrollment Cards 1898-1914

RESIDENCE: Tobucksy COUNTY. **Choctaw Nation** **Choctaw Roll** CARD No.
POST OFFICE: Kiowa, I.T. *(Not Including Freedmen)* FIELD No. **3215**

Dawes' Roll No.	NAME	Relationship to Person First Named	AGE	SEX	BLOOD	TRIBAL ENROLLMENT Year	County	No.
9294	1 Wesley, Lucy Ann 17	First Named	14	F	1/2	1896	Gaines	12931
9295	2 " Henry 15	Bro	12	M	1/2	1896	"	12932
9296	3 " Millie 6	Sister	3	F	1/2	1896	"	12933
9697	4 " Jane 4	"	10mo	"	1/2			
	5							
	6							
	7							
	8							
	9							
	10	ENROLLMENT OF NOS. 1,2,3 and 4 HEREON						
	11	APPROVED BY THE SECRETARY						
	12	OF INTERIOR Feb 4 1903						
	13							
	14							
	15							
	16							
	17							

TRIBAL ENROLLMENT OF PARENTS

	Name of Father	Year	County	Name of Mother	Year	County
1	Abel Wesley		Chickasaw	Polly Wesley	Dead	Tobucksy
2	" "		"	" "	"	"
3	" "		"	" "	"	"
4	" "		"	" "	"	"
5						
6						
7						
8	No1 on 1896 roll as Louisiana Wesley					
9						
10						
11						
12						
13						
14					Date of Application for Enrollment.	
15					Aug 3/99	
16						
17						

Choctaw By Blood Enrollment Cards 1898-1914

RESIDENCE: Gaines   COUNTY. **Choctaw Nation**   **Choctaw Roll**   CARD NO.
POST OFFICE: Hartshorne, I.T.   (Not Including Freedmen)   FIELD NO. **3216**

Dawes' Roll No.	NAME		Relationship to Person	AGE	SEX	BLOOD	TRIBAL ENROLLMENT		
							Year	County	No.
9298	1 Wilson, Sarah	50	First Named	47	F	1/4	1896	Skullyville	12834
9299	2 " Mary	20	Dau	17	F	1/8	1896	"	12835
9300	3 " Eva	17	"	14	"	1/8	1896	"	12836
9301	4 " Horace	14	Son	11	M	1/8	1896	"	12867
DEAD	5 " Kelly B DEAD		"	4	"	1/8	1896	"	12838
	6								
	7	ENROLLMENT							
	8	OF NOS. 1,2,3 and 4 HEREON APPROVED BY THE SECRETARY							
	9	OF INTERIOR Feb 4 1903							
	10	No.5 hereon dismissed under							
	11	order of the Commission to the							
	12	Five Civilized Tribes of March 31, 1900.							
	13								
	14	For child of No2 see NB (Apr 26-06) Card #357							
	15	" " " " " " (Mar 3-05) " #135							
	16								
	17								

TRIBAL ENROLLMENT OF PARENTS

	Name of Father	Year	County	Name of Mother	Year	County
1	Joseph Merkel	Dead	Non Citz	Elizabeth Merkel	Dead	Nashoba
2	John H Wilson		" "	No1		
3	" " "		" "	No1		
4	" " "		" "	No1		
5	" " "		" "	No1		
6						
7						
8						
9	No.5 Died in March 1901. Proof of death filed Dec 24 1902					
10	No4 on 1896 roll as Harvey Wilson					
11	No5 born on Aug 13, 1894. On 1896					
12	roll as Kelly Wilson, also admitted by					
13	Dawes Com. Case No 956					
14	All but No5 were admitted by an Act of Council, approved Oct. 30/90.				Date of Application for Enrollment.	
15	Act No 17 of regular Session of 1890				Aug 3/99	
16	Citizenship, of all, is questioned.					
17						

RESIDENCE: Gaines	COUNTY.	Choctaw Nation	Choctaw Roll	CARD No.
POST OFFICE: Wilburton, I.T.			(Not Including Freedmen)	FIELD No. 3217

Dawes' Roll No.	NAME	Relationship to Person First Named	AGE	SEX	BLOOD	Year	County	No.
DEAD.	1 Brown, Newton DEAD	Named	44	M	1/2	1896	Gaines	856
I.W. 920	2 " Lou ③⑦	Wife	34	F	I.W.			
9302	3 " Abel 19	Son	16	M	3/4	1896	Gaines	857
9303	4 " William 14	"	11	"	3/4	1896	"	858
	5							
	6							
	7	ENROLLMENT						
	8	OF NOS. 3 and 4 HEREON APPROVED BY THE SECRETARY						
	9	OF INTERIOR FEB 4 1903						
	10	ENROLLMENT						
	11	OF NOS. 2 HEREON APPROVED BY THE SECRETARY						
	12	OF INTERIOR AUG 3 1904						
	13	No. 1 HEREON DISMISSED UNDER						
	14	ORDER OF THE COMMISSION TO THE FIVE						
	15	CIVILIZED TRIBES OF MARCH 31, 1905.						
	16							
	17							

TRIBAL ENROLLMENT OF PARENTS

	Name of Father	Year	County	Name of Mother	Year	County
1	Geo. Brown	Dead	Chickasaw	Mary Lomer		Gaines
2	Reynolds	"	Non Citz	Sallie Reynolds		Non Citz
3	No1			Lizzie Brown	Dead	Gaines
4	No1			" "	"	"
5						
6						
7						
8						
9						
10	No4 on 1896 roll as Wᵐ Brown					
11						
12	No1 Citizenship of mother, Mary Lomer, questioned. If shown she has no					
13	right he will be enrolled as a Chick-				Date of Application for Enrollment.	
14	asaw – following his father					
15	No1 died January 4 1901. See letter of wife filed March 13, 1901				Aug 3/99	
16	Evidence of divorce between Nº1 and former wife Melissa Brown received and filed Jany 19, 1903					
17	Nº1 Died Jany 5[sic], 1901, proof of death filed Feby 5, 1903					

Choctaw By Blood Enrollment Cards 1898-1914

RESIDENCE:	Gaines	COUNTY.	**Choctaw Nation**				Choctaw Roll		CARD NO.	
POST OFFICE:	Wilburton, I.T.						*(Not Including Freedmen)*		FIELD NO. 3218	

Dawes' Roll No.	NAME		Relationship to Person First Named	AGE	SEX	BLOOD	TRIBAL ENROLLMENT		
							Year	County	No.
DEAD.	1 Tom, Jackson	DEAD.		33	M	Full	1896	Gaines	11994
9304	2 " Bynie	43	Wife	40	F	"	1896	"	11995
9305	3 " Renie	12	Dau	9	"	"	1896	"	11996
	4								
	5								
	6	ENROLLMENT							
	7	OF NOS. 2 and 3 HEREON APPROVED BY THE SECRETARY							
	8	OF INTERIOR FEB 4 1903							
	9								
	10	No. 1 HEREON DISMISSED UNDER							
	11	ORDER OF THE COMMISSION TO THE FIVE							
	12	CIVILIZED TRIBES OF MARCH 31, 1905.							
	13								
	14								
	15								
	16								
	17								

TRIBAL ENROLLMENT OF PARENTS

Name of Father	Year	County	Name of Mother	Year	County
1 Ok-tha-chubbee	Dead	Sugar Loaf		Dead	Jacks Fork
2 Hom-bey	"	" "	Millie Hombey	"	Sans Bois
3 No1			No2		
4					
5					
6					
7					
8 No1 died March 2, 1901; proof of death filed Dec 19 1902					
9					
10					
11					
12					
13					
14			Date of Application for Enrollment.	Aug 3/99	
15					
16					
17					

Choctaw By Blood Enrollment Cards 1898-1914

RESIDENCE: Gaines	COUNTY.								
POST OFFICE: Hartshorne, I.T.	**Choctaw Nation**					**Choctaw Roll** (Not Including Freedmen)		CARD NO. FIELD NO. 3219	

Dawes' Roll No.	NAME		Relationship to Person First Named	AGE	SEX	BLOOD	TRIBAL ENROLLMENT		
							Year	County	No.
9306	1 James, Gaines	26	First Named	23	M	Full	1896	Gaines	6568
	2								
	3								
	4	ENROLLMENT OF NOS. 1 HEREON							
	5	APPROVED BY THE SECRETARY							
	6	OF INTERIOR FEB 4 1903							
	7								
	8								
	9								
	10								
	11								
	12								
	13								
	14								
	15								
	16								
	17								

TRIBAL ENROLLMENT OF PARENTS

Name of Father	Year	County	Name of Mother	Year	County
1 Bason James	Dead	Sugar Loaf	Sabile James		Sugar Loaf
2					
3					
4					
5					
6					
7					
8					
9					
10					
11					
12					
13					
14					
15			Date of Application for Enrollment.	Aug 3/99	
16					
17					

Choctaw By Blood Enrollment Cards 1898-1914

RESIDENCE: Gaines COUNTY. **Choctaw Nation** Choctaw Roll CARD NO.
POST OFFICE: Damon, I.T. (Not Including Freedmen) FIELD NO. 3220

Dawes' Roll No.	NAME		Relationship to Person	AGE	SEX	BLOOD	TRIBAL ENROLLMENT		
							Year	County	No.
9307	1 Taylor, Wilkin	29	First Named	26	M	Full	1896	Gaines	11985
9308	2 " Malinda	36	Wife	33	F	"	1896	"	11986
DEAD.	3 Thompson, Sisen DEAD.		S.Dau	12	"	"	1896	"	11987
9309	4 " Harris		S.Son	10	M	"	1896	"	11988
	5								
	6								
	7	ENROLLMENT							
	8	OF NOS. 1,2 and 4 HEREON APPROVED BY THE SECRETARY							
	9	OF INTERIOR FEB 4 1903							
	10								
	11	No. 3 HEREON DISMISSED UNDER							
	12	ORDER OF THE COMMISSION TO THE FIVE CIVILIZED TRIBES OF MARCH 31, 1905.							
	13								
	14								
	15								
	16								
	17								

TRIBAL ENROLLMENT OF PARENTS

	Name of Father	Year	County	Name of Mother	Year	County
1	Ya-ho-nubbee	Dead	Gaines	Becky Hicks		Gaines
2	To-ko-bey	"	Bok Tuklo	Mollie	Dead	Bok Tuklo
3	Thompson Wesley	"	Gaines	No2		
4	" "	"	"	No2		
5						
6						
7						
8			No2 on 1896 roll as Mintee Taylor			
9			No3 " 1896 " " Sisen "			
10			No4 " 1896 " " Harrie "			
11	No3 died April, 1900: proof of death filed Dec 6 1902		No's 1 and 2 are divorced			
12						
13						
14					Date of Application for Enrollment.	
15					Aug 3/99	
16						
17						

220

RESIDENCE: Gaines	COUNTY.					**Choctaw Roll**	CARD NO.	
POST OFFICE: Damon, I.T.	**Choctaw Nation**					*(Not Including Freedmen)*	FIELD NO. 3221	

Dawes' Roll No.	NAME	Relationship to Person First Named	AGE	SEX	BLOOD	TRIBAL ENROLLMENT		
						Year	County	No.
	1 Taylor, William	Named	43	M	Full	1896	Gaines	12003
9310	2 " Mary 27	Wife	24	F	"	1896	"	6614
9311	3 " Elum 19	Nephew	16	M	"	1896	"	12000
9312	4 " Johnson 5	"	3	"	"	1896	"	12001
	5							
	6							
	7	ENROLLMENT OF NOS. 2,3 and 4 HEREON						
	8	APPROVED BY THE SECRETARY OF INTERIOR FEB 4 1903						
	9							
	10							
	11	No. 1 HEREON DISMISSED UNDER						
	12	ORDER OF THE COMMISSION TO THE FIVE CIVILIZED TRIBES OF MARCH 31, 1905.						
	13							
	14							
	15							
	16							
	17							

TRIBAL ENROLLMENT OF PARENTS

Name of Father	Year	County	Name of Mother	Year	County
1 Ya-ho-nubbee	Dead	Gaines	Ba-yo-nah	Dead	Gaines
2 Thos. Jones	"	Sugar Loaf	Silsie Carney	"	"
3 Simon Taylor	"	Gaines	Elizabeth Taylor	"	"
4 " "	"	"	" "	"	"
5					
6					
7					
8					
9	No2 on 1896 roll as Mary Jones				
10	No4 " 1896 " " John Taylor				
11					
12	No1 is dead see testimony in allotment jackets #9311-9312 see letter				
13	of No2 in G. O files #10095-64				
14					Date of Application for Enrollment.
15	No1 Died Sept 23 1900. Proof of death filed Jan 26, 1905				Aug 3/99
16					
17					

RESIDENCE:	Gaines	COUNTY.	**Choctaw Nation**				**Choctaw Roll**	CARD NO.	
POST OFFICE:	Vireton, I.T.						*(Not Including Freedmen)*	FIELD NO.	3222

Dawes' Roll No.	NAME	Relationship to Person First Named	AGE	SEX	BLOOD	TRIBAL ENROLLMENT		
						Year	County	No.
✓ ※	1 Miller, Henry E	Named	56	M	1/4			
✓ ※	2 " Sarah	Wife	55	F	I.W.			
✓ ※	3 " Jesse O	Son	15	M	1/8			
✓ ※	4 " Virginia	Dau	12	F	1/8			
	5							
	6							
	7							
	8							
	9							
	10							
	11							
	12							
	13							
	14							
	15							
	16							
	17							

TRIBAL ENROLLMENT OF PARENTS

Name of Father	Year	County	Name of Mother	Year	County
1 Edward Miller	Dead	Non Citz	Catherine Miller	Dead	Choctaw
2 Nath Stubblefield	"	"	Mary Stubblefield	"	Non Citz
3 No1			No2		
4 No1			No2		
5					
6					
7					
8 Nos1 to 4 incl' denied in 96 Case #1282					
9 Admitted by U.S. Court, Central Dist, Aug 25/97 Case No.121. As to residence, see testimony of No1.					
10 Judgment of U.S. Court admitting Nos 1 to 4 inclusive set aside by Decree of Choctaw Chickasaw Cit Court Dec 17/02					
11 Nos 1 to 4 [illegible] C.C.C.C. Case #61					
12 Nos 1 to 4 [illegible] C.C.C.C. Case #61 March 3 '04					
13				Date of Application for Enrollment.	
14					
15				Aug 3/99	
16					
17					

| RESIDENCE: | Gaines | COUNTY. | **Choctaw Nation** | Choctaw Roll | CARD No. |
| POST OFFICE: | Vireton, I.T. | | | *(Not Including Freedmen)* | FIELD No. 3223 |

Dawes' Roll No.	NAME	Relationship to Person	AGE	SEX	BLOOD	TRIBAL ENROLLMENT		
						Year	County	No.
✓ * 1	Miller, Edward	First Named	29	M	1/8			
✓ * 2	" Lillie	Wife	25	F	I.W			
✓ * 3	" Arrie	Dau	8	"	1/16			
✓ * 4	" Maud	"	6	"	1/16			
✓ * 5	" Lodie	"	4	"	1/16			
* 6	" Thadeus	Son	3	M	1/16			
✓ 7	" Burrel	"	7mo	"	1/16			
✓ 8	" Patsy E	Dau	18mo	F	1/16			
9								
10								
11	DISMISSED							
12	MAY 25 1904							
13								
14								
15	DENIED CITIZENSHIP BY THE CHOCTAW AND							
16	CHICKASAW CITIZENSHIP COURT						Mar 9 '04	
17								

TRIBAL ENROLLMENT OF PARENTS

	Name of Father	Year	County	Name of Mother	Year	County
1	Henry E Miller		Choctaw	Sarah Miller		white woman
2	James Wagner	Dead	Non Citz	Ruthie Wagner		Non Citz
3	No1			No2		
4	No1			No2		
5	No1			No2		
6	No1			No2		
7	No1			No2		
8	No1			No2		
9	Nos 1 to 6 incl denied in 96 Case #1282					
10	Admitted by U.S. Court, Central Dist. Aug 1896					
11	Case No 121. As to residence and birth of No7 see testimony of No1					
12	Judgment of U.S. Court admitting Nos 1 to 6 incl vacated and set aside by Decree of Choctaw Chickasaw Cit Court Dec 17 '02					
13	No7 Affidavit of birth to be supplied: Filed Nov 2/99					
14	No8 Born March 15, 1901; enrolled Oct. 2, 1902				Date of Application for Enrollment.	
15	Nos 1 to 6 incl denied by C.C.C. Case #61 March 9 '04				Aug 3/99	
16						
17	P.O. Owl 12/2/02					

223

Choctaw By Blood Enrollment Cards 1898-1914

RESIDENCE: Gaines   P.O. Coalgate IT
POST OFFICE: Vireton, I.T.   COUNTY. **Choctaw Nation**   Choctaw Roll (Not Including Freedmen)   CARD NO.
FIELD NO. 3224

Dawes' Roll No.	NAME	Relationship to Person First Named	AGE	SEX	BLOOD	TRIBAL ENROLLMENT Year	County	No.
✓ *	1 Miller, James N.	Named	34	M	1/8			
✓ *	2 " Jennie	Wife	22	F	I.W			
✓ *	3 " William	Son	10	M	1/16			
✓ *	4 " Warnie	"	5	"	1/16			
✓	5 " Sarah Louisa B	Dau	1½	F	1/16			
✓	6 " Thomas Franklin	Son	3mo	M	1/16			
✓	7 " Carrie Ethel	Dau	1mo	F	1/16			
	8							
Nos 5-6 &7	9							
	10	DISMISSED						
	11	MAY 25 1904						
	12							
	13	Nos 1 to 4 incl now in C.C.C. Case #61						
*	14	Nos 1 to 4 incl denied by C.C.C. Case #61 March 9 '04						
	15							
	16							
	17							

DENIED CITIZENSHIP BY THE CHOCTAW AND CHICKASAW CITIZENSHIP COURT Mar 9 '04

TRIBAL ENROLLMENT OF PARENTS

Name of Father	Year	County	Name of Mother	Year	County
1 Henry E Miller		Choctaw	Sarah Miller		white woman
2 William Meek	Dead	Non Citz	Louisa Meek		Non Citz
3 No 1			Cynthia Miller	Dead	" "
4 No 1			No 2		
5 No 1			No 2		
6 No. 1			No. 2		
7 Nº 1			Nº 2		
8					
9 Present address of parties is Coalgate, I.T.					
10 Nos 1 to 4 incl denied by Com in 96 Case #1282					
11 Admitted by U.S. Court Central Dist Aug 25/97, Case No 121. As to residence					
12 and birth of No5, see testimony of No1					
13 Judgment of U.S. Court admitting Nos 1 to 4 incl vacated and set aside by Decree of Choctaw Chickasaw Cit Court Dec 17 '02					
14 No5 Affidavit of birth to be supplied: Recd Dec 18/99. Irregular and			Date of Application for Enrollment.		
15 returned for correction. Returned corrected and filed 10/26, 1900.		Aug 3/99			
16 No6 Enrolled June 29th, 1900					
17 No.7 Born July 20, 1902. Enrolled Aug. 30, 1902					

224

Choctaw By Blood Enrollment Cards 1898-1914

RESIDENCE: Gaines COUNTY. **Choctaw Nation** Choctaw Roll CARD NO.
POST OFFICE: Vireton, I.T. *(Not Including Freedmen)* FIELD NO. 3225

Dawes' Roll No.	NAME	Relationship to Person First Named	AGE	SEX	BLOOD	TRIBAL ENROLLMENT		
						Year	County	No.
1	Flinn, Laura	Named	17	F	1/8			
2								
3								
4								
5								
6								
7								
8								
9								
10								
11								
12								
13								
14								
15								
16								
17								

TRIBAL ENROLLMENT OF PARENTS

	Name of Father	Year	County	Name of Mother	Year	County
1	Henry E Miller		Choctaw	Sarah Miller		white woman
2						
3						
4						
5						
6						
7	No1 denied in 96 Case #1282					
8	Admitted by U.S. Court, Central Dist.					
9	Aug 25/97, Case No 121, as Laura					
10	Miller. As to residence see her testimony.					
11	Judgement of US Court admitting No1 vacated and set aside by Decree of Choctaw Chickasaw Cit Court Dec 17/02					
12	No1 now in C.C.C. Case #61					
13	No1 denied by C.C.C.C. Case #61 March 7/03					
14						
15					Date of Application for Enrollment. Aug 3/99	
16						
17						

225

RESIDENCE:	Gaines	COUNTY.							

RESIDENCE: Gaines COUNTY. **Choctaw Nation** Choctaw Roll — CARD No.
POST OFFICE: Featherston, I.T. (Not Including Freedmen) — FIELD No. **3226**

Dawes' Roll No.	NAME	Relationship to Person	AGE	SEX	BLOOD	TRIBAL ENROLLMENT		
						Year	County	No.
I.W. 301	1 Featherston, Lucius C	(49) First Named	38	M	I.W.	1896	Gaines	14521
9313	2 " Mittie A 29	Wife	26	F	1/8	1896	"	3992
9314	3 " Charles C 10	Son	7	M	1/16	1896	"	3993
9315	4 " Willis F 8	"	5	"	1/16	1896	"	3994
9316	5 " Lucius C Jr 7	"	4	"	1/16	1896	"	3995
9317	6 " Henry B 6	"	3	"	1/16	1896	"	3911
9318	7 " James T 4	"	8mo	"	1/16			
9319	8 " Edward M 2	"	1	"	1/16			
	9							
	10	ENROLLMENT						
	11	OF NOS. 2,3,4,5,6,7 and 8 HEREON APPROVED BY THE SECRETARY						
	12	OF INTERIOR Feb 4 1903						
	13	ENROLLMENT OF NOS 1 HEREON						
	14	APPROVED BY THE SECRETARY OF INTERIOR Sep 12 1903						
	15							
	16 For child of Nos 1&2 see NB (Mar 3-05) Card #578							
	17 For child of Nos 1&2 see NB (Apr 26-06) Card #524							

TRIBAL ENROLLMENT OF PARENTS

Name of Father	Year	County	Name of Mother	Year	County
1 C. H. Featherston	Dead	Non Citz	Nancy Featherston	Dead	Non Citz
2 J. W. Vaile	"	" "	Fannie Vaile		Atoka
3 No1			No2		
4 No1			No2		
5 No1			No2		
6 No1			No2		
7 No1			No2		
8 No.1			No.2		
9					
10 No1 was admitted by Dawes Com Case No 473 as					
11 L.C. Featherstone On 1896 roll as Luther B. Featherstone.					
12 No2 on 1896 roll as Mattie A. Featherstone					
12 No3 " 1896 " " Chas. C. "					
13 No4 " 1896 " " Willy F "				#1 to 7 inc.
14 No5 " 1896 " " Lucius C "			Date of Application for Enrollment.	
15 Nos 6-7 Affidavits of birth to be supplied:- Recd Oct 7/99			Aug 3/99	
16 No.8 born Sept 23d, 1900: Enrolled Oct 18th, 1901				
17					

Choctaw By Blood Enrollment Cards 1898-1914

RESIDENCE: Gaines COUNTY. **Choctaw Nation** Choctaw Roll CARD No.
POST OFFICE: Featherston, I.T. *(Not Including Freedmen)* FIELD No. 3227

Dawes' Roll No.	NAME	Relationship to Person	AGE	SEX	BLOOD	TRIBAL ENROLLMENT		
						Year	County	No.
9320	1 Hancock, Albert 24	First Named	21	M	3/4	1896	Gaines	5315
9321	2 " Doy Lee 2	Son	2mo	M	3/8			
9322	3 " William J Bryan 1	Son	2mo	M	3/8			
I.W. 1322	4 " Viola 22	Wife	22	F	I.W.			
	5							
	6 ENROLLMENT							
	7 OF NOS. 1, 2 and 3 HEREON							
	APPROVED BY THE SECRETARY							
	8 OF INTERIOR FEB 4 1903							
	9							
	10							
	11 ENROLLMENT							
	OF NOS. 4 HEREON							
	12 APPROVED BY THE SECRETARY							
	13 OF INTERIOR MAR 14 1905							
	14							
	15 For child of Nos 1&4 see NB (Apr 26-06) Card #328							
	16 " " " " " " " " (Mar 3-05) " #1403							
	17							

TRIBAL ENROLLMENT OF PARENTS

Name of Father	Year	County	Name of Mother	Year	County
1 Jonas Hancock	Dead	Sans Bois	Sophie Hancock	Dead	Sans Bois
2 No.1			Viola Hancock		Non-citizen
3 No.2			" "		" "
4 Sam Forgee	dead	noncitizen	Maggie Forgee	dead	" "
5					
6					
7					
8					
9					
10					
11 No.2 Enrolled June 27th, 1900					
12 No.3 Born Feby 26, 1902: Enrolled April 8, 1902					
13 Nº1 is husband of Viola Hancock Choctaw card #D.981					
Nos 1 and 4 were married Oct. 1, 1899					Date of Application for Enrollment.
14 No.4 originally listed for enrollment on Choctaw card D-					
15 981 Dec. 24, 1902: transferred to this card Jan 29, 1905			Aug 3/99		
16 See decision of Jan. 13, 1905.					
17					

Choctaw By Blood Enrollment Cards 1898-1914

RESIDENCE: Gaines   COUNTY. **Choctaw Nation**   **Choctaw Roll**   CARD NO.
POST OFFICE: Damon, I.T.   *(Not Including Freedmen)*   FIELD NO. 3228

Dawes' Roll No.	NAME		Relationship to Person	AGE	SEX	BLOOD	TRIBAL ENROLLMENT		
							Year	County	No.
9323	1 Davis, Minnie	18	First Named	15	F	Full	1896	Gaines	3272
	2								
	3								
	4								
	5	ENROLLMENT OF NOS. 1 HEREON							
	6	APPROVED BY THE SECRETARY OF INTERIOR FEB 4 1903							
	7								
	8								
	9								
	10								
	11								
	12								
	13								
	14								
	15								
	16								
	17								

TRIBAL ENROLLMENT OF PARENTS

	Name of Father	Year	County	Name of Mother	Year	County
1	William Davis	Dead	Gaines	Siney Davis	Dead	Gaines
2						
3						
4						
5						
6	For child of No.1 see NB (March 2, 1905) #869					
7						
8						
9						
10						
11						
12						
13						Date of Application for Enrollment.
14						
15						Aug 3/99
16						
17	P.O. Hartshorne IT 4/8/05					

228

Choctaw By Blood Enrollment Cards 1898-1914

RESIDENCE:	Sans Bois	COUNTY.								
POST OFFICE:	Sans Bois, I.T.	**Choctaw Nation**					Choctaw Roll (Not Including Freedmen)		CARD NO. FIELD NO. 3229	

Dawes' Roll No.	NAME		Relationship to Person	AGE	SEX	BLOOD	TRIBAL ENROLLMENT		
							Year	County	No.
9324	1 McGilberry, Abel	31	First Named	28	M	Full	1896	Sans Bois	8981
I.W. 302	2 " Nora	20	Wife	17	F	I.W.			
9325	3 " Charlie	9	Son	6	M	Full	1896	Sans Bois	8982
9326	4 " Pearl E	3	Dau	2mo	F	1/2			
9327	5 " Sampson	2	Son	2mo	M	1/2			
	6								
	7	ENROLLMENT OF NOS. 1,3,4 and 5 HEREON APPROVED BY THE SECRETARY OF INTERIOR FEB 4 1903							
	8								
	9								
	10	ENROLLMENT OF NOS. 2 HEREON APPROVED BY THE SECRETARY OF INTERIOR SEP 12 1903							
	11								
	12								
	13								
	14								
	15								
	16								
	17								

TRIBAL ENROLLMENT OF PARENTS

	Name of Father	Year	County	Name of Mother	Year	County
1	Chas McGilberry	Dead	Sans Bois	Annie McGilberry	Dead	Sans Bois
2	Frank Kelton		Non Citz	Emiline Kelton		Non Citz
3	No 1			Kittie McGilberry	Dead	Sans Bois
4	No 1			No 2		
5	No.1			No.2		
6						
7						
8	No.5 Enrolled March 15th, 1901					
9						
10						
11	No. 1 is in Pendetentiary [sic] at Leavenworth, Ks 12/28 '02					
12						
13						
14						Date of Application for Enrollment.
15						Aug 3/99
16						
17	P.O. Hartshorne I.T. 3/23/07					

RESIDENCE: Gaines COUNTY.								
POST OFFICE: Damon, I.T.								

Choctaw Nation — Choctaw Roll (Not Including Freedmen) — CARD NO. / FIELD NO. **3230**

Dawes' Roll No.	NAME		Relationship to Person First Named	AGE	SEX	BLOOD	TRIBAL ENROLLMENT Year	County	No.
9328	1 Taylor Charley	32	Named	29	M	Full	1893	Gaines	550
9329	2 " Rosa	35	Wife	32	F	"	1894	"	551
9330	3 " Ben	8	Son	5	M	"			
9331	4 " Jacob	6	"	3	"	"			
9332	5 Paxton Islan	16	S.Son	13	"	"	1893	Gaines	552
14797	6 Taylor Tracy	1	Dau	7mo	F	"			
	7								
	8	ENROLLMENT OF NOS. 1,2,3,4 and 5 HEREON APPROVED BY THE SECRETARY OF INTERIOR Feb 4 1903							
	9								
	10								
	11								
	12	ENROLLMENT OF NOS. 6 HEREON APPROVED BY THE SECRETARY OF INTERIOR May 20 1903							
	13								
	14								
	15								
	16								
	17								

TRIBAL ENROLLMENT OF PARENTS

	Name of Father	Year	County	Name of Mother	Year	County
1	Ya-ho-nubbee	Dead	Gaines	Beckey Hicks		Gaines
2	William Paxton	"	Sugar Loaf	Tennessee Taylor		"
3	No1			No2		
4	No1			No2		
5	Philip Paxton		Gaines	No2		
6	No1			No2		
7						
8	No1 on 1893 roll Page 59, No 550, Gaines Co.					
9	No2 " 1893 " " 59 " 551 " " as Rosy Taylor					
10	No5 " 1893 " " 59 " 552 " " as Islum Paxton					
11	No6 Born May 21, 1902, enrolled Dec. 24, 1902					
12	For child of Nos 1&2 see NB (Apr 26-06) Card #856					
13						#1 to 5
14					Date of Application for Enrollment.	
15					Aug 3/99	
16						
17	Wilburton					

Choctaw By Blood Enrollment Cards 1898-1914

RESIDENCE: Gaines	COUNTY.	**Choctaw Nation**	**Choctaw Roll** *(Not Including Freedmen)*	CARD NO.
POST OFFICE: Damon, I.T.				FIELD NO. 3231

Dawes' Roll No.	NAME	Relationship to Person	AGE	SEX	BLOOD	TRIBAL ENROLLMENT		
						Year	County	No.
9333	1 Taylor, Thomas ⁵³	First Named	50	M	Full	1896	Gaines	12002
9334	2 " Tennessee ⁵⁵	Wife	52	F	"	1893	"	541
	3							
	4							
	5	ENROLLMENT						
	6	OF NOS. 1 and 2 HEREON APPROVED BY THE SECRETARY						
	7	OF INTERIOR FEB 4 1903						
	8							
	9							
	10							
	11							
	12							
	13							
	14							
	15							
	16							
	17							

TRIBAL ENROLLMENT OF PARENTS

	Name of Father	Year	County	Name of Mother	Year	County
1	Ya-ho-nubbee	Dead	Gaines	Ba-o-na	Dead	Gaines
2	Chan-tubbee	"	Sugar Loaf	Char-la-hoke	"	"
3						
4						
5						
6						
7			See card # 37[?] & 3230			
8			No2 on 1892 Pay Roll, Page 58, No 541, Gaines Co			
9						
10						
11						
12						
13						
14					Date of Application for Enrollment.	
15					Aug 3/99	
16						
17						

Choctaw By Blood Enrollment Cards 1898-1914

RESIDENCE:	Tobucksy	COUNTY.		Choctaw Nation			Choctaw Roll		CARD NO.	
POST OFFICE:	Hartshorne, I.T.						(Not Including Freedmen)		FIELD NO.	3232

Dawes' Roll No.	NAME		Relationship to Person First Named	AGE	SEX	BLOOD	TRIBAL ENROLLMENT		
							Year	County	No.
DEAD.	₁ Carter, Jesse	DEAD.		47	M	Full	1896	Tobucksy	2314
9335	₂ " Rosa	20	Dau	17	F	"	1896	"	2317
15579	₃ Nail Eva	1	Dau of N°2	2½	F	1/2			
	4								
	5	ENROLLMENT OF NOS. 2 HEREON APPROVED BY THE SECRETARY							
	6	OF INTERIOR FEB 4 1903							
	7								
	8	ENROLLMENT OF NOS. 3 HEREON APPROVED BY THE SECRETARY							
	9	OF INTERIOR SEP 22 1904							
	10								
	11	No. 1 HEREON DISMISSED UNDER							
	12	ORDER OF THE COMMISSION TO THE FIVE							
	13	CIVILIZED TRIBES OF MARCH 31, 1905.							
	14								
	15								
	16								
	17								

TRIBAL ENROLLMENT OF PARENTS

Name of Father	Year	County	Name of Mother	Year	County
₁ Ah-tok-cubbee	Dead	Bok Tuklo	Me-a-le-hu-na	Dead	Bok Tuklo
₂ No1			Lucinda Carter	"	Gaines
₃ Silas W Nail	1896	Chickasaw	N°2		
4					
5					
6	N°2 on 1896 roll as Rosie Carter				
7	Wife and one child on Chickasaw Card #696				
8	Evidence of Death of Wife filed May 9th 1901				
9	Now husband of Frances Gardner In Choctaw Card #4827				
10	N°1 Died June 26, 1902: proof of death filed Aug 25, 1902				
11	N°3 Born June 29, 1901, application made at So M⁰Alester I.T. Dec 23, 1902. Proof of birth filed and N°3 enrolled April 23, 1904.				
12					
13	For child of No2 see NB (Mar 3-1905) Card #215.				
14				Date of Application for Enrollment.	
15				Aug 3/99	
16					
17					

Choctaw By Blood Enrollment Cards 1898-1914

RESIDENCE: Tobucksy COUNTY. **Choctaw Nation** Choctaw Roll CARD NO.
POST OFFICE: Hartshorne, I.T. (Not Including Freedmen) FIELD NO. 3233

Dawes' Roll No.	NAME		Relationship to Person First Named	AGE	SEX	BLOOD	TRIBAL ENROLLMENT		
							Year	County	No.
9336	1 Carter, Fannie	22	First Named	19	F	Full	1896	Tobucksy	2316
9337	2 " Julia	5	Dau	1	"	1/2			
9338	3 " Charlie	3	Son	2mo	M	3/4			
	4								
	5								
	6								
	7								
	8								
	9								
	10								
	11								
	12								
	13								
	14								
	15								
	16								
	17								

ENROLLMENT OF NOS. 1,2 and 3 HEREON APPROVED BY THE SECRETARY OF INTERIOR FEB 4 1903

TRIBAL ENROLLMENT OF PARENTS

Name of Father	Year	County	Name of Mother	Year	County
1 Jesse Carter		Tobucksy	Lucinda Carter	Dead	Tobucksy
2 Coleman Perry	Dead	Chickasaw	No1		
3 Silas Nail		Gaines	No1		
4					
5					
6					
7					
8					
9		[Illegible] Office letter Aug 24, 1910 D.C. #11051910			
10					
11		Nos2-3 Affidavits of birth			
12		to be supplied: Recd Aug 4/99.			
13					
14				Date of Application for Enrollment	
15			Date of Application for Enrollment.	Aug 3/99	
16					
17					

233

RESIDENCE:	Sans Bois	COUNTY.	**Choctaw Nation**	**Choctaw Roll**	CARD NO.	
POST OFFICE:	Enterprise, I.T.			*(Not Including Freedmen)*	FIELD NO.	3234

Dawes' Roll No.	NAME	Relationship to Person First Named	AGE	SEX	BLOOD	TRIBAL ENROLLMENT Year	County	No.
1	Smith, Mary E	Named	33	F	1/8			
2	" Nancy C	Dau	15	"	1/16			
3	" Minnie B	"	13	"	1/16			
4	" Mariah E	"	10	"	1/16			
5	" Viola	"	7	"	1/16			
6	" George A	Son	5	M	1/16			
7	" Sylvia L	"	3	"	1/16			
8	" Ethel L	Dau	1 1/2	F	1/16			
9	" Joicephine[sic]	Dau	1 3/4	F	1/16			
10	" Ida	Dau	6mo	F	1/16			
11								
12	Nos 1 to 7 inclusive denied in 96 Case #780							
13	Nos 1 to 7 incl No Appeal to C.C.C.C							
14								
15								
16								
17								

No.1 drd 8-6-0?

DISMISSED SEP 22 1904

TRIBAL ENROLLMENT OF PARENTS

	Name of Father	Year	County	Name of Mother	Year	County
1	F. A. Massey		Non Citz	Margaret Massey	Dead	Choctaw
2	Albert H Smith		" "	No 1		
3	" " "		" "	No 1		
4	" " "		" "	No 1		
5	" " "		" "	No 1		
6	" " "		" "	No 1		
7	" " "		" "	No 1		
8	" " "		" "	No 1		
9	" " "		" "	Nº 1		
10	" " "		" "	Nº 1		
11	Admitted by U.S. Court, Central Dist, Sept 10/99					
12	Case No 110. As to residence and birth of No8,					
13	see testimony of No1					
14	Judgment of U.S. Court admitting Nos 1 to 7 incl vacated and set aside by Decree of Choctaw Chickasaw Cir Court Dec 17/02					
15	No8 Affidavit of birth to be supplied·					
16	Recd Oct 7/99					
17	Nº9 Born April 1, 1900: enrolled Jan. 11, 1902. Nº10 Born Feby 19, 1902: enrolled Sept 4, 1902.				Date of Application for Enrollment. Aug 4/99	

Choctaw By Blood Enrollment Cards 1898-1914

RESIDENCE:	Sugar Loaf	COUNTY.							

Choctaw Nation

Choctaw Roll *(Not Including Freedmen)*

POST OFFICE: Cavanal, I.T.

CARD NO. FIELD NO. **3235**

Dawes' Roll No.	NAME	Relationship to Person First Named	AGE	SEX	BLOOD	TRIBAL ENROLLMENT		
						Year	County	No.
✓ * 1	McFarland, Sarah		38	F	1/8			
* 2	Walters, Thomas	Son	19	M	1/16			
3								
4	Denied Citizenship by the Choctaw-Chickasaw Citizenship							
5	Court Feb 1 '04							
6								
7								

Judgement[sic] of U.S. Court C.D. admitting Nos 1&2 vacated and set aside
by Decree of Choctaw Chickasaw Citizenship Court Decr 17 '02   Nos 1&2
Denied by Choctaw-Chickasaw Citizenship Court Feb 1st 1904 – Case #13

10								
11								
12								
13								
14								
15								
16								
17								

TRIBAL ENROLLMENT OF PARENTS

	Name of Father	Year	County	Name of Mother	Year	County
1	J. A. Webb	Dead	Non Citz	Elizabeth Deaton		Choctaw
2	Thos Walters		" "	No 1		
3						
4						
5						
6						
7						
8						
9						
10	Nos 1&2 Denied by Dawes Com in 1896 Choc Cit Case #598					
11	Admitted by U.S. Court, Central Dist,					
12	July 24/97 Case No 94. As to residence					
13	see testimony of No.1					
14	The above notation is an error, No.2 was admitted as a citizen by blood by U.S. Court, Central District, South McAlester					
15	I.T. January 19, 1898, Court Case #94. No1 was denied in the same case				Date of Application for Enrollment.	
16	but by a nunc protune order was admitted by U.S. Court July 24 1899				Aug 4/99	
17	as Sarah E McFarland					

235

Choctaw By Blood Enrollment Cards 1898-1914

RESIDENCE: Gaines COUNTY. **Choctaw Nation** Choctaw Roll CARD NO.
POST OFFICE: Hartshorne, I.T. (Not Including Freedmen) FIELD NO. 3236

Dawes' Roll No.	NAME	Relationship to Person First Named	AGE	SEX	BLOOD	TRIBAL ENROLLMENT Year	County	No.
I.W. 303	1 Stallings, Jared A ㉜		28	M	I.W			
9339	2 " Carrie M 22	Wife	19	F	1/8	1896	Gaines	10729
9340	3 " Isabelle 4	Dau	9mo	"	1/16			
	4							
	5							
	6	ENROLLMENT OF NOS. 2 and 3 HEREON						
	7	APPROVED BY THE SECRETARY						
	8	OF INTERIOR FEB 4 1903						
	9	ENROLLMENT OF NOS. 1 HEREON						
	10	APPROVED BY THE SECRETARY						
	11	OF INTERIOR SEP 12 1903						
	12							
	13							
	14							
	15							
	16							
	17							

TRIBAL ENROLLMENT OF PARENTS

	Name of Father	Year	County	Name of Mother	Year	County
1	Jas E Stallings	Dead	Non Citz	Malissa H Stallings		Non Citz
2	A. Frank Ross		Blue	Emma Ross		" "
3	No1			No2		
4						
5						
6	No2 on 1896 roll as Carrie May Ross					
7						
8	No2 Parents were admitted by Act of Council of Nov 7 1888					
9	No proof of marriage therefore necessary					
10	No3 Affidavit of birth to be supplied: Recd					
11	Aug 9/99					
12	For child of Nos 1&2 see NB (March 3-1905) #137					
13						
14					Date of Application for Enrollment.	
15					Aug 4/99	
16						
17						

Choctaw By Blood Enrollment Cards 1898-1914

RESIDENCE:	Gaines	COUNTY.							
POST OFFICE:	Hartshorne, I.T.								

Choctaw Nation

Choctaw Roll (Not Including Freedmen)

CARD NO. FIELD NO. 3237

Dawes' Roll No.	NAME		Relationship to Person First Named	AGE	SEX	BLOOD	TRIBAL ENROLLMENT		
							Year	County	No.
I.W. 304	1 Wallace, Robert	24	First Named	21	M	I.W			
9341	2 " Myrtle	20	Wife	17	F	1/8	1896	Gaines	834
	3								
	4								
	5	ENROLLMENT							
	6	OF NOS. 2 HEREON APPROVED BY THE SECRETARY							
	7	OF INTERIOR FEB 4 1903							
	8	ENROLLMENT							
	9	OF NOS. 1 HEREON APPROVED BY THE SECRETARY							
	10	OF INTERIOR SEP 12 1903							
	11								
	12								
	13								
	14								
	15								
	16								
	17								

TRIBAL ENROLLMENT OF PARENTS

Name of Father	Year	County	Name of Mother	Year	County
1 Jno Wallace	Dead	Non Citz	Sarah Wallace	Dead	Non Citz
2 Allen Beagles		" "	Annie Beagles		Gaines
3					
4					
5					
6					
7	No2 on 1896 roll as Myrtle Beagles				
8	For child of Nos 1 and 2 see NB (March 3,1905) #1254				
9					
10					
11					
12	No1 See his testimony as to remarriage				
13					
14				Date of Application for Enrollment.	
15				Aug 4/99	
16					
17	P.O. Legal, I.T. 11/19/02				

Choctaw By Blood Enrollment Cards 1898-1914

RESIDENCE: **Sans Bois** COUNTY. **Choctaw Nation** **Choctaw Roll** CARD NO.
POST OFFICE: **Sans Bois,** I.T. *(Not Including Freedmen)* FIELD NO. **3238**

Dawes' Roll No.	NAME	Relationship to Person First Named	AGE	SEX	BLOOD	TRIBAL ENROLLMENT Year	County	No.
9342	1 Hischa, Sampson 21		18	M	Full	1896	Sans Bois	5079
	2							
	3							
	4							
	5							
	6							
	7							
	8							
	9							
	10							
	11							
	12							
	13							
	14							
	15							
	16							
	17							

ENROLLMENT
OF NOS. 1 HEREON
APPROVED BY THE SECRETARY
OF INTERIOR FEB 4 1903

TRIBAL ENROLLMENT OF PARENTS

	Name of Father	Year	County	Name of Mother	Year	County
1	Chas Hischa	Dead	Sans Bois	Rachel King		Sans Bois
2						
3						
4						
5						
6			On 1896 roll as Sampson Hecha			
7						
8						
9						
10						
11						
12						
13						
14				Date of Application for Enrollment.		
15						
16						
17						

RESIDENCE:	Sans Bois	COUNTY.							CARD NO.	
POST OFFICE:	Featherston, I.T.	**Choctaw Nation**				**Choctaw Roll** *(Not Including Freedmen)*			FIELD NO.	3239

Dawes' Roll No.	NAME		Relationship to Person	AGE	SEX	BLOOD	TRIBAL ENROLLMENT		
							Year	County	No.
9343	₁ Hancock, Loran	21	First Named	18	M	Full	1896	Gaines	5267
	2								
	3								
	4	ENROLLMENT							
	5	OF NOS. 1 HEREON APPROVED BY THE SECRETARY							
	6	OF INTERIOR FEB 4 1903							
	7								
	8								
	9								
	10								
	11								
	12								
	13								
	14								
	15								
	16								
	17								

TRIBAL ENROLLMENT OF PARENTS

Name of Father	Year	County	Name of Mother	Year	County
₁ Jonas Hancock	Dead	Sans Bois	Sophie Hancock	Dead	Sans Bois
2					
3					
4					
5					
6					
7					
8					
9	On 1896 roll as Lorin Hancock				
10					
11					
12					
13	No.1 is now husband of Jane Nelson on Choc Card #309				
14				Date of Application for Enrollment.	
15				Aug 4/99	
16					
17					

Choctaw By Blood Enrollment Cards 1898-1914

RESIDENCE:	Chickasaw Natn ~~COUNTY.~~								

Choctaw Nation

POST OFFICE: Atlee, I.T. **Choctaw Roll** *(Not Including Freedmen)* CARD No. FIELD No. 3240

Dawes' Roll No.	NAME	Relationship to Person	AGE	SEX	BLOOD	TRIBAL ENROLLMENT Year	County	No.
9344	1 Woods, Hattie 26	First Named	23	F	1/8	1893	Kiamitia	41
~~9345~~	2 ~~DIED PRIOR TO SEPTEMBER 25,1902 Mollie L~~	~~Dau~~	~~5~~	"	~~1/16~~			
9346	3 " Willie M 7	Son	3	M	1/16			
9347	4 " Edgar 6	"	1	"	1/16			

ENROLLMENT
OF NOS. 1,2,3 and 4 HEREON
APPROVED BY THE SECRETARY
OF INTERIOR FEB 4 1903

TRIBAL ENROLLMENT OF PARENTS

	Name of Father	Year	County	Name of Mother	Year	County
1	Stewart	Dead	Wade	Siss Stewart	Dead	Wade
2	~~George Woods~~		~~Non Citz~~	~~No 1~~		
3	" "		" "	No 1		
4	" "		" "	No 1		

No1 on 1893 Pay Roll, Page 116, No 41, Kiamitia County, as Hattie Stewart
No2 died April 2, 1900; Enrollment cancelled by Department July 8, 1904
Nos 2-3-4 Affidavits of birth to be supplied; Recd Oct 7/99
For child of No.1 see NB (March 3 1905) #1451

Date of Application for Enrollment. Aug 4/99

240

Choctaw By Blood Enrollment Cards 1898-1914

RESIDENCE: Jacks Fork COUNTY.
POST OFFICE: Stringtown, I.T.

Choctaw Nation

Choctaw Roll (Not Including Freedmen)

CARD NO.
FIELD NO. **3241**

Dawes' Roll No.	NAME		Relationship to Person	AGE	SEX	BLOOD	TRIBAL ENROLLMENT		
							Year	County	No.
9348	1 Baker Logan	47	First Named	44	M	Full	1896	Jacks Fork	1936
9349	2 " Mary A	24	Wife	21	F	"	1896	Gaines	6580
9350	3 Doctor Levina	23	Dau	20	"	"	1896	Jacks Fork	1938
9351	4 Baker Siney	18	"	15	"	"	1896	" "	1940
9352	5 " Annie	15	"	12	"	"	1896	" "	1941
9353	6 " Jane	13	"	10	"	"	1896	" "	1942
9354	7 " Lena	9	"	6	"	"	1896	" "	1943
9355	8 " Winnie	3	"	4mo	"	"			
9356	9 " Emma	1	"	4mo	"	"			
9357	10 Doctor Rosa	1	Dau of No3	1	F	1/2			
	11								
	12								
	13								
	14								
	15								
	16								
	17								

ENROLLMENT
OF NOS. 1,2,3,4,5,6,7,8,9 and 10 HEREON
APPROVED BY THE SECRETARY
OF INTERIOR Feb 4 1903

See Cards 3100 & 4217
& & NB 1154

TRIBAL ENROLLMENT OF PARENTS

	Name of Father	Year	County	Name of Mother	Year	County
1		Dead	in Mississippi	Sukey Baker	Dead	Jacks Fork
2	Sam James	"	Jacks Fork	Julia James	"	Gaines
3	No1			Millie Baker	"	Jacks Fork
4	No1			" "	"	" " "
5	No1			" "	"	" " "
6	No1			" "	"	" " "
7	No1			" "	"	" " "
8	No.1			No. 2		
9	Nº1			Nº 2		
10	James Doctor		Chickasaw	No 3		
11	No2 on 1896 roll as Mary A James					
12	No3 " 1896 " ' Leona Baker					
13	No7 " 1896 " ' Millie "				#1 to 7 inc	
14	No.8 Enrolled June 4th, 1900				Date of Application for Enrollment.	
15	Nº9 Born Dec 2 1901: enrolled May 1, 1902				Aug 4/99	
16	No10 born Nov 11, 1901: enrolled December 15, 1902					
16	No3 now wife of James Doctor on Chick Freedman Card 970: evidence of marriage filed Dec 29, 1902					
17	No3 PO Ti IT 4/10/05 For child of No 3 see NB (March 3, 1905) #836					

No1 PO Ti IT 4/10/05 " " " Nos1&2 " " " " " #1154

241

Choctaw By Blood Enrollment Cards 1898-1914

RESIDENCE:	Tobucksy	COUNTY.						CARD NO.	
POST OFFICE:	Hartshorne, I.T.		Choctaw Nation (Not Including Freedmen)	Choctaw Roll				FIELD NO. 3242	

Dawes' Roll No.	NAME	Relationship to Person	AGE	SEX	BLOOD	TRIBAL ENROLLMENT		
						Year	County	No.
9358	1 Harmby, Anderson 18	First Named	15	M	Full	1896	Tobucksy	5334
	2							
	3							
	4							
	5							
	6							
	7							
	8							
	9							
	10	ENROLLMENT OF NOS. 1 HEREON APPROVED BY THE SECRETARY OF INTERIOR FEB 4 1903						
	11							
	12							
	13							
	14							
	15							
	16							
	17							

TRIBAL ENROLLMENT OF PARENTS

	Name of Father	Year	County	Name of Mother	Year	County
1	Louis Harmby	Dead	Bok Tuklo	Melinda Taylor		Gaines
2						
3						
4						
5						
6						
7						
8						
9						
10						
11						
12						
13						
14				Date of Application for Enrollment.	Aug 4/99	
15						
16						
17						

Choctaw By Blood Enrollment Cards 1898-1914

RESIDENCE: Tobucksy COUNTY.	POST OFFICE: Alderson, I.T.

Choctaw Nation

Choctaw Roll
(Not Including Freedmen)

CARD NO.
FIELD NO. 3243

Dawes' Roll No.	NAME	Relationship to Person First Named	AGE	SEX	BLOOD	TRIBAL ENROLLMENT		
						Year	County	No.
1	Quinn, Patrick W		52	M	I.W	1896	Tobucksy	14953
2								
3								
4	Can't locate							
5								
6	See O. A. [illegible]							
7								
8								
9								
10	DISMISSED DEC 11 1906							
11								
12								
13								
14								
15								
16								
17								

TRIBAL ENROLLMENT OF PARENTS

	Name of Father	Year	County	Name of Mother	Year	County
1	James Quinn	Dead	Non Citz	Elizabeth Quinn	Dead	Non Citz
2						
3						
4						
5						
6						
7			On 1896 roll as P. W. Queen. Admitted by			
8			Dawes Com as an intermarried citizen Case			
9			No 1150 as P. W. Quinn			
10						
11			No1 died October 3, 1901: Proof of death filed Dec 10 1906			
12						
13						
14					Date of Application for Enrollment.	
15					Aug 4/99	
16						
17						

Choctaw By Blood Enrollment Cards 1898-1914

RESIDENCE: Gaines   COUNTY. **Choctaw Nation**   **Choctaw Roll**   CARD No.
POST OFFICE: Kiowa, I.T.   (Not Including Freedmen)   FIELD NO. 3244

Dawes' Roll No.	NAME	Relationship to Person First Named	AGE	SEX	BLOOD	TRIBAL ENROLLMENT		
						Year	County	No.
9359	1 Baker, Solomon 62		59	M	Full	1896	Jacks Fork	1917
	2							
	3							
	4							
	5	ENROLLMENT OF NOS. 1 HEREON APPROVED BY THE SECRETARY OF INTERIOR FEB 4 1903						
	6							
	7							
	8							
	9							
	10							
	11							
	12							
	13							
	14							
	15							
	16							
	17							

TRIBAL ENROLLMENT OF PARENTS

Name of Father	Year	County	Name of Mother	Year	County
1 Bob Baker	Dead	Blue		Dead	in Mississippi
2					
3					
4					
5					
6					
7					
8					
9					
10					
11					
12					
13					
14				Date of Application for Enrollment.	
15				Aug 4/99	
16					
17 P.O. Blanco, I.T. 12/24/02					

Choctaw By Blood Enrollment Cards 1898-1914

| RESIDENCE: Gaines COUNTY. | | | **Choctaw Nation** | | | **Choctaw Roll** (Not Including Freedmen) | | CARD No. FIELD No. 3245 | |
| POST OFFICE: Kiowa, I.T. | | | | | | | | | |

Dawes' Roll No.	NAME		Relationship to Person	AGE	SEX	BLOOD	TRIBAL ENROLLMENT		
							Year	County	No.
14798	1 Baker Sarah	32	First Named	29	F	Full	1896	Jacks Fork	1895
14799	2 " Rose	5	Dau	2	"	"			
	3								
	4	ENROLLMENT							
	5	OF NOS. 1 and 2 HEREON							
	6	APPROVED BY THE SECRETARY OF INTERIOR MAY 20 1903							
	7								
	8								
	9								
	10								
	11								
	12								
	13								
	14								
	15								
	16								
	17								

TRIBAL ENROLLMENT OF PARENTS

Name of Father	Year	County	Name of Mother	Year	County
1 Solomon Baker		Gaines	Un-na-he-ma	Dead	Blue
2 Namon Fobb		Jacks Fork	No1		
3					
4					
5					
6					
7					
8					
9					
10					
11					
12					
13					
14					
15			Date of Application for Enrollment.	Aug 4/99	
16					
17					

Choctaw By Blood Enrollment Cards 1898-1914

RESIDENCE:	Gaines	COUNTY.	**Choctaw Nation**	**Choctaw Roll** (Not Including Freedmen)	CARD NO.
POST OFFICE:	Damon, I.T.				FIELD NO. 3246

Dawes' Roll No.	NAME		Relationship to Person	AGE	SEX	BLOOD	TRIBAL ENROLLMENT		
							Year	County	No.
9360	1 Hicks, Smith M	53	First Named	50	M	Full	1896	Gaines	5275
DEAD.	2 " Becky		Wife	50	F	"	1896	"	5276
	3								
	4								
	5								
	6								
	7								
	8								
	9								
	10								
	11								
	12								
	13								
	14								
	15								
	16								
	17								

ENROLLMENT
OF NOS. 1 HEREON
APPROVED BY THE SECRETARY
OF INTERIOR FEB 4 1903

No. 2 HEREON DISMISSED UNDER
ORDER OF THE COMMISSION TO THE FIVE
CIVILIZED TRIBES OF MARCH 31, 1905.

TRIBAL ENROLLMENT OF PARENTS

	Name of Father	Year	County	Name of Mother	Year	County
1	John Smith		Mississippi	E-la-le-sa-ho-ke		Wade
2	Wallace McGilberry	Dead	Gaines	Ho-te-ma	Dead	Gaines
3						
4						
5						
6						
7		No1 on 1896 roll as Smith Mc Hicks				
8						
9		No2 died Sept 5, 1899; proof of death filed Dec 19 1902				
10						
11		No.1 died about Jany 27, 1905.				
12						
13						
14					Date of Application for Enrollment.	
15					Aug 4/99	
16						
17						

Choctaw By Blood Enrollment Cards 1898-1914

	RESIDENCE: Gaines COUNTY.	POST OFFICE: Damon, I.T.

Choctaw Nation   Choctaw Roll (Not Including Freedmen)

CARD NO. FIELD NO. **3247**

Dawes' Roll No.	NAME		Relationship to Person	AGE	SEX	BLOOD	Year	County	No.
9361	1 Harvey, Green	36	First Named	33	M	Full	1896	Gaines	5268
9362	2 " Willy	20	Son	17	"	"	1896	"	5270
9363	3 " Jonas	17	"	14	"	"	1896	"	5271
9364	4 " Sissie	16	Dau	13	F	"	1896	"	5272
9365	5 " Beard	12	Son	9	M	"	1896	"	5273
9266	6 " Clydas	9	Dau	6	F	"	1896	"	5274
	7								
	8								
	9	ENROLLMENT OF NOS. 1,2,3,4,5 and 6 HEREON							
	10	APPROVED BY THE SECRETARY OF INTERIOR FEB 4 1903							
	11								
	12								
	13								
	14								
	15								
	16								
	17								

TRIBAL ENROLLMENT OF PARENTS

	Name of Father	Year	County	Name of Mother	Year	County
1	E-la-pa-ha-nubbee	Dead	Gaines	Chum-pa	Dead	Gaines
2	No1			Ellen Harvey	"	"
3	No1			" "	"	"
4	No1			" "	"	"
5	No1			" "	"	"
6	No1			" "	"	"
7						
8	No5 on 1896 roll as Johnnie Harvey					
9	No6 " 1896 " " Clatis		"			
10	Correct age of No2 is 21 See his testimony taken May 26, 1903					
11						
12	No.6 Name changed from "Gladys" to "Clydas"					
13	under Departmental authority of March 24, 1906					
14	(I.T.D. 4766-1906) D.C. 11750-1906)				Date of Application for Enrollment.	
15					Aug 4/99	
16						
17	No1 P.O. Hugo OK 4/29/0?					

Choctaw By Blood Enrollment Cards 1898-1914

RESIDENCE: Gaines   COUNTY. **Choctaw Nation**   Choctaw Roll   CARD NO.
POST OFFICE: Damon, I.T.   *(Not Including Freedmen)*   FIELD NO. **3248**

Dawes' Roll No.	NAME		Relationship to Person First Named	AGE	SEX	BLOOD	TRIBAL ENROLLMENT Year	County	No.
9367	1	Pusley, Adam	DIED PRIOR TO SEPTEMBER 25 1902	34	M	Full	1896	Gaines	10192
9368	2	" Elizabeth ²⁷	Wife	24	F	"	1896	Sugar Loaf	6551
9369	3	" Murtie ¹⁵	Dau	12	"	"	1896	Gaines	10194
9370	4	" George ¹³	Son	10	M	"	1896	"	10195
9371	5	" Cornelia ⁹	Dau	6	F	"	1896	"	10197
9372	6	Cephus	DIED PRIOR TO SEPTEMBER 25 1902 Son	4	M	"	1896	"	10198
9373	7	Lewis Harriet ⁷	S.Dau	4	F	"	1896	Sugar Loaf	7778
9374	8	Pusley Lou ²	Dau	19mo	F	"			
	9								
	10								
	11	ENROLLMENT							
	12	OF NOS. 1,2,3,4,5,6,7 and 8 HEREON APPROVED BY THE SECRETARY							
	13	OF INTERIOR Feb 4 1903							
	14								
	15								
	16								
	17								

TRIBAL ENROLLMENT OF PARENTS

	Name of Father	Year	County	Name of Mother	Year	County
1	Calvin Pusley	Dead	Gaines	Sa-to-na	Dead	Sugar Loaf
2	Jim Jones		Sugar Loaf	Lizann Jones	"	" "
3	No1			Sillie Pusley	"	Gaines
4	No1			" "	"	"
5	No1			" "	"	"
6	No1			" "	"	"
7	Alick Lewis		Sugar Loaf	No2		
8	Nº1			Nº2		
9						
10						
11	No2 on 1896 roll as Elizabeth Jones					
12	No3 ' 1896 " " Mattie Pusley					
13	No6 ' 1896 " " Cephas "					
	Nº8 Born Oct 3, 1900. enrolled May 16, 1902					
14	Nº1 Died June 17, 1900: proof of death filed Dec 20 1902 filed Dec 31, 1902					
15	No.1 died June 17, 1900: No6 died Oct - 1900: Enrollment cancelled by Department #1 to 7 inc.					
16	July 8, 1904				Date of Application for Enrollment.	
17					Aug 4/99	

Choctaw By Blood Enrollment Cards 1898-1914

RESIDENCE: Gaines COUNTY.								
POST OFFICE: Wilburton, I.T.	**Choctaw Nation**		Choctaw Roll *(Not Including Freedmen)*			CARD NO. FIELD NO. 3249		

Dawes' Roll No.	NAME	Relationship to Person First Named	AGE	SEX	BLOOD	TRIBAL ENROLLMENT		
						Year	County	No.
9375	1 Hunter, Cicilia 50	First Named	47	F	3/8	1896	Gaines	5304
DEAD.	2 " William W DEAD.	Son	19	M	3/16	1896	"	5306
DEAD.	3 " Scaly C DEAD.	Dau	15	F	3/16	1896	"	5308
9376	4 " Pearly J 15	"	12	"	3/16	1896	"	5309
9377	5 " Bernina 13	"	10	"	3/16	1896	"	5310
9378	6 " Clayton W 11	Son	8	M	3/16	1896	"	5311
	7							
	8							
	9 ENROLLMENT OF NOS. 1,4,5 and 6 HEREON							
	10 APPROVED BY THE SECRETARY OF INTERIOR FEB 4 1903							
	11							
	12							
	13 No. 2 and 3 HEREON DISMISSED UNDER							
	14 ORDER OF THE COMMISSION TO THE FIVE							
	15 CIVILIZED TRIBES OF MARCH 31, 1905.							
	16							
	17							

TRIBAL ENROLLMENT OF PARENTS

	Name of Father	Year	County	Name of Mother	Year	County
1	Ward Folsom	Dead	Skullyville	Eliz. Folsom	Dead	Skullyville
2	Wallace Hunter		Non Citz	No1		
3	" "		" "	No1		
4	" "		" "	No1		
5	" "		" "	No1		
6	" "		" "	No1		
7						
8						
9						
10	No1 on 1896 roll as Sissilia Hunter					
11	No2 " 1896 " " Wm W. "					
12	No3 " 1896 " " Silvey P. "					
13	No4 " 1896 " " Pearl J "					
14	No5 " 1896 " " Perriney "			Date of Application for Enrollment.		
15	No.2 Died Sept 15, 1899: Proof of death filed Dec 23, 1902					
16	No.3 " Oct. 12, 1899: " " " " " 23, 1903			Aug 4/99		
17	as "Saly"					

249

Choctaw By Blood Enrollment Cards 1898-1914

RESIDENCE: Gaines   COUNTY. **Choctaw Nation**   **Choctaw Roll**   CARD NO.
POST OFFICE: Wilburton, I.T.   *(Not Including Freedmen)*   FIELD NO.   3250

Dawes' Roll No.	NAME	Relationship to Person First Named	AGE	SEX	BLOOD	TRIBAL ENROLLMENT		
						Year	County	No.
9379	1 Fetter, Abigail 24	First Named	21	F	3/16	1896	Gaines	5305
9380	2 " Ema Pocahontas 3	dau	3mo	F	3/32			
9381	3 " Nora Cecelia 1	dau	1mo	F	3/32			
	4							
	5							
	6							
	7							
	8							
	9							
	10							
	11							
	12							
	13							
	14							
	15							
	16							
	17							

ENROLLMENT
OF NOS. 1,2 and 3 HEREON
APPROVED BY THE SECRETARY
OF INTERIOR FEB 4 1903

TRIBAL ENROLLMENT OF PARENTS

	Name of Father	Year	County	Name of Mother	Year	County
1	Wallace Hunter		Non Citz	Cicilia Hunter		Gaines
2	O B Fetter		" "	No1		
3	Oliver B Fetter		non-citizen	No. 1		
4						
5						
6						
7						
8	On 1896 roll as Abigail Hunter.					
9						
10	No.3 born Dec. 30, 1901: Enrolled Jany. 20, 1902					
11	For child of No1 see NB (Mar 3-1905) Card #222					
12						
13						Date of Application for Enrollment.
14						
15			No2 enrolled 6/5/1900		Aug 4/99	
16						
17	P.O. Lutie, I.T. 12/9/02					

Choctaw By Blood Enrollment Cards 1898-1914

RESIDENCE: Gaines COUNTY. **Choctaw Nation** Choctaw Roll CARD No.
POST OFFICE: Wilburton, I.T. (Not Including Freedmen) FIELD No. 3251

Dawes' Roll No.	NAME	Relationship to Person	AGE	SEX	BLOOD	TRIBAL ENROLLMENT		
						Year	County	No.
9382	1 Graham, Emma E 20	First Named	17	F	3/16	1896	Gaines	5307
9383	2 " Artemissa 3	Dau	1mo	"	3/32			
DEAD.	3 " Mintissa	"	1mo	"	3/32			
9384	4 " Bessie Cicilia 1	"	3mo	"	3/32			
	5							
	6							
	7							
	8	ENROLLMENT						
	9	OF NOS. 1,2 and 4 HEREON APPROVED BY THE SECRETARY						
	10	OF INTERIOR FEB 4 1903						
	11							
	12	No. 3 HEREON DISMISSED UNDER						
	13	ORDER OF THE COMMISSION TO THE FIVE CIVILIZED TRIBES OF MARCH 31, 1905						
	14							
	15							
	16							
	17							

TRIBAL ENROLLMENT OF PARENTS

Name of Father	Year	County	Name of Mother	Year	County
1 Wallace Hunter		Non Citz	Cicilia Hunter		Gaines
2 E. L. Graham		" "	No1		
3 " " "		" "	No1		
4 " " "		" "	No1		
5					
6					
7					
8		No1 on 1896 roll as Emily I. Hunter			
9		No4 Enrolled Aug 6, 1901			
10		No.3 Died Dec. 5, 1899: Proof of death filed Dec 24 1902			
11		For child of No1 see NB (Apr 26-06) Card #60 " " " " " (Mar 3-1905) " #1206			
12					
13					
14				Date of Application for Enrollment.	
15				Aug 4/99	
16					
17 P.O. Wapanucka 1/22/05					

Choctaw By Blood Enrollment Cards 1898-1914

RESIDENCE: Gaines COUNTY. **Choctaw Nation** Choctaw Roll CARD NO.
POST OFFICE: Hartshorne, I.T. 3252 (Not Including Freedmen) FIELD NO.

Dawes' Roll No.	NAME		Relationship to Person	AGE	SEX	BLOOD	TRIBAL ENROLLMENT		
							Year	County	No.
9385	1 Nelson, Jackson F	33	First Named	30	M	7/8	1896	Gaines	9590
9386	2 " Emma C	23	Wife	20	F	1/2	1896	"	9591
15580	3 " Garrett E	5	Son	3	M	11/16			
15581	4 " Roy M	3	"	7mo	"	11/16			
9387	5 " Richard	17	Bro	14	M	1/2	1896	Gaines	9594
9388	6 " Alice	14	Sister	11	F	1/2	1896	"	9595
9389	7 " Adolphus B	3	Son	1yr 8mo	M	11/16			
9390	8 " Andrew J	1	"	3 "	"	11/16			
	9								
	10					ENROLLMENT			
	11	ENROLLMENT			OF NOS. 3 and 4 HEREON APPROVED BY THE SECRETARY				
	12	OF NOS. 1,2,5,6,7 and 8 HEREON APPROVED BY THE SECRETARY			OF INTERIOR SEP 22 1904				
	13	OF INTERIOR FEB 4 1903							
	14								
	15	N°3 Born Jany 27, 1897: proof of birth filed May 20, 1904							
	16	N°4 Born Jany 1, 1899: proof of birth filed May 20, 1904							
	17								

TRIBAL ENROLLMENT OF PARENTS

	Name of Father	Year	County	Name of Mother	Year	County
1	Simon Nelson	Dead	Gaines	Elizabeth Nelson	Dead	Gaines
2	Jos Pitchlynn	"	"	Rebecca Pitchlynn	"	"
3	No1			No.2		
4	No1			No. 2		
5	Simon Nelson	Dead	Gaines	Rebecca Nelson	Dead	Gaines
6	" "	"	"	" "	"	"
7	No.1			No 2		
8	No.1			No. 2		
9						
10	No1 on 1896 roll as Jack F Nelson					
11	No5 " 1896 " ' Johnnie "					
12	No6 " 1896 " ' Allie "					
13	Nos 3-4 Affidavits of birth to be					
14	supplied: For child of Nos 1&2 see NB (March 3,1905) #1425					
15	No.7 Born April 4,1901: Application made Dec 24/02			Date of Application for Enrollment.		Aug 4/99
16	No.8 " Sept 19,1902: " " 24/02					↘1 to 6 inc
17	Proof of birth of Nos 7 and 8 filed March 7, 1903.					
	PO Coleman IT 5/1/05					

'Craig I.T.

252

RESIDENCE: **Gaines** COUNTY. **Choctaw Nation** **Choctaw Roll** *(Not Including Freedmen)* CARD NO.
POST OFFICE: **Hartshorne, I.T.** FIELD NO. **3253**

Dawes' Roll No.	NAME		Relationship to Person	AGE	SEX	BLOOD	TRIBAL ENROLLMENT		
							Year	County	No.
9391	₁ James, Mary A.	32	First Named	29	F	Full	1896	Gaines	6579
9392	₂ " William S	9	Son	6	M	3/4	1896	"	6581
9393	₃ " Samuel M	8	"	5	"	3/4	1896	"	6582
9394	₄ " Yancey L	6	"	3	"	3/4	1896	"	6583
9395	₅ " George G	4	"	1	"	3/4			
	6								
	7								
	8	ENROLLMENT							
	9	OF NOS. 1,2,4 and 5 HEREON APPROVED BY THE SECRETARY							
	10	OF INTERIOR Feb 4 1903							
	11								
	12								
	13	No.1 = "Died prior to September 25, 1902;							
	14	not entitled to land or money."							
	15	(See Indian Office letter of July 23 1910, D.C. #1045-1910)							
	16								
	17								

TRIBAL ENROLLMENT OF PARENTS

	Name of Father	Year	County	Name of Mother	Year	County
₁	Solomon Baker		Gaines	Sophia Baker	Dead	Atoka
₂	Samuel James	Dead	"	No 1		
₃	" "	"	"	No 1		
₄	" "	"	"	No 1		
₅	" "	"	"	No 1		
₆						
₇						
₈			No1 on 1896 roll as Mary Ann James			
₉			No2 1896 " " Wᵐ Solomon "			
₁₀			No4 1896 " " Roy "			
₁₁						
₁₂						
₁₃						
₁₄					Date of Application for Enrollment.	
₁₅					Aug 4/99	
₁₆						
₁₇						

Choctaw By Blood Enrollment Cards 1898-1914

RESIDENCE:	Atoka	COUNTY.					Choctaw Roll	CARD NO.	
POST OFFICE:	Citra, I.T.	**Choctaw Nation**					(Not Including Freedmen)	FIELD NO.	3254

Dawes' Roll No.	NAME	Relationship to Person	AGE	SEX	BLOOD	TRIBAL ENROLLMENT		
						Year	County	No.
9396	1 Frazier, Amanda 22	First Named	19	F	1/2	1896	Atoka	4492
9397	2 " Thompson 20	Bro	17	M	1/2	1896	"	4490
9398	3 " Impson 18	Bro	15	"	1/2	1896	"	4491
	4							
	5							
	6 ENROLLMENT							
	7 OF NOS. 1-2 and 3 HEREON APPROVED BY THE SECRETARY							
	8 OF INTERIOR FEB 4 1903							
	9							
	10							
	11							
	12							
	13							
	14							
	15							
	16							
	17							

TRIBAL ENROLLMENT OF PARENTS

Name of Father	Year	County	Name of Mother	Year	County
1 Andy Frazier		Freedman	Susan Frazier	Dead	Atoka
2 " "		"	" "	"	"
3 " "		"	" "	"	"
4					
5					
6					
7					
8 No 1 on 1896 roll as Maudie Frazier					
9 N°2 is now the husband of Lona Mishontombe on Choctaw card #3263	Nov. 19, 1902.				
10 For child of No2 see NB (Mar 3 1905) #640					
11					
12					
13					
14				Date of Application for Enrollment.	
15				Aug 7/99	
16					
17					

Choctaw By Blood Enrollment Cards 1898-1914

RESIDENCE: Atoka COUNTY.		Choctaw Nation	Choctaw Roll (Not Including Freedmen)	CARD NO.	
POST OFFICE: Citra, I.T.				FIELD NO. 3255	

Dawes' Roll No.	NAME	Relationship to Person	AGE	SEX	BLOOD	TRIBAL ENROLLMENT		
						Year	County	No.
9399	1 Frazier, Susan 33	First Named	30	F	Full	1896	Atoka	4489
	2							
	3							
	4	ENROLLMENT						
	5	OF NOS. 1 APPROVED BY THE SECRETARY HEREON						
	6	OF INTERIOR FEB 4 1903						
	7							
	8							
	9							
	10							
	11							
	12							
	13							
	14							
	15							
	16							
	17							

TRIBAL ENROLLMENT OF PARENTS

Name of Father	Year	County	Name of Mother	Year	County
1 Edmund Lewis	Dead	Atoka	Melvina Lewis	Dead	Atoka
2					
3					
4					
5					
6					
7		Also on 1896 roll as Susan Perkins,			
8		Page 269, No 10562, Atoka Co.			
9					
10					
11					
12					
13					
14					
15			Date of Application for Enrollment.	Aug 7/99	
16					
17					

Choctaw By Blood Enrollment Cards 1898-1914

RESIDENCE:	Atoka	COUNTY.							
POST OFFICE:	Guertie, I.T.								

Choctaw Nation

Choctaw Roll *(Not Including Freedmen)*

CARD NO.

FIELD NO. 3256

Dawes' Roll No.	NAME		Relationship to Person First Named	AGE	SEX	BLOOD	TRIBAL ENROLLMENT		
							Year	County	No.
9400	1 Walton, Nancy	43	First Named	40	F	Full	1896	Atoka	14022
	2								
	3								
	4								
	5	ENROLLMENT							
	6	OF NOS. 1 APPROVED BY THE SECRETARY	HEREON						
	7	OF INTERIOR FEB 4 1903							
	8								
	9								
	10								
	11								
	12								
	13								
	14								
	15								
	16								
	17								

TRIBAL ENROLLMENT OF PARENTS

	Name of Father	Year	County	Name of Mother	Year	County
1	Tom Ellis	Dead	Blue	Sallie Ellis	Dead	Blue
2						
3						
4						
5						
6						
7						
8						
9						
10						
11						
12						
13					Date of Application for Enrollment.	
14						
15					Aug 7/99	
16						
17						

256

Choctaw By Blood Enrollment Cards 1898-1914

RESIDENCE:	Atoka	COUNTY.							
POST OFFICE:	Citra, I.T.								

Choctaw Nation — Choctaw Roll (*Not Including Freedmen*)

CARD NO. FIELD NO. **3257**

Dawes' Roll No.	NAME		Relationship to Person	AGE	SEX	BLOOD	TRIBAL ENROLLMENT		
							Year	County	No.
9401	1 Lewis, George	30	First Named	27	M	Full	1896	Atoka	8329
9402	2 " Nancy	29	Wife	26	F	"	1893	"	1188
9403	3 " Houston	5	Son	1	M	"			
9404	4 Carpenter, Ellis	13	S.Son	9	"	"	1896	Atoka	2956
9405	5 Lewis, Ben	1	Son	3mo	M	"			
	6								
	7								
	8								
	9								
	10	ENROLLMENT							
	11	OF NOS. 1,2,3,4 and 5 HEREON APPROVED BY THE SECRETARY							
	12	OF INTERIOR Feb 4 1903							
	13								
	14								
	15								
	16								
	17								

TRIBAL ENROLLMENT OF PARENTS

Name of Father	Year	County	Name of Mother	Year	County
1 Edmund Lewis	Dead	Atoka	Finie Lewis	Dead	Atoka
2 Simon Peter	"	"	Rhoda Peter	"	"
3 No1			No2		
4 Solomon Carpenter		Atoka	No2		
5 No1			No2		
6					
7					
8					
9	No2 on 1893 Pay Roll, Page 17, No 188, Atoka				
10	County, as Nancy Carpenter.				
11					
12	No3 Affidavit of birth to be supplied:				
13	Recd Oct 7/99			#1 to 4	
14	No.5 Enrolled Oct 9, 1901			Date of Application for Enrollment.	
15	For child of Nos 1&2 see NB (Mar 3-1905) Card #650			Aug 7/99	
16					
17					

Choctaw By Blood Enrollment Cards 1898-1914

RESIDENCE: Atoka COUNTY.	POST OFFICE: Gurtie[sic], I.T.	**Choctaw Nation**	Choctaw Roll _(Not Including Freedmen)_	CARD NO. FIELD NO. 3258

Dawes' Roll No.	NAME	Relationship to Person	AGE	SEX	BLOOD	TRIBAL ENROLLMENT Year	County	No.
9406	1 Lawrence, Osborne S 30	First Named	27	M	1/2	1896	Atoka	8292
9407	2 " Pikey 29	Wife	26	F	3/4	1896	"	4495
9408	3 " Green D 5	Son	1½	M	5/8			
9409	4 " Gilbert M 2	Son	5mo	M	5/8			
9410	5 " Rosa 1	Dau	4mo	F	5/8			
	6							
	7							
	8							
	9	ENROLLMENT						
	10	OF NOS. 1-2-3-4 and 5 HEREON APPROVED BY THE SECRETARY						
	11	OF INTERIOR FEB 4 1903						
	12							
	13							
	14							
	15							
	16							
	17							

TRIBAL ENROLLMENT OF PARENTS

Name of Father	Year	County	Name of Mother	Year	County
1 Sidney S Lawrence		Choctaw residing in Chick Natn	Annie Lawrence		Atoka
2 Jos. Frazier	Dead	Atoka	Wima Frazier	Dead	"
3 No1			No2		
4 No. 1			No. 2		
5 No.1			No.2		
6					
7					
8					
9 No1 on 1896 roll as O S. Lawrence					
10 No2 " 1896 " " Pinky Frazier					
11					
12 No3 Affidavit of birth to be supplied:					
13 Filed Nov 2/99					
14 No.4 Enrolled Feby 25. 1901					
No.5 Born Sept. 3, 1902. Proof of birth received Dec 24, 1902.				For Nos	Date of Application for Enrollment.
15				1,2 &3 –	Aug 7/99
16					
17 Legal I.T. 12/29/02					

258

Choctaw By Blood Enrollment Cards 1898-1914

RESIDENCE: Atoka COUNTY.	**Choctaw Nation**	Choctaw Roll (Not Including Freedmen)	CARD NO.
POST OFFICE: Gurtie[sic], I.T.			FIELD NO. 3259

Dawes' Roll No.	NAME	Relationship to Person First Named	AGE	SEX	BLOOD	TRIBAL ENROLLMENT		
						Year	County	No.
9411	1 Lawrence, Frank 24	First Named	21	M	1/2	1896	Atoka	8325
	2							
	3							
	4							
	5							
	6							
	7							
	8							
	9							
	10							
	11							
	12							
	13							
	14							
	15							
	16							
	17							

ENROLLMENT OF NOS. 1 HEREON APPROVED BY THE SECRETARY OF INTERIOR FEB 4 1903

TRIBAL ENROLLMENT OF PARENTS

Name of Father	Year	County	Name of Mother	Year	County
1 Sidney S Lawrence		Choctaw residing in Chick Natn	Annie Frazier		Atoka
2					
3					
4					
5					
6					
7					
8					
9					
10					
11					
12					
13					
14				Date of Application for Enrollment.	
15				Aug 7/99	
16					
17 P.O. Legal I.T. 1/26/03					

Choctaw By Blood Enrollment Cards 1898-1914

RESIDENCE:	Atoka	COUNTY.	**Choctaw Nation**			**Choctaw Roll**		CARD NO.	
POST OFFICE:	Guertie, I.T.					*(Not Including Freedmen)*		FIELD NO.	3260

Dawes' Roll No.	NAME		Relationship to Person First Named	AGE	SEX	BLOOD	TRIBAL ENROLLMENT		
							Year	County	No.
9412	1 Frazier, Annie	56	First Named	53	F	3/4	1896	Atoka	4496
	2								
	3								
	4								
	5	ENROLLMENT							
	6	OF NOS. 1 HEREON APPROVED BY THE SECRETARY							
	7	OF INTERIOR FEB 4 1903							
	8								
	9								
	10								
	11								
	12								
	13								
	14								
	15								
	16								
	17								

TRIBAL ENROLLMENT OF PARENTS

	Name of Father	Year	County	Name of Mother	Year	County
1	Benj. Frazier	Dead	Atoka		Dead	Atoka
2						
3						
4						
5						
6						
7						
8						
9						
10						
11						
12						
13				Date of Application for Enrollment.		
14						
15				Aug 7/99		
16						
17						

Choctaw By Blood Enrollment Cards 1898-1914

RESIDENCE:	Chickasaw Natn	~~COUNTY.~~		**Choctaw Nation**		**Choctaw Roll** *(Not Including Freedmen)*	CARD NO.	
POST OFFICE:	Wayne, I.T.						FIELD NO.	**3261**

Dawes' Roll No.	NAME		Relationship to Person	AGE	SEX	BLOOD	TRIBAL ENROLLMENT		
							Year	County	No.
I.W.4000	1 Marcum, John W	37	First Named	34	M	I.W	1896	Tobucksy	14816
DEAD	2 " ~~Ellen~~ ~~DEAD~~		~~Wife~~	~~26~~	~~F~~	~~1/2~~	~~1896~~	"	~~8553~~
9413	3 " Rosa	6	Dau	3	"	1/4	1896	"	8555
9414	4 " Henry Clay	5	Son	2	M	1/4			
	5								
	6	ENROLLMENT							
	7	OF NOS. 3 and 4	HEREON						
	8	~~APPROVED BY THE SECRETARY~~ OF INTERIOR Feb 4 1903							
	9								
	10	ENROLLMENT							
	11	OF NOS. ~~~ 1 ~~~	HEREON						
	12	APPROVED BY THE SECRETARY ~~OF INTERIOR~~ ~~Oct 21 1904~~							
	13								
	14	~~No.2 hereon dismissed under~~							
	15	order of the Commission to							
	16	the Five Civilized Tribes of							
	17	~~March 31, 1905~~							

TRIBAL ENROLLMENT OF PARENTS

	Name of Father	Year	County	Name of Mother	Year	County
1	Randolph Marcum	Dead	Non Citz	Eliz. Marcum	Dead	Non Citz
2	~~Ross Frazier~~	"	~~Jacks Fork~~	~~Selina Frazier~~	"	~~Jacks Fork~~
3	No1			No2		
4	No1			No2		
5						
6						
7						
8						
9				Bingham and Apple Attys for No1.		
10	As to marriage and remarriage see his					
11	testimony					
12	No4 Affidavit of birth to be supplied:					
13	Filed Nov 2/99					
14	No.2 died December 17, 1899. Proof of death filed July 31, 1901				Date of Application for Enrollment.	
15					Aug 7/99	
16						
17						

Choctaw By Blood Enrollment Cards 1898-1914

RESIDENCE:	Chickasaw Natn	~~COUNTY.~~	**Choctaw Nation**	**Choctaw Roll**	CARD NO.	
POST OFFICE:	Frank, I.T.			*(Not Including Freedmen)*	FIELD NO.	3262

Dawes' Roll No.	NAME		Relationship to Person	AGE	SEX	BLOOD	TRIBAL ENROLLMENT		
							Year	County	No.
I.W 1323	1 Victor, Mary J	36	First Named	36	F	I.W			
	2								
	3								
	4								
	5								
	6								
	7								
	8								
	9								
	10								
	11								
	12								
	13	ENROLLMENT OF NOS. 1 HEREON APPROVED BY THE SECRETARY OF INTERIOR MAR 14 1905							
	14								
	15								
	16								
	17								

TRIBAL ENROLLMENT OF PARENTS

	Name of Father	Year	County	Name of Mother	Year	County
1	A. J. Cotner	Dead	Non Citz	Rebecca Cotner	Dead	Non Citz
2						
3						
4						
5						
6						
7		As to marriage see her testimony				
8		See additional testimony of Nº1 taken October 22, 1902				
9		No1 is the wife of Alfred Victor Choctaw card No61 – 10-22/02				
10		~~Alfred Victor on final Choctaw roll as a citizen by blood, No 15034,~~ ~~approved by the Secretary of the Interior on February 16, 1904~~				
11						
12						
13						
14				Date of Application for Enrollment		
15				Aug 7/99		
16						
17						

Choctaw By Blood Enrollment Cards 1898-1914

RESIDENCE: Atoka	COUNTY.							
POST OFFICE: Citra, I.T.	**Choctaw Nation**					**Choctaw Roll** (Not Including Freedmen)	CARD NO. FIELD NO. 3263	

Dawes' Roll No.	NAME	Relationship to Person First Named	AGE	SEX	BLOOD	TRIBAL ENROLLMENT		
						Year	County	No.
9415	1 Mishontambe, Betsy 28	First Named	25	F	3/4	1896	Atoka	8852
9416	2 Frazier Lona 19	Sister	16	"	Full	1896	"	8855
9417	3 Mishontambe Daniel 15	Bro	13	M	"	1896	"	8853
9418	4 " Loman 12	"	9	"	3/4	1896	"	8854
9419	5 Frazier Lula	Dau of Nº2	17mo	F	3/4			
	6							
	7							
	8	ENROLLMENT OF NOS. 1,2,3,4 and 5 APPROVED BY THE SECRETARY OF INTERIOR FEB 4 1903 HEREON						
	9							
	10							
	11							
	12							
	13							
	14							
	15							
	16							
	17							

TRIBAL ENROLLMENT OF PARENTS

	Name of Father	Year	County	Name of Mother	Year	County
1	Joshua Wade	Dead	Atoka	Bicey Shields	Dead	Atoka
2	Bob Shields	"	"	" "	"	"
3	Lewis Jackson	"	"	" "	"	"
4	Andy Frazier	"	"	" "	"	"
5	Thompson Frazier	1896	"	Nº2		
6						
7						
8	No2 on 1896 roll as Leona Mishontambe					
9	Nº2 is also known as Lona Shields. See letter of V. M. Wallace filed herein. Nov. 19,1902					
10	Nº2 is now the wife of Thompson Frazier on Choctaw card #3254. Certified copy of marriage certificate filed Nov. 19, 1902.					
11	Nº5 Born June 12, 1901, enrolled Nov. 19, 1902					
12	For child of No.2 see NB (Mar 3,1905) #640					
13						#1 to 4
14					Date of Application for Enrollment.	
15					Aug 7/99	
16						
17						

Choctaw By Blood Enrollment Cards 1898-1914

RESIDENCE: Tobucksy   COUNTY. **Choctaw Nation**   **Choctaw Roll**   CARD NO.
POST OFFICE: Calvin, I.T.   *(Not Including Freedmen)*   FIELD NO. **3264**

Dawes' Roll No.	NAME	Relationship to Person	AGE	SEX	BLOOD	TRIBAL ENROLLMENT Year	County	No.
9420	1 Perry, Calvin C 65	First Named	62	M	1/4	1896	Tobucksy	10265
9421	2 " Phoebe 50	Wife	47	F	1/2	1896	"	10266
9422	3 " Calvin C Jr 13	Son	10	M	3/8	1896	"	10268
9423	4 Sampson, Angeline 13	G.Dau	10	F	3/16	1896	"	11294
	5							
	6							
	7	ENROLLMENT						
	8	OF NOS. 1,2,3 and 4 HEREON APPROVED BY THE SECRETARY						
	9	OF INTERIOR FEB 4 1903						
	10							
	11							
	12							
	13							
	14							
	15							
	16							
	17							

TRIBAL ENROLLMENT OF PARENTS

	Name of Father	Year	County	Name of Mother	Year	County
1	Moses Perry	Dead	Non Citz	Hettie Perry	Dead	Red River
2	Gabriel Burris	"	Atoka	Casey Burris	"	Atoka
3	No1			No2		
4	Perry Sampson		Non Citz	Simie Sampson	Dead	Tobucksy
5						
6						
7						
8	For child of No3 see NB (Apr 26 '06) Card No 1303					
9						
10						
11						
12						
13						
14					Date of Application for Enrollment.	
15					Aug 7/99	
16						
17						

Choctaw By Blood Enrollment Cards 1898-1914

RESIDENCE: Tobucksy	COUNTY.				
POST OFFICE: Calvin, I.T.	**Choctaw Nation**		Choctaw Roll *(Not Including Freedmen)*	CARD NO. FIELD NO.	3265

Dawes' Roll No.	NAME		Relationship to Person	AGE	SEX	BLOOD	TRIBAL ENROLLMENT		
							Year	County	No.
9424	₁ Frazier, Johnson	38	First Named	35	M	Full	1893	Tobucksy	332
9425	₂ Anolatubbi, Lizzie	16	Niece	13	F	1/2	1893	"	335
	3								
	4								
	5	ENROLLMENT							
	6	OF NOS. 1 and 2 HEREON APPROVED BY THE SECRETARY							
	7	OF INTERIOR FEB 4 1903							
	8								
	9								
	10								
	11								
	12								
	13								
	14								
	15								
	16								
	17								

TRIBAL ENROLLMENT OF PARENTS

	Name of Father	Year	County	Name of Mother	Year	County
1	Davis Frazier	Dead	Cedar	Wa-te-ma	Dead	Atoka
2	Jas. Anolatubbi	"	Chick Roll	Annie Anolatubbi	"	"
3						
4						
5						
6						
7						
8						
9						
10	No1 on 1893 Pay Roll, Page 35, No 332 Tobucksy Co					
11	No2 " 1893 " " " 35 " 335 " " as Lizzie Anolatubbee					
12	No2 also on 1896 Roll Page 243, No 9605 " Anoletubbe					
13	Tobucksy Co.					
14	Alice Frazier daughter of N°1 on Creek card #3783					
15					Date of Application for Enrollment.	Aug 7/99
16						
17						

Choctaw By Blood Enrollment Cards 1898-1914

RESIDENCE: Chickasaw Natn ~~COUNTY.~~ **Choctaw Nation**   Choctaw Roll   CARD NO.
POST OFFICE: White Bead, I.T.   *(Not Including Freedmen)*   FIELD NO. **3266**

Dawes' Roll No.	NAME		Relationship to Person	AGE	SEX	BLOOD	TRIBAL ENROLLMENT		
							Year	County	No.
9426	1 Garvin, Robert H	26	First Named	23	M	1/8	1896	Chick Dist	5014
I.W. 305	2 " Mattie M	27	Wife	22	F	I.W			
9427	3 " Vashti	3	Dau	2mo	"	1/16			
9428	4 " Robert H Jr	1	Son	3mo	M	1/16			
	5								
	6								
	7	ENROLLMENT OF NOS. 1, 3 and 4 HEREON							
	8	APPROVED BY THE SECRETARY							
	9	OF INTERIOR Feb 4 1903							
	10								
	11	ENROLLMENT OF NOS. 2 HEREON							
	12	APPROVED BY THE SECRETARY OF INTERIOR Sep 12 1903							
	13								
	14								
	15								
	16								
	17								

TRIBAL ENROLLMENT OF PARENTS

Name of Father	Year	County	Name of Mother	Year	County
1 S. J. Garvin		Intermarried	Susan Garvin		Choctaw residing in ~~Chick Natn~~
2 J. T. Flemming		Non Citz	Mattie Flemming		Non Citz
3 No1			No2		
4 No.1			No.2		
5					
6					
7		No.4 born July 14, 1901 Enrolled Oct. 22d, 1901.			
8		See testimony of N°1 taken October 22, 1902			
9					
10					
11					
12					
13					Date of Application for Enrollment.
14					
15				No2 enrolled Aug 7/99	
16				No1 " Sept 12/99	
17 Pauls Valley I.T. 10/22/02				No3 " Dec 14/99	

Choctaw By Blood Enrollment Cards 1898-1914

RESIDENCE: Chickasaw Natn COUNTY.
POST OFFICE: Conway, I.T.

Choctaw Nation

Choctaw Roll
(Not Including Freedmen)

CARD NO.
FIELD NO. 3267

Dawes' Roll No.	NAME		Relationship to Person First Named	AGE	SEX	BLOOD	TRIBAL ENROLLMENT		
							Year	County	No.
9429	1 Bowlin, Susa	19	First Named	16	F	1/2	1896	Atoka	8286
9430	2 " Edna	3	dau	2mo	F	1/4			
	3								
	4	ENROLLMENT							
	5	OF NOS. 1 and 2 HEREON APPROVED BY THE SECRETARY							
	6	OF INTERIOR FEB 4 1903							
	7								
	8								
	9								
	10								
	11								
	12								
	13								
	14								
	15								
	16								
	17								

TRIBAL ENROLLMENT OF PARENTS

	Name of Father	Year	County	Name of Mother	Year	County
1	David Lawrence		Atoka	Elphie Lawrence		Atoka
2	R. M. Bowlin			No.1		
3						
4						
5						
6						
7			On 1896 roll as Susa Lawrence			
8						
9			Husband on Card No D297			
			For children of No.1 see NB (March 3,1905) #1308			
10						
11						
12						
13						
14				#1		
15				Date of Application for Enrollment.	Aug 7/99	
16			No.2 Enrolled May 24, 1900			
17						

Choctaw By Blood Enrollment Cards 1898-1914

RESIDENCE:	Atoka	COUNTY.	**Choctaw Nation**	Choctaw Roll	CARD NO.
POST OFFICE:	Citra, I.T.			*(Not Including Freedmen)*	FIELD NO. **3268**

Dawes' Roll No.	NAME	Relationship to Person First Named	AGE	SEX	BLOOD	TRIBAL ENROLLMENT		
						Year	County	No.
15918	1 Mishontambe, Bency 5		1½	F	1/2			
	2							
	3							
	4							
	5							
	6							
	7							
	8							
	9							
	10							
	11							
	12	ENROLLMENT OF NOS. One HEREON APPROVED BY THE SECRETARY OF INTERIOR Aug 23 1905						
	13							
	14							
	15							
	16							
	17							

TRIBAL ENROLLMENT OF PARENTS

	Name of Father	Year	County	Name of Mother	Year	County
1	Robert Richardson		Colored	Jennie Clark	Dead	Atoka
2						
3						
4						
5						
6	Mother of No.1 on 1893 Pay Roll, Atoka County, page 16, No 179 as Jenny Clark					
7	No definite information as to when this					
8	child was born could be obtained. Is said to be about 18 months of age. Child					
9	was present when enrolled.					
10	No.1 proof of birth filed July 7, 1905.					
11						
12						
13						
14					Date of Application for Enrollment.	
15					Aug 7/99	
16						
17						

268

Choctaw By Blood Enrollment Cards 1898-1914

RESIDENCE:	Atoka	COUNTY.									

RESIDENCE: Atoka **COUNTY.**   **Choctaw Nation**   **Choctaw Roll** *(Not Including Freedmen)* CARD NO.
POST OFFICE: Gurtie[sic], I.T.   FIELD NO. **3269**

Dawes' Roll No.	NAME		Relationship to Person	AGE	SEX	BLOOD	TRIBAL ENROLLMENT		
							Year	County	No.
9431	1 Lawrence, Dave	37	First Named	34	M	1/2	1896	Atoka	8282
	2								
	3								
	4								
	5								
	6								
	7								
	8								
	9								
	10								
	11								
	12								
	13								
	14								
	15								
	16								
	17								

ENROLLMENT OF NOS. 1 HEREON APPROVED BY THE SECRETARY OF INTERIOR Feb 4 1903

TRIBAL ENROLLMENT OF PARENTS

Name of Father	Year	County	Name of Mother	Year	County
1 Sidney S Lawrence		Choctaw residing in Chick Natn	Zonie Lawrence	Dead	Atoka
2					
3					
4					
5					
6					
7					
8					
9					
10					
11					
12					
13				Date of Application for Enrollment.		
14					
15				Aug 7/99		
16					
17					

Choctaw By Blood Enrollment Cards 1898-1914

RESIDENCE: Atoka COUNTY. **Choctaw Nation** Choctaw Roll CARD NO.
POST OFFICE: Gurtie[sic] I.T. *(Not Including Freedmen)* FIELD NO. 3270

Dawes' Roll No.	NAME		Relationship to Person	AGE	SEX	BLOOD	TRIBAL ENROLLMENT		
							Year	County	No.
9432	1 Robeson Joe	36	First Named	33	M	Full	1896	Atoka	11002
	2								
	3								
	4								
	5	ENROLLMENT							
	6	OF NOS. 1 HEREON APPROVED BY THE SECRETARY							
	7	OF INTERIOR FEB 4 1903							
	8								
	9								
	10								
	11								
	12								
	13								
	14								
	15								
	16								
	17								

TRIBAL ENROLLMENT OF PARENTS

	Name of Father	Year	County	Name of Mother	Year	County
1	Robinson[sic]	Dead	Atoka	Charity Robinson	Dead	Atoka
2						
3						
4						
5						
6	No. 1 Correct name of this person appears to be Joseph Robeson See letter #11904-1902 G.O. Files					
7	July 24/02 also evidence of marriage filed in Chickasaw #339					
8	No1 is the husband of Jane Lewis on Chickasaw card #339					
	For child of No1 see Chick NB (Mar 3,1905) #517					
9						
10						
11						
12						
13						
14						
15				Date of Application for Enrollment.	Aug 7/99	
16						
17	Stonewall I.T.					

Choctaw By Blood Enrollment Cards 1898-1914

RESIDENCE:	Atoka	COUNTY.					CARD NO.	3271
POST OFFICE:	Gertie[sic] I.T.						FIELD NO.	

Choctaw Nation — Choctaw Roll *(Not Including Freedmen)*

Dawes' Roll No.	NAME		Relationship to Person	AGE	SEX	BLOOD	TRIBAL ENROLLMENT		
							Year	County	No.
9433	1 Pusley Lyman	53	First Named	50	M	Full	1896	Gaines	10179
9434	2 " Lizzie	25	Wife	22	F	"	1896	"	10180
9435	3 " Ida	7	Dau	4	"	"	1896	"	10181
9436	4 " Evalena	4	"	1	"	"			
9437	5 " Osborne	21	Son	18	M	1/2	1896	"	10163
9438	6 " Bertha Andre	2	Dau	3wks	F	Full			
	7								
	8								
	9								
	10	ENROLLMENT OF NOS. 1,2,3,4,5 and 6 HEREON APPROVED BY THE SECRETARY OF INTERIOR FEB 4 1903							
	11								
	12								
	13								
	14								
	15								
	16								
	17								

TRIBAL ENROLLMENT OF PARENTS

	Name of Father	Year	County	Name of Mother	Year	County
1	Edmond Pusley	Dead	Tobucksy	Susan Pusley	1896	Atoka
2	Tom James	"	Gaines	Unknown	Dead	Gaines
3	No.1			No 2		
4	No 1			No. 2		
5	No 1			Mary Pusley	Dead	Sugarloaf Non Citz
6	No. 1			No.2		
7						
8						
9						
10	As to proof of marriage of father and mother					
11	of Nos see testimony.					
12	No.6 Enrolled January 5th, 1901					
13	For child of Nos 1 and 2 see NB (Mar 3,1905) #475					
14						
15						
16				Date of Application for Enrollment.	For Nos 1-to-5 Incl	
17					Aug 7/99	

271

Choctaw By Blood Enrollment Cards 1898-1914

RESIDENCE: Pickens COUNTY. **Choctaw Nation** Choctaw Roll CARD NO. 3272
POST OFFICE: Purdy I.T. (Not Including Freedmen) FIELD NO.

Dawes' Roll No.	NAME		Relationship to Person	AGE	SEX	BLOOD	TRIBAL ENROLLMENT		
							Year	County	No.
I.W. 306	1 Price William E	25	First Named	22	M	I.W.			
DEAD.	2 " Willie M DEAD.		Wife	18	F	1/4	1896	Tobucksy	5366
9439	3 " Cora May	2	Dau	2	F	1/8			
	4 No. 2 HEREON DISMISSED UNDER								
	5 ORDER OF THE COMMISSION TO THE FIVE CIVILIZED TRIBES OF MARCH 31, 1905.								
	6								
	7 ENROLLMENT								
	8 OF NOS. 3 HEREON APPROVED BY THE SECRETARY								
	9 OF INTERIOR FEB 4 1903								
	10 ENROLLMENT								
	11 OF NOS. 1 HEREON APPROVED BY THE SECRETARY								
	12 OF INTERIOR SEP 12 1903								
	13								
	14								
	15								
	16								
	17								

TRIBAL ENROLLMENT OF PARENTS

	Name of Father	Year	County	Name of Mother	Year	County
1	J. W. Price		U.S.	Rachel Price		U.S.
2	Charley Hathaway	Dead	Pickens	Celia Hathaway	Dead	Tobucksy
3	Nº1			Nº2		
4						
5						
6						
7						
8	No 2 on roll as Willy M Hathaway					
9	Nº3 Born Aug 20, 1900: enrolled Sept 3, 1902					
10	Nº2 is dead: See affidavits accompanying proof of birth of Nº3 Sept 3, 1902					
11	Affidavits of J.A. and N.C. Thomas stating that Nº2 had never been married previous to her marriage to Nº1, filed May 9, 1903,					
12						
13					Date of Application for Enrollment.	
14						
15					Sept 12/98	
16						
17						

RESIDENCE:	Atoka	COUNTY.	**Choctaw Nation**				Choctaw Roll		CARD NO.	3273
POST OFFICE:	Coalgate I.T.						*(Not Including Freedmen)*		FIELD NO.	

Dawes' Roll No.	NAME	Relationship to Person	AGE	SEX	BLOOD	TRIBAL ENROLLMENT		
						Year	County	No.
I.W.307 ₁	Lankford Thomas N ⁴¹	First Named	38	M	I.W.			
9440 ₂	" Mary ²⁷	Wife	24	F	1/4	1896	Tobucksy	6656
9441 ₃	" William F ⁴	Son	1	M	1/8			
DEAD. ₄	" Richard Young	Son	4mo	M	1/8			
9442 ₅	" Lucretia Bell ¹	Dau	5mo	F	1/8			
₆								
₇								
₈	ENROLLMENT OF NOS. 2 3 and 5 HEREON							
₉	APPROVED BY THE SECRETARY OF INTERIOR FEB 4 1903							
₁₀								
₁₁	ENROLLMENT OF NOS. 1 HEREON							
₁₂	APPROVED BY THE SECRETARY OF INTERIOR SEP 12 1903							
₁₃								
₁₄								
₁₅	No 4 HEREON DISMISSED UNDER							
₁₆	ORDER OF THE COMMISSION TO THE FIVE							
₁₇	CIVILIZED TRIBES OF MARCH 31, 1905.							

TRIBAL ENROLLMENT OF PARENTS

	Name of Father	Year	County	Name of Mother	Year	County
₁	Wᵐ Lankford		U.S.	Ura I Lankford		U.S.
₂	William Johnson	1896	Tobucksy	Christiana McCann	Dead	Tobucksy
₃	No 1			No 2		
₄	No. 1			No. 2		
₅	Nº 1			Nº 2		
₆						
₇	No.1 admitted by Dawes Commission No. 1220 as Thomas U. Lankford					
₈	No2 on roll as Mary Johnson					
₉	Evidence of birth of No.3 to be supplied. Recd Oct 7/99					
₁₀						
₁₁	For child of Nos 1&2 see NB (Mar 3-1905) Card #134					
₁₂						
₁₃	No.4 Enrolled May 24, 1900					
₁₄	Nº5 Born Nov 23, 1901; enrolled April 23, 1902					
₁₅					Date of Application for Enrollment: Aug 7/99	
₁₆	No4 died October 7, 1900; proof of death filed Nov 26, 1902					
₁₇	Cairo I.T. 11/21/02					

#1 to 3

Choctaw By Blood Enrollment Cards 1898-1914

RESIDENCE: Tobucksy COUNTY. **Choctaw Nation** Choctaw Roll CARD NO. 3274
POST OFFICE: Calvin I.T. Tandy (Not Including Freedmen) FIELD NO.

Dawes' Roll No.	NAME		Relationship to Person	AGE	SEX	BLOOD	TRIBAL ENROLLMENT		
							Year	County	No.
9443	1 Choate David	33	First Named	30	M	3/4	1896	Tobucksy	2326
I.W.308	2 " Belle D	29	Wife	25	F	I.W.	1896	"	14389
9444	3 " William D	6	Son	3	M	3/8	1896	"	2327
9445	4 " Joseph E	4	Son	1	M	3/8			
9446	5 " Naoma Adilira	2	Dau	5mo	F	3/8			
	6								
	7	ENROLLMENT							
	8	OF NOS. 1,3,4 and 5 HEREON APPROVED BY THE SECRETARY							
	9	OF INTERIOR FEB 4 1903							
	10	ENROLLMENT							
	11	OF NOS. 2 HEREON APPROVED BY THE SECRETARY							
	12	OF INTERIOR SEP 12 1903							
	13								
	14								
	15								
	16								
	17								

TRIBAL ENROLLMENT OF PARENTS

	Name of Father	Year	County	Name of Mother	Year	County
1	Jno. Choate	Dead	Tobucksy	Emily Choate	Dead	Jackson
2	Edward Towry		U.S.	Milly Towry		U.S.
3	No.1			No 2		
4	No 1			No 2		
5	No.1			No.2		
6						
7						
8						
9	For children of Nos 1&2 see NB (Mar 3 1905) #677					
10	No2 on roll Belle D Choat					
11	No3 " " Wᵐ D Choate					
12	Evidence of birth of No4 to be supplied. Recd					
13	Dec 18/99. Irregular and returned for correction. Recd & filed Jany 17, 1900					Date of Application for Enrollment.
14	No.2 admitted as an intermarried citizen and No.3 as a citizen by blood by Dawes Commission in 1896: Choctaw case #731: no appeal					
15	No.5 Enrolled June 18, 1901.					Aug 7 – 99
16						
17	PO Celestine IT 4/3/05					

For 1 to 4

RESIDENCE:	Tobucksy	COUNTY.		
POST OFFICE:	Calvin I.T.			

Choctaw Nation

Choctaw Roll
(Not Including Freedmen)

CARD NO. 3275
FIELD NO.

Dawes' Roll No.	NAME	Relationship to Person First Named	AGE	SEX	BLOOD	TRIBAL ENROLLMENT		
						Year	County	No.
1	Leader Edward		58	M	Full			
2								
3								
4								
5								
6								
7								
8								
9								
10								
11								
12								
13								
14								
15								
16								
17								

TRIBAL ENROLLMENT OF PARENTS

	Name of Father	Year	County	Name of Mother	Year	County
1	Jim Leader	Dead	James	Nancy Leader	Dead	Tobucksy
2						
3						
4						
5						
6						
7			On Page 71 Chickasaw Roll			
8			is father of Hepsie Leader on Creek Indian Card Field Nº 2486			
	No1 "	" "	Nancy Leader "	" " " "	"	2300
9	No1 "	" "	Emma Leader "	" " " "	"	2299
10	No1 "	" "	Barney Leader "	" " " "	"	2236
11						
12						
13						
14						
15						
16				Date of Application for Enrollment.		
17				8 – 7 – 99		

[CANCELLED]

[Cancelled and transferred [remainder illegible]]

RESIDENCE:	Tobucksy	COUNTY.	**Choctaw Nation**	Choctaw Roll	CARD NO.	
POST OFFICE:	Calvin I.T.			(Not Including Freedmen)	FIELD NO.	**3276**

Dawes' Roll No.	NAME		Relationship to Person	AGE	SEX	BLOOD	TRIBAL ENROLLMENT		
							Year	County	No.
9447	1 Atwood Patsy N	35	First Named	32	F	1/2	1896	Tobucksy	126
9448	2 " Ottie	19	Dau	16	"	1/4	1896	"	127
9449	3 " Arra	17	"	14	"	1/4	1896	"	128
9450	4 " Benjamin	15	Son	12	M	1/4	1896	"	129
9451	5 " Ollie	13	Dau	10	F	1/4	1896	"	130
9452	6 " Coleman	11	Son	8	M	1/4	1896	"	131
9453	7 " Lizzie	9	Dau	6	F	1/4	1896	"	132
9454	8 " Ambrosia	7	"	4	"	1/4	1896	"	133
I.W. 1409	9 " Chester C		Husband	41	M	I.W.	1896	"	14256
	10								
	11	ENROLLMENT OF NOS. 1,2,3,4,5,6,7 and 8 HEREON APPROVED BY THE SECRETARY OF INTERIOR Feb 4 1903							
	12								
	13								
	14	ENROLLMENT OF NOS. ~~~ 9 ~~~ HEREON APPROVED BY THE SECRETARY OF INTERIOR Jun 12 1905							
	15								
	16								
	17								

TRIBAL ENROLLMENT OF PARENTS

Name of Father	Year	County	Name of Mother	Year	County
1 Ben Burris	Dead	Tobucksy	Sallie Burris	Dead	Tobucksy
2 Chester C. Atwood	1896	"	No 1		
3 "			No 1		
4 "			No 1		
5 "			No 1		
6 "			No 1		
7 "			No 1		
8 "			No 1		
9 Eli Atwood		noncitizen	Katie Atwood		noncitizen
10					
11 No9 restored to roll by Departmental authority of January 19, 1909 (File 5-51)					
Enrollment of No.9 cancelled by order of Department March 4, 1907					
12 No1 on roll as Patsy Atwood					
13 Husband of No1 on Choctaw Card D-298					
No.9 on 1885 Choc Census Roll Tobucksy Co, #195					
14 No.9 originally listed for enrollment on Choc Card #D-298					
15 Transferred to this card May 15, 1905. See decision of March 28 1905				#1 to 8	
16 No9 denied by Commission in 1896 Choctaw case No 1127. No appeal.				Date of Application for Enrollment.	
17 P.O. No9-Newburg I.T. 3/28/05				Aug 7/99	

RESIDENCE: Pontotoc COUNTY.	Choctaw Nation	Choctaw Roll (Not Including Freedmen)	CARD No. 3277 FIELD No.
POST OFFICE: Center I.T.			

Dawes' Roll No.	NAME	Relationship to Person First Named	AGE	SEX	BLOOD	TRIBAL ENROLLMENT		
						Year	County	No.
0	1 Adams Lucy	Named	21	F	1/8		Court	
0	2 " Mabel	Dau	4	F	1/16			
DP	3 " Earnest P.	Son	2mo	M	1/16			
DP	4 " Ida Vadis	Dau	2mo	F	1/16			
	5							
#3-4-	6 DISMISSED							
	8 JAN 19 1905							
	9							
	10							
	11							
	12							
	13							
	14							
1-2	15 DENIED CITIZENSHIP BY THE CHOCTAW AND							
	16 CHICKASAW CITIZENSHIP COURT							
	17							

TRIBAL ENROLLMENT OF PARENTS

	Name of Father	Year	County	Name of Mother	Year	County
1	Preston Early		US	Sophy Early	1896	Pontotoc
2	Gus Adams		US	No1		
3	"		"	No1		
4	A. M. Adams		non-citizen	No.1		
5						
6						
7						
8						
9						
10	Nos 1 and 2 Denied in Case #850					
11	No.1 Admitted by US Court at South McAlester, I.T.					
12	January 19th, 1898 No 101. As to residence and birth of child (No3) see her testimony					
13	No.2 also admitted by above judgment					
14	No.4 Born Dec 12, 1901; enrolled Feby 24, 1902					
15	Judgment of US Court admitting Nos 1&2 vacated and set aside by Decree of Choctaw Chickasaw Cit Court Decr 17'02					
16	Nos 1 and 2 now in C. C. C. C. Case #05.58					
17	For child of No1 see N.B. #953 (Act Apr 26-06)					

Date of Application for Enrollment.
8-7-99

Choctaw By Blood Enrollment Cards 1898-1914

RESIDENCE:	Tobucksy	COUNTY.				CARD NO. 3278
POST OFFICE:	Newberg I.T.					FIELD NO.

Choctaw Nation — Choctaw Roll *(Not Including Freedmen)*

Dawes' Roll No.	NAME		Relationship to Person	AGE	SEX	BLOOD	TRIBAL ENROLLMENT		
							Year	County	No.
9455	1 Hallmark, Sarah	37	First Named	34	F	1/2	1896	Gaines	5281
9456	2 " Mary M	15	Dau	12	"	1/4	1896	"	5282
9457	3 " Jennie	12	"	9	"	1/4	1896	"	5283
9458	4 " Uriah	12	Son	9	M	1/4	1896	"	5284
9459	5 " Samuel	10	"	7	"	1/4	1896	"	5285
9460	6 " Lillie	6	Dau	3	F	1/4	1896	"	5286
9461	7 " John F	2	Son	6mo	M	1/4			
I.W. 309	8 " John J	45	Hus	45	M	I.W.	1896	Gaines	14609
9462	9 " Ottie	1	Dau	1mo	F	1/4			
9463	10 " Henry	1	Son	1mo	M	1/4			
	11								
	12 ENROLLMENT								
	13 OF NOS. 1,2,3,4,5,6,7,9,10 HEREON APPROVED BY THE SECRETARY								
	14 OF INTERIOR FEB 4 1903								
	15 ENROLLMENT								
	16 OF NOS. 8 HEREON APPROVED BY THE SECRETARY								
	17 OF INTERIOR SEP 12 1903								

TRIBAL ENROLLMENT OF PARENTS

	Name of Father	Year	County	Name of Mother	Year	County
1	Simon James	Dead	Tobucksy		Dead	Tobucksy
2	Jno. J. Hallmark		Non Citz	No1		
3	" " "		" "	No1		
4	" " "		" "	No1		
5	" " "		" "	No1		
6	" " "		" "	No1		
7	" " "		" "	No1		
8	John B. Hallmark	dead	non-citizen	~~~~ Hallmark	dead	non-citizen
9	No.8			No.1		
10	No.8			No.1		
11	No8 admitted by Dawes Commission in 1896 as an intermarried citizen. Case #189: no appeal					
12	Surnames on 1896 roll as Halmark					
13	For child of Nos 1 and 8 see NB (Apr 26,1906) No 526				#1 to 7 inc	
13	No7 Affidavit of birth to be				Date of Application for Enrollment.	
14	supplied: Recd Oct 7/99					
15	No.8 Enrolled March 16, 1901.				Aug 8/99	
16	Nos 9 and 10 are twins: Enrolled June 13th 1901					
16	For child of Nos 1 and 8 see NB (Mar 3 1905) #501					
17	Jeff I.T. 11/15/02					

Choctaw By Blood Enrollment Cards 1898-1914

RESIDENCE: Chickasaw Natn ~~COUNTY.~~
POST OFFICE: Bebee, I.T.

Choctaw Nation

Choctaw Roll *(Not Including Freedmen)*

CARD NO. 32~~79~~
FIELD NO.

Dawes' Roll No.	NAME	Relationship to Person First Named	AGE	SEX	BLOOD	TRIBAL ENROLLMENT Year	County	No.
0	1 Early, Zora S	Named	41	M	1/4			
0	2 " Nellie	Dau	18	F	1/8			
DP	3 Goodwin, Albert Clarence	Grandson	2mo	M	1/16			
	4							
	5							
	6							
No2 Denied by C.C.C.C. as Nellie Goodwin or Nellie Early								
	8							
	~~DISMISSED~~ 9							
	10 JAN 21 1905							
	11							
	12							
	13							
	14							
	15							
	16							
	17							

~~DENIED CITIZENSHIP BY THE CHOCTAW AND CHICKASAW CITIZENSHIP COURT~~

TRIBAL ENROLLMENT OF PARENTS

	Name of Father	Year	County	Name of Mother	Year	County
1	Jas M Lewis	Dead	Choctaw	Zora P Lewis		Choctaw
2	Preston Early		Non Citz	No1		
3	John Goodwin		non-citizen	No2		
4						
5						
6						
7	Nos1 and 2 denied by Com in 96 Case #850					
8	Admitted by U.S. Court, Central Dist. Jany 19/98 Case No 101 As to residence, see testimony of					
9	No1.					
10	No.2 is now the wife of John Goodwin, a non-citizen June 14, 1901					
11	No.3 Enrolled June 14th, 1901					
12	Nos 1 and 2 now in f. C.C.C. Case #6558					
13	For child of No2 see NB 991 (Act Apr 26-06)					
14					Date of Application for Enrollment.	
15					Aug 7/99	
16						
17						

RESIDENCE: Chickasaw Natn ~~COUNTY.~~ **Choctaw Nation** Choctaw Roll CARD NO. 3280
POST OFFICE: Bebee, I.T. *(Not Including Freedmen)* FIELD NO.

Dawes' Roll No.	NAME	Relationship to Person First Named	AGE	SEX	BLOOD	TRIBAL ENROLLMENT		
						Year	County	No.
0	Lewis, Zora P		75	F	1/8			
2								
3								
4								
5								
6								
7								
8								
9								
10								
11								
12								
13								
14								
15								
16								
17								

TRIBAL ENROLLMENT OF PARENTS

	Name of Father	Year	County	Name of Mother	Year	County
1	Wᵐ Patterson	Dead	Non Cit.	Rhoda Patterson	Dead	Choctaw
2						
3						
4						
5						
6						
7	No1 Denied in 96 Case #850					
8	Admitted by U.S. Court, Central Dist, Jany 19/98					
	Case No 101. As to residence, see testimony of					
9	Zora S. Early					
10	Judgment of U.S. Court admitting No1 vacated and set aside by Decree of Choctaw Chickasaw Cit Court Decr 17'02					
11	No1 now in C.C.C.C. Case #5[illegible]					
12						
13						
14					Date of Application for Enrollment.	
15					Aug 7/99	
16						
17	PO Okemah IT 1/12/05	Pet #C 130	Duplicate record bound			

| RESIDENCE: Atoka | COUNTY: **Choctaw Nation** | **Choctaw Roll** | CARD NO. 3281 |
| POST OFFICE: Guertie, I.T. | | *(Not Including Freedmen)* | FIELD NO. |

Dawes' Roll No.	NAME	Relationship to Person First Named	AGE	SEX	BLOOD	TRIBAL ENROLLMENT		
						Year	County	No.
9464	₁ Anderson, William P ²⁵	First Named	22	M	1/2	1896	Atoka	452
9465	₂ Cunnish Martha ²³	Wife	20	F	Full	1896	Gaines	9149
DEAD.	₃ " Jesse DEAD	Son	9mo	M	3/4			
9466	₄ Cunnish Joel ¹	Son of Nº2	7mo	M	7/8			
	5							
	6							
	7							
	8	ENROLLMENT						
	9	OF NOS. 1,2 and 4 HEREON APPROVED BY THE SECRETARY						
	10	OF INTERIOR FEB 4 1903						
	11							
	12	No 3 HEREON DISMISSED UNDER						
	13	ORDER OF THE COMMISSION TO THE FIVE						
	14	CIVILIZED TRIBES OF MARCH 31, 1905.						
	15							
	16							
	17							

TRIBAL ENROLLMENT OF PARENTS

Name of Father	Year	County	Name of Mother	Year	County
₁ W. H. Anderson		Non Citz	Jensey Jackson	Dead	Atoka
₂ Basil McKans	Dead	Kiamitia	Phoebe McKans	"	Tobucksy
₃ No1			No2		
₄ Webster Cunnish	1896	Atoka	Nº2		
5					
6					
7					
8					
9	No1 on 1896 roll as Wᵐ P Anderson				
10	No2 " 1896 " " Martha McKans				
11	Nos 1 and 2 are separated				
12	No3 died January 29, 1901; proof of death filed Dec 5 1902				
13	No1 is now husband of Micey Wilkins Choc #4882				
14	Nº4 Born June 26 1902. Enrolled Dec 24, 1902			For Nos 1,2 &3	
15	Evidence of marriage between Nº2 and Webster Cunnish on Choctaw Card #4065 filed Dec. 26, 1902		Date of Application for Enrollment		
16	For child of No.2 see NB (March 3, 1905) #1447		Aug 7/99		
17	P.O. of Nº2 Lehigh I.T. Dec 26/02				

Choctaw By Blood Enrollment Cards 1898-1914

RESIDENCE: Atoka	COUNTY.	CARD NO. 3282

RESIDENCE: Atoka COUNTY. **Choctaw Nation** **Choctaw Roll** CARD NO. 3282
POST OFFICE: Guertie, I.T. *(Not Including Freedmen)* FIELD NO.

Dawes' Roll No.	NAME		Relationship to Person	AGE	SEX	BLOOD	TRIBAL ENROLLMENT		
							Year	County	No.
I.W. 310	1 Hembree, William	31	First Named	29	M	I.W			
9467	2 " Amy	22	Wife	19	F	1/2	1896	Atoka	5992
9468	3 " Edward	6	Son	2	M	1/4			
9469	4 " Lucy	4	Dau	6mo	F	1/4			
9470	5 " Elmer	1	Son	1/2	M	1/4			
	6								
	7								
	8	ENROLLMENT							
	9	OF NOS. 2,3,4 and 5 HEREON APPROVED BY THE SECRETARY							
	10	OF INTERIOR FEB 4 1903							
	11	ENROLLMENT							
	12	OF NOS. I HEREON APPROVED BY THE SECRETARY							
	13	OF INTERIOR SEP 12 1903							
	14								
	15	For child of Nos 1&2 see NB (Apr 26-06) Card #631							
	16	" " " " " " (Mar 3-05) " #223							
	17								

TRIBAL ENROLLMENT OF PARENTS

	Name of Father	Year	County	Name of Mother	Year	County
1	Ezekial Hembee[sic]		Non Citz	Brazilley Hembee		Non Citz
2	W. H Anderson		" "	Rebecca Anderson	Dead	Atoka
3	No1			No2		
4	No1			No2		
5	No1			No2		
6						
7			No2 on 1896 roll as Amy Hembra			
8						
9			As to marriage see testimony of No1			
10						
11			Evidence of marriage to be supplied: Recd Oct 7/99			
12			Nos 3-4 Affidavits of birth to be supplied: Recd Oct 7/99			
13			No.5 Enrolled April 10, 1902	#1 to 4 inc		
14				Date of Application for Enrollment.		
15				Aug 7/99		
16						
17	PO Farris, IT 3/15/05					

| RESIDENCE: | Tobucksy | COUNTY. | **Choctaw Nation** | Choctaw Roll | CARD No. 3283 |
| POST OFFICE: | Stewart, IT | | | (Not Including Freedmen) | FIELD No. |

Dawes' Roll No.	NAME		Relationship to Person	AGE	SEX	BLOOD	TRIBAL ENROLLMENT		
							Year	County	No.
9471	1 Case, Lucy	31	First Named	28	F	Full	1896	Atoka	2957
9472	2 " Lillie M	13	Dau	10	"	1/2	1896	"	2958
9473	3 " Emma	9	"	6	"	1/2	1896	"	2959
DEAD.	4 " Walter DEAD.		Son	1½	M	1/2			
void	5 Baldwin, Mary		Sister	14	F	Full	1896	Atoka	1870
9474	6 Case Joseph H		Son	3m	M	1/2			
I.W. 826	7 " Lee		Hus	38	M	IW			
	8								
	9								
	10	ENROLLMENT							
	11	OF NOS. 1,2,3 and 6 HEREON APPROVED BY THE SECRETARY							
	12	OF INTERIOR FEB 4 1903							
	13	For child of Nos 1&7 see NB (Apr 26-06) Card #447							
	14	ENROLLMENT							
	15	OF NOS. 7 HEREON APPROVED BY THE SECRETARY							
	16	OF INTERIOR MAY 21 1904							
	17								

No. 4 HEREON DISMISSED UNDER ORDER OF THE COMMISSION TO THE FIVE CIVILIZED TRIBES OF MARCH 31, 1905.

TRIBAL ENROLLMENT OF PARENTS

	Name of Father	Year	County	Name of Mother	Year	County
1	Wash Baldwin		Atoka	Jane	Dead	Citra
2	Lee Case		Non Citz	No 1		
3	" "		" "	No 1		
4	" "		" "	No 1		
5	Wash Baldwin		Atoka	Selina Baldwin		Jacks Fork
6	Lee Case		Non Citz	No 1		
7	Samuel Case	Dead	" "	Matilda Case	Dead	noncitizen
8						
9						
10						
11						
12	No 5 on 1896 Roll a Mary Balwin					
13	No.6 Enrolled January 16, 1901					
14	No 5 is duplicate enrollment of No4 on Choctaw card #1696					
	No.4 died January 20, 1900; proof of death filed Dec [?] 1902					#1 to 5 inc
15	Husband of N°1 and father of children				Date of Application for Enrollment.	Aug 7/99
16	hereon is Lee Case on Choctaw Card #D944					
17	No2 transferred from Choctaw card D944 April 16 1904 See decision of March 15, 1904					

Choctaw By Blood Enrollment Cards 1898-1914

RESIDENCE:	Atoka	COUNTY.					

Choctaw Nation — Choctaw Roll (Not Including Freedmen)

RESIDENCE: Atoka COUNTY.
POST OFFICE: Guertie, I.T.
CARD NO. 3284
FIELD NO.

Dawes' Roll No.	NAME	Relationship to Person First Named	AGE	SEX	BLOOD	TRIBAL ENROLLMENT Year	TRIBAL ENROLLMENT County	TRIBAL ENROLLMENT No.
9475	1 Pusley, Susan ⁶⁶	First Named	63	F	1/2	1896	Tobucksy	10221
	2							
	3							
	4							
	5	ENROLLMENT						
	6	OF NOS. 1 HEREON APPROVED BY THE SECRETARY						
	7	OF INTERIOR FEB 4 1903						
	8							
	9							
	10							
	11							
	12							
	13							
	14							
	15							
	16							
	17							

TRIBAL ENROLLMENT OF PARENTS

	Name of Father	Year	County	Name of Mother	Year	County
1	Geo Murphey[sic]	Dead	Non Citz		Dead	Kiamitia
2						
3						
4						
5						
6						
7						
8						
9						
10						
11						
12						
13						
14					Date of Application for Enrollment.	
15					Aug 7/99	
16						
17	Legal I.T.					

| RESIDENCE: | Gaines | COUNTY. | **Choctaw Nation** | | | **Choctaw Roll** *(Not Including Freedmen)* | | CARD NO. 3285 |
| POST OFFICE: | Hartshorne I.T | | | | | | | FIELD NO. |

Dawes' Roll No.		NAME		Relationship to Person First Named	AGE	SEX	BLOOD	TRIBAL ENROLLMENT		
								Year	County	No.
DEAD.	1	York, Charley		Named	52	M	Full	1896	Gaines	14202
14939	2	" Sarah	48	Wife	45	F	3/4	1896	"	14203
15455	3	" Roscoe	18	Son	15	M	Full	1896	"	14204
15456	4	" John	15	"	12	"	"	1896	"	14205
15457	5	" Lillie	14	Dau	11	F	"	1896	"	14206
9476	6	Jefferson, Ellis	16	S.Son	13	M	Full	1896	"	6574
	7									
	8									
	9	ENROLLMENT								
	10	OF NOS. 6		HEREON						
	11	APPROVED BY THE SECRETARY OF INTERIOR FEB 4 1903								
	12	ENROLLMENT								
	13	OF NOS. ~ 2 ~		HEREON						
	14	APPROVED BY THE SECRETARY OF INTERIOR OCT 15 1903						ENROLLMENT		HEREON
	15	No. 1 HEREON DISMISSED UNDER						OF NOS. 3 – 4 – 5 APPROVED BY THE SECRETARY		
	16	ORDER OF THE COMMISSION TO THE FIVE						OF INTERIOR MAY 9 1904		
	17	CIVILIZED TRIBES OF MARCH 31, 1905.								

TRIBAL ENROLLMENT OF PARENTS

	Name of Father	Year	County	Name of Mother	Year	County
1	Thos York	Dead	Tobucksy	Minie York		Tobucksy
2	Bill Blue		Sugar Loaf	Joana Holson	Dead	Sugar Loaf
3	No1			Nicie York		
4	No1			" "		
5	No1			" "		
6	Thos Jefferson	Dead	Gaines	No2		
7						
8	No5 is duplicate of Lillie York (No2) on Choctaw card #4646 Roll No. #12848					
9	Enrollment cancelled under Departmental instructions of July 15-1904 (D.C. #25572-1904)					
10	Name of parents of Nos 3-4-5 to be supplied:					
11	No.1 Died Dec 26, 1900: Proof of death filed Dec 30, 1902					
12						
13	See affidavit of Saven York as to name of mother of Nos 3,4 and 5 and amount of Choctaw blood possessed by them.					
14						
15					Date of Application for Enrollment.	Aug 7/99
16						
17						

Choctaw By Blood Enrollment Cards 1898-1914

RESIDENCE:	Atoka	COUNTY.					CARD NO.	
POST OFFICE:	Guertie, I.T.	**Choctaw Nation**		**Choctaw Roll** (Not Including Freedmen)			FIELD NO. 3286	

Dawes' Roll No.	NAME	Relationship to Person First Named	AGE	SEX	BLOOD	TRIBAL ENROLLMENT		
						Year	County	No.
9477	1 Adams, Melvina 76		73	F	Full	1896	Gaines	86
	2							
	3							
	4							
	5							
	6							
	7							
	8							
	9							
	10							
	11							
	12							
	13							
	17							

ENROLLMENT
OF NOS. 1 HEREON
APPROVED BY THE SECRETARY
OF INTERIOR FEB 4 1903

TRIBAL ENROLLMENT OF PARENTS

Name of Father	Year	County	Name of Mother	Year	County
1 Ma-lon-te-cubbee	Dead	Skullyville	Ta-lon-sey	Dead	Gaines
2					
3					
4					
5					
6					
7					
8					
9					
10					
11					
12					
13					
14			Date of Application for Enrollment.	Aug 7/99	
15					
16					
17					

RESIDENCE:	Atoka	COUNTY.							
POST OFFICE:	Guertie, I.T.								

Choctaw Nation

Choctaw Roll
(Not Including Freedmen)

CARD NO. 3287
FIELD NO.

Dawes' Roll No.		NAME	Relationship to Person First Named	AGE	SEX	BLOOD	TRIBAL ENROLLMENT		
							Year	County	No.
DEAD	1	Hunter, Tecumseh DEAD		26	M	Full	1896	Atoka	6044
DEAD	2	" Elsie DEAD	Wife	35	F	"	1896	"	6045
9478	3	" Andel	Son	12	M	"	1896	"	6046
9479	4	" Tandy	"	9	"	"	1896	"	6047
	5								
	6								
	7								
	8	ENROLLMENT OF NOS. 3 and 4 HEREON APPROVED BY THE SECRETARY OF INTERIOR FEB 4 1903							
	9								
	10								
	11								
	12	No. 1 and 2 HEREON DISMISSED UNDER ORDER OF THE COMMISSION TO THE FIVE CIVILIZED TRIBES OF MARCH 31, 1905.							
	13								
	14								
	15								
	16								
	17								

TRIBAL ENROLLMENT OF PARENTS

	Name of Father	Year	County	Name of Mother	Year	County
1	Andrew Hunter	Dead	Cedar	Jincey Hunter	Dead	Cedar
2	Ka-ah-kin-ta	"	Jacks Fork	Ok-la-hu-na	"	Jacks Fork
3	No 1			No 2		
4	No 1			No 2		
5						
6						
7			No 3 on 1896 roll as Andle Hunter			
8			Nº1 Died Aug 9, 1901. Proof of death filed Dec 24, 1902			
9			Nº2 Died April 28, 1901. Proof of death filed Dec 24, 1902			
10						
11						
12						
13						
14					Date of Application for Enrollment.	
15					Aug 7/99	
16						
17						

Choctaw By Blood Enrollment Cards 1898-1914

RESIDENCE: Chickasaw Natn ~~COUNTY.~~ **Choctaw Nation**   **Choctaw Roll** (*Not Including Freedmen*)   CARD NO. 3288

POST OFFICE: Ada, I.T.   1/6/04   FIELD NO.

Dawes' Roll No.	NAME		Relationship to Person	AGE	SEX	BLOOD	TRIBAL ENROLLMENT		
							Year	County	No.
IW 1118	1 Allen, John C	37	First Named	34	M	IW			
Void	2 " Randle M		Son	6mo	"	1/32			
	3								
	4								
	5								
	6								
	7								
	8								
	9								
	10								
	11								
	12								
	13								
	14								
	15								
	16								
	17								

ENROLLMENT OF NOS. ~~1~~ HEREON APPROVED BY THE SECRETARY OF INTERIOR NOV 16 1904

No2 transferred to Choc 46 Oct 28, 1902

TRIBAL ENROLLMENT OF PARENTS

	Name of Father	Year	County	Name of Mother	Year	County
1	John M Allen	Dead	Non Citz	Arzella Allen	Dead	Non Citz
2	No1			Mary I. Allen		Choctaw residing in Chickasaw Natn
3						
4						
5						
6	See decision in 7-46					
7	Wife and one other child on Choctaw Card No 46					
8	No1 was admitted by Dawes Com. Case No 1129.					
9	As to residence see his testimony. No appeal					
10						
11	Post office now seems to be Brady, I.T. 12/12/02					
12						
13						
14						
15				Date of Application for Enrollment.	Aug 7/99	
16						
17						

Choctaw By Blood Enrollment Cards 1898-1914

RESIDENCE: **Atoka** COUNTY. **Choctaw Nation** **Choctaw Roll** CARD NO. **3289**
POST OFFICE: **Guertie, I.T.** *(Not Including Freedmen)* FIELD NO.

Dawes' Roll No.	NAME	Relationship to Person First Named	AGE	SEX	BLOOD	Year	County	No.
9480	1 Carpenter, Solomon 35	First Named	32	M	Full	1896	Atoka	2954
9481	2 " Kitsy 33	Wife	30	F	"	1896	"	2955
9482	3 " Mary 1	Dau	2mo	F	"			
	4							
	5							
	6	ENROLLMENT						
	7	OF NOS. 1,2 and 3 HEREON APPROVED BY THE SECRETARY						
	8	OF INTERIOR FEB 4 1903						
	9							
	10							
	11							
	12							
	13							
	14							
	15							
	16							
	17							

TRIBAL ENROLLMENT OF PARENTS

	Name of Father	Year	County	Name of Mother	Year	County
1	Freeman Carpenter	Dead	Jacks Fork	Okla-hu-na	Dead	Jacks Fork
2	Jos Buchanan	"	Cedar		"	Towson
3	No.1			No2		
4						
5						
6						
7			No.3 Enrolled Aug 8, 1901			
8			For child of Nos 1&2 see NB (March 3,1905) #758			
9						
10						
11						
12						
13						
14					Date of Application for Enrollment.	
15					Aug 7/99	
16						
17						

RESIDENCE: Tobucksy COUNTY. **Choctaw Nation** Choctaw Roll CARD No. 3290
POST OFFICE: Calvin, I.T. *(Not Including Freedmen)* FIELD No.

Dawes' Roll No.	NAME	Relationship to Person First Named	AGE	SEX	BLOOD	TRIBAL ENROLLMENT		
						Year	County	No.
DEAD. 1	Perry, Benjamin	Named	22	M	5/8	1896	Tobucksy	10267
2								
3								
4								
5	No. 1 HEREON DISMISSED UNDER							
6	ORDER OF THE COMMISSION TO THE FIVE CIVILIZED TRIBES OF MARCH 11, 1905							
7								
8								
9								
10								
11								
12								
13								
14								
15								
16								
17								

TRIBAL ENROLLMENT OF PARENTS

	Name of Father	Year	County	Name of Mother	Year	County
1	Calvin C Perry		Tobucksy	Phoebe Perry		Tobucksy
2						
3						
4						
5						
6			N°1 is the husband of Dixie Perry Choctaw card #4356			
7			N°1 Died Sept 3, 1900: proof of death filed Nov. 12 1902			
8						
9						
10						
11						
12						
13						
14					Date of Application for Enrollment.	
15					Aug 7/99	
16						
17						

CANCELLED

Approved and filed prior to ratification of Choctaw-Chickasaw agreement Sept 25, 1902

| RESIDENCE: Atoka | | | | | | | | |
| POST OFFICE: Citra, I.T. | COUNTY. **Choctaw Nation** | | | **Choctaw Roll** (Not Including Freedmen) | | CARD NO. 3291 FIELD NO. | | |

Dawes' Roll No.	NAME	Relationship to Person	AGE	SEX	BLOOD	TRIBAL ENROLLMENT		
						Year	County	No.
I.W.311 ₁	Gulley, Eugene A ⁽⁴⁸⁾	First Named	45	M	I.W	1896	Atoka	14427
9483 ₂	" Cora ²⁸	Wife	25	F	1/4	1896	Atoka	4957
9484 ₃	" Lillie O ¹¹	Dau	8	"	1/8	1896	"	4960
9485 ₄	" Tandy F ⁸	Son	5	M	1/8	1896	"	4958
9486 ₅	" Theodore ⁶	"	3	"	1/8	1896	"	4959
9487 ₆	" Jewell H ¹	Dau	12das	F	1/8			
	₇							
	₈							
	₉	ENROLLMENT OF NOS. 2,3,4,5 and 6 HEREON APPROVED BY THE SECRETARY OF INTERIOR FEB 4 1903						
	₁₀							
	₁₁							
	₁₂	ENROLLMENT OF NOS. 1 HEREON APPROVED BY THE SECRETARY OF INTERIOR SEP 12 1903						
	₁₃							
	₁₄							
	₁₅							
	₁₆							
	₁₇							

TRIBAL ENROLLMENT OF PARENTS

Name of Father	Year	County	Name of Mother	Year	County
₁ John Gulley	Dead	Non Citz	Sarah Gulley	Dead	Non Citz
₂ Impson	"	Blue	Matilda Freeney		Blue
₃ No1			No2		
₄ No1			No2		
₅ No1			No2		
₆ Nº1			Nº2		
₇					
₈ No1 was admitted by Dawes Com Case No 1013					
₉ On 1896 roll as Eugene Cullie					
₁₀ No3 on 1896 roll as Ona Gulley					
₁₁ No5 " 1896 " " Willy "					
No4 " 1896 " " Folsom "					
₁₂ Nº6 Born Sept 10, 1902: enrolled Sept 22, 1902					
₁₃					
₁₄					
₁₅					
₁₆					
₁₇ Guertie I.T.					

| RESIDENCE: | Tobucksy | COUNTY. | **Choctaw Nation** | | | | Choctaw Roll | | CARD NO. | 3292 |
| POST OFFICE: | Guertie, I.T. | | | | | | (Not Including Freedmen) | | FIELD NO. | |

Dawes' Roll No.		NAME		Relationship to Person	AGE	SEX	BLOOD	TRIBAL ENROLLMENT		
								Year	County	No.
DEAD.	1	Flinchum, James W	DEAD Named	First Named	40	M	IW	1896	Tobucksy	14525
9488	2	" Julia A	42	Wife	39	F	1/2	1896	"	4026
See 5344	3	" William		Son	19	M	1/4	1896	"	4027
9489	4	" Columbus	18	"	15	"	1/4	1896	"	4029
9490	5	" James M	13	"	10	"	1/4	1896	"	4030
9491	6	" Leroy	12	"	9	"	1/4	1896	"	4031
9492	7	" Mary A K	10	Dau	7	F	1/4	1896	"	4032
9493	8	" Nora E	8	"	5	"	1/4	1896	"	4033
9494	9	" John B	5	Son	2	M	1/4			
9495	10	" Samma R	3	Dau	4mo	F	1/4			
	11	No9 Affidavit of birth to be								
	12	supplied:- Recd Oct 7/99								
	13	No6 on 1896 roll as Leroy A Flinchum								
	14	No.10 Enrolled June 23d, 1900								
	15	ENROLLMENT								
	16	OF NOS. 2,4,5,6,7,8,9 and 10 HEREON								
	17	OF INTERIOR FEB 4 1903								

No. 1 HEREON DISMISSED UNDER ORDER OF THE COMMISSION TO THE FIVE CIVILIZED TRIBES OF MARCH 31, 1905.

APPROVED BY THE SECRETARY

TRIBAL ENROLLMENT OF PARENTS

	Name of Father	Year	County	Name of Mother	Year	County
1	Wash Flinchum	Dead	Non Citz	Mary Flinchum	Dead	Non Citz
2	Turner B Turnbull	"	Blue	Jerrico Turnbull	"	Blue
3	No1			No2		
4	No1			No2		
5	No1			No2		
6	No1			No2		
7	No1			No2		
8	No1			No2		
9	No1			No2		
10	No.1			No.2		
11	No3 transferred to Choctaw card [remainder illegible]					
12	No1 on 1896 roll as James Flinchum – Also					
13	admitted by Dawes Com, Case 442 as James Flinchum					
14	No3 on 1896 roll as Wᵐ Flinchum			No.1 Died October 17,1899 See testimony		
15	No5 " 1896 " Jas M "			of William N Flinchum July 16		
16	No7 " 1896 " Marcum K "					
17	No8 " 1896 " Nora "			For child of No.1 see NB (Mar 3-05) #464		

Date of Application for Enrollment. 1 to 9 inc Aug 7/99

Date of Application for Enrollment

P.O. Raydon, Okla   12/17/08

RESIDENCE:	Tobucksy	COUNTY.	**Choctaw Nation**		Choctaw Roll	CARD NO. 3293
POST OFFICE:	Guertie, I.T.				(Not Including Freedmen)	FIELD NO.

Dawes' Roll No.	NAME		Relationship to Person First Named	AGE	SEX	BLOOD	TRIBAL ENROLLMENT		
							Year	County	No.
9496	1 Wilson Fannie	18	First Named	15	F	1/4	1896	Tobucksy	4028
9497	2 Wilson Eddie	1	~~Son~~ Dau	1mo	~~M~~ F	1/8			
	3								
	4								
	5								
	6	ENROLLMENT							
	7	OF NOS. 1 and 2 HEREON APPROVED BY THE SECRETARY							
	8	OF INTERIOR FEB 4 1903							
	9								
	10	10/4/21							
	11	(x) Correction of Sex of No2 made							
	12	in accordance with (Dept'l letter							
	13	IO No 5659-1921)							
	14								
	15								
	16								
	17								

TRIBAL ENROLLMENT OF PARENTS

	Name of Father	Year	County	Name of Mother	Year	County
1	Jas. W. Flinchum		Intermarried	Julia A Flinchum		Tobucksy
2	R. M. Wilson		noncitizen	No.1		
3						
4						
5						
6						
7						
8	On 1896 roll as Fannie Flinchum					
9	No.1 is now the wife of R.M. Wilson a noncitizen. Evidence of					
10	marriage filed Aug 29, 1901.					
11	No.2 Enrolled Aug 29, 1901. For child of No.1 see N.B. (Apr 26 1906) Card No 212.					
12						
13						
14					#1	
15				Date of Application for Enrollment.	Aug 7/99	
16						
17	P.O. Raydon, Okla. 3/23/09					

Choctaw By Blood Enrollment Cards 1898-1914

RESIDENCE: Tobucksy   COUNTY. **Choctaw Nation**   **Choctaw Roll**   CARD No. 32__

POST OFFICE: Legal, I.T.   *(Not Including Freedmen)*   FIELD No.

Dawes' Roll No.	NAME	Relationship to Person First Named	AGE	SEX	BLOOD	TRIBAL ENROLLMENT		
						Year	County	No.
0	1 Lewis, Edward M	Named	57	M	1/4			
0	2 " Sarah E	Wife	42	F	I.W			
0	3 " Gail B	Dau	20	"	1/8			
0	4 " Edward H	Son	10	M	1/8			
	5							
	6							
	7							
	8							
	9							
	10 #1 DISMISSED							
	11 JAN 26 1905							
	12				No			
	13							
	14							
	15							
	16							
	17							

TRIBAL ENROLLMENT OF PARENTS

	Name of Father	Year	County	Name of Mother	Year	County
1	Jas M Lewis	Dead	Choctaw	Zora P Lewis		Choctaw
2	Littleton Adams	"	Non Citz	Lucretia Adams	Dead	Non Citz
3	No1			No2		
4	No1			No2		
5						
6						
7	Nos 1 to 4 incl denied in 96 Case #850					
8	Admitted by U.S. Court, Central Dist, Jany 19/98					
9	Case No 101. As to residence, see testimony of No1					
10	Nos 1 to 4 incl were in C.C.C.C. #58					
11						
12						
13						Date of Application for Enrollment.
14						
15						Aug 7/99
16						
17	For child of No3 see NB 970 (Act Apr 26-06)					

Choctaw By Blood Enrollment Cards 1898-1914

RESIDENCE: COUNTY. **Choctaw Nation**   **Choctaw Roll**   CARD NO. 3295
POST OFFICE: Shawnee, Oklahoma   (Not Including Freedmen)   FIELD NO.

Dawes' Roll No.	NAME	Relationship to Person First Named	AGE	SEX	BLOOD	TRIBAL ENROLLMENT Year	County	No.
0	1 Guyer, Zora A		18	F	1/8			
DP	2 " Lindley Blaine	Son	8mo	M	1/16			
DP	3 " Edith May	Dau	2mo	F	1/16			
DP	4 " Fielding Lewis	Son	1mo	M	1/16			
	6							
	7							
	8 No1 Denied by C.C.C.C. as Zora A Lewis							
	9							
	10 #2-3-4							
	11							
	12							
	13 Sept 20- 1902							
	14 P.O. Center I.T.							
	15 See Pet #CC-130							
	16							
	17							

DENIED CITIZENSHIP BY THE CHOCTAW AND
CHICKASAW CITIZENSHIP COURT

DISMISSED

JAN 21 1905

Duplicate record found

TRIBAL ENROLLMENT OF PARENTS

Name of Father	Year	County	Name of Mother	Year	County
1 Edw M Lewis		Choctaw	Sarah E Lewis		Intermarried
2 W. H. Guyer		I.M. citizen	No.1		
3 " " "		" "	No.1		
4 " " "		" "	N⁰ 1		
5					
6					
7 No1 Denied in 96 Case #850					
Admitted by U.S. Court, Central Dist, Jany 19/98					
8 Case No 101, as Zora A. Lewis					
9 Judgment of U.S. Court admitting No1 vacated and set aside by Decree of Choctaw Chickasaw Citizenship Court Decr 17-02					
As to residence, see testimony of her father, Edw.					
10 M. Lewis					
11 No.1 is the wife of William H. Guyer on Choctaw card #D425					
12 No.2 Enrolled July 16, 1900					
No.3 Enrolled June 7th, 1901					
13 N⁰ 4 Born Aug 20, 1902: enrolled Sept 24, 1902					
14 No1 now in C.C.C.C. Case #58				Date of Application for Enrollment.	
15 For children of No1 see NB #992 (Act Apr 26-06)				Aug 7/99	
16					
17					

Choctaw By Blood Enrollment Cards 1898-1914

RESIDENCE:	Tobucksy	COUNTY.								
POST OFFICE:	Legal, I.T.									

Choctaw Nation — Choctaw Roll (Not Including Freedmen) — CARD NO. 3296 — FIELD NO.

Dawes' Roll No.	NAME	Relationship to Person First Named	AGE	SEX	BLOOD	TRIBAL ENROLLMENT Year	County	No.
0 DP	1 McKibben Sarah J		44	F	1/4			
0	2 " George L	Son	18	M	1/8		D	
0	3 " Cassie O	Dau	10	F	1/8		D	
0	4 " Claude	"	6	"	1/8		D	
0	5 " Thomas P	Son	3	M	1/8		D	
DP	6 " Grant	"	15mo	"	1/8			
	7							
2, 3, 4 & 5	8							
	9							
	10							
	11							
	12	Nos 1 to 5 incl now in C.C.C. Case #6558						
	13	#1-6						
	14	JAN 26 1905						
	15							
	16	See Pet #C-130						
	17	Duplicate record bound						

DENIED CITIZENSHIP BY THE CHOCTAW AND CHICKASAW CITIZENSHIP COURT

Judgment of U.S. Ct. admitting Nos 1 to 5 incl. vacated and set aside by Decree of Choctaw Chickasaw Citizenship Court Decr 17 '02

DISMISSED

TRIBAL ENROLLMENT OF PARENTS

Name of Father	Year	County	Name of Mother	Year	County
1 Jas M Lewis	Dead	Choctaw	Zora P Lewis		Choctaw
2 Geo W McKibben		Non Citz	No1		
3 " " "		" "	No1		
4 " " "		" "	No1		
5 " " "		" "	No1		
6 " " "		" "	No1		
7					
8					
9	Nos 1 to 5 incl denied in 96 Case #850				
10	All but No6 were admitted by the U.S. Court,				
11	Central Dist, Jany 19/98, Case No 101.				
12	No1 was admitted as Sarah Jane McKibben				
13	No2 " " " George Lewis "				
14	No3 " " " Casie O.			As to residence and birth of No6, see	Date of Application for Enrollment.
15	testimony of Edw. M. Lewis				
16	No6 Affidavit of birth to be supplied:-			Aug 7/99	
17	Red Oct. 7/99				

Choctaw By Blood Enrollment Cards 1898-1914

RESIDENCE: Tobucksy   COUNTY. **Choctaw Nation**   **Choctaw Roll** *(Not Including Freedmen)*   CARD NO. 3297
POST OFFICE: Legal, I.T.   FIELD NO.

Dawes' Roll No.	NAME	Relationship to Person First Named	AGE	SEX	BLOOD	TRIBAL ENROLLMENT Year	County	No.
1	Clark, Lydia	Named	23	F	1/8			
2								
3								
4								
5								
6								
7								
8								
9								
10								
11								
12								
13								
14								
15								
16								
17								

TRIBAL ENROLLMENT OF PARENTS

	Name of Father	Year	County	Name of Mother	Year	County
1	Thos P Lewis		Choctaw	Amanda Lewis	Dead	Non Citz
2						
3						
4						
5						
6						
7	No1 Denied in 96 Case #850					
8	Admitted by the US. Court Central Dist					
9	Jany 19/98, Case No 101. As to residence, see her testimony.					
10	Judgment of U.S Court affirmed by decree by the Dawson Choctaw Chickasaw Cit Court Dec 1702					
11	No1 is wife of No1 on Choctaw card #5604					
12	No1 now in C.C.C.C. Case # 58					
13						
14					Date of Application for Enrollment.	
15					Aug 7/99	
16						
17						

Choctaw By Blood Enrollment Cards 1898-1914

RESIDENCE: Chickasaw Natn COUNTY. **Choctaw Nation** Choctaw Roll CARD NO. 3298
POST OFFICE: Bebee, I.T. (Not Including Freedmen) FIELD NO.

Dawes' Roll No.	NAME	Relationship to Person First Named	AGE	SEX	BLOOD	TRIBAL ENROLLMENT		
						Year	County	No.
0 ✓ 1	Cowart, Virgil		33	M	1/4			
0 ✓ 2	" Anna	Wife	24	F	I.W.			
3								
4								
5								
6								
7								
8								
9								
10								
11								
12								
13								
14								
15								
16								
17								

TRIBAL ENROLLMENT OF PARENTS

	Name of Father	Year	County	Name of Mother	Year	County
1	Saml J Cowart	Dead	Non Citz	Rhoda T Cowart	Dead	Choctaw
2	J L Rowland	" "	Augusta Rowland	"	Non Citz
3						
4						
5						
6	Nos 1&2 Denied in 96 Case #850					
7	Admitted by U.S. Court, Central Dist, Jan 19/99					
8	Case No 101. As to residence, see testimony of No1					
9	Nos 1&2 now on ((((Case #45 58					
10						
11						
12						
13						
14				Date of Application for Enrollment.		
15				Aug 7/99		
16						
17						

298

Choctaw By Blood Enrollment Cards 1898-1914

RESIDENCE: Atoka	COUNTY. Choctaw Nation	Choctaw Roll (Not Including Freedmen)	CARD No. 3299
POST OFFICE: Colgate, I.T.			FIELD No.

Dawes' Roll No.	NAME	Relationship to Person First Named	AGE	SEX	BLOOD	TRIBAL ENROLLMENT Year	County	No.
1	McCarty, Everett E	Named	58	M	1/4			
2	" Evelyn E	Wife	54	F	I.W			
3	" Jennie F	Dau	22	"	1/8			
4	" Carroll C	Son	18	M	1/8			
5								
6								
7								
8								
9								
10								
11								
12								
13								
14								
15								
16								
17								

DENIED CITIZENSHIP BY THE CHOCTAW AND
CHICKASAW CITIZENSHIP COURT
Nos 2 & 4   Case #29 Apr 20-04

No1 claims right as I.W
See testimony of 12/22/04

No1
DISMISSED
APR 19 1906

TRIBAL ENROLLMENT OF PARENTS

	Name of Father	Year	County	Name of Mother	Year	County
1	Bryant McCarty	Dead	Non Citz	Annie McCarty	Dead	Choctaw
2	J. J. Greenwade	"	" "	Mary Greenwade	"	Non Citz
3	No1			No2		
4	No1			No2		
5						
6						
7						
8	Nos 1 to 4 Denied in 96 Case #1275					
9	Admitted by U.S. Court Central Dist Aug 26/97					
10	Case No 59 As to residence see testimony of No1					
11						
12						
13	No4 now claims as intermarried citizen by reason of					
14	his marriage to Delta R Davis Choctaw 4296 #7705			Date of Application for Enrollment.		
	For record see Choctaw 43302 Also see Lula West Pet #88					
15					Aug 8/99	
16						
17	P.O. of No4 McGee I.T. Dec 22 '04					
	No4 PO Durant IT 1/5/05					

RESIDENCE: Atoka COUNTY. **Choctaw Nation** Choctaw Roll CARD NO. 3300
POST OFFICE: Colgate, I.T. *(Not Including Freedmen)* FIELD NO.

Dawes' Roll No.	NAME	Relationship to Person First Named	AGE	SEX	BLOOD	TRIBAL ENROLLMENT		
						Year	County	No.
✓	1 McCarty, Theron B		26	M	1/8			
DP	2 " Everett B	Son	10mo	"	1/16			
DP	3 " Stewart Milton	Son	2mo	"	1/16			
	4							
	5							
2.3	6 DISMISSED MAY 27 1904							
	7							
	8							
	9							
	10							
	11							
	12							
	13							
	14							
	15	DENIED CITIZENSHIP BY THE CHOCTAW AND						
	16	CHICKASAW CITIZENSHIP COURT						
	17							

TRIBAL ENROLLMENT OF PARENTS

	Name of Father	Year	County	Name of Mother	Year	County
1	Everett McCarty		Choctaw	Evelyn McCarty		Intermarried
2	No1			Annie McCarty		Non Citz
3	No1			" "		" "
4						
5						
6						
7						
8	No1 Denied in 96 Case #1275					
9	Admitted by U.S. Court Central Dist. Aug 26/97					
10	Case No 59. As to residence and birth of No2 see testimony of No1					
11						
12	No2 Affidavit of birth to be supplied: Recd Oct 7/99					
13	No3 Enrolled February 16, 1901					
14	Wife of No1 – Annie L. McCarty Choctaw Card #D405				Date of Application for Enrollment.	
15					Aug 8/99	
16						
17